✺ TRAVELS AND TALES OF MIRIAM GREEN ELLIS

# TRAVELS AND TALES OF MIRIAM GREEN ELLIS

Pioneer Journalist of the Canadian West

MIRIAM GREEN ELLIS

Edited and with an Introduction by
PATRICIA DEMERS

THE UNIVERSITY OF ALBERTA PRESS

Published by

The University of Alberta Press
Ring House 2
Edmonton, Alberta, Canada T6G 2E1
www.uap.ualberta.ca

Introduction copyright © 2013 Patricia Demers
Copyright © 2013 Miriam Green Ellis

LIBRARY AND ARCHIVES CANADA
CATALOGUING IN PUBLICATION

Ellis, Miriam Green
    Travels and tales of Miriam Green Ellis :
pioneer journalist of the Canadian West / Miriam
Green Ellis ; edited and with an introduction by
Patricia Demers.

Includes bibliographical references and index.
Issued also in electronic formats.
ISBN 978-0-88864-626-2

    1. Ellis, Miriam Green. 2. Women journalists—
Alberta—Biography. 3. Feminists—Alberta—
Biography. 4. Suffragists—Alberta—Biography.
5. Alberta—Biography. 6. Alberta—Social
conditions—20th century. 7. Canada, Western—
Biography. 8. Canada, Western—Social conditions—
20th century. I. Demers, Patricia, 1946– II. Title.
III. Title: Miriam Green Ellis.

PN4913.E44A3 2013   070.92   C2012-908220-1

First edition, first printing, 2013.
Printed and bound in Canada by Houghton
Boston Printers, Saskatoon, Saskatchewan.
Copyediting by Lisa LaFramboise.
Proofreading by Lesley Peterson.
Map by Wendy Johnson.
Indexing by Elizabeth Macfie.

All rights reserved. No part of this publication may be produced, stored in a retrieval system, or transmitted in any form or by any means (electronic, mechanical, photocopying, recording, or otherwise) without prior written consent. Contact the University of Alberta Press for further details.

The University of Alberta Press is committed to protecting our natural environment. As part of our efforts, this book is printed on Enviro Paper: it contains 100% post-consumer recycled fibres and is acid- and chlorine-free.

The University of Alberta Press gratefully acknowledges the support received for its publishing program from The Canada Council for the Arts. The University of Alberta Press also gratefully acknowledges the financial support of the Government of Canada through the Canada Book Fund (CBF) and the Government of Alberta through the Alberta Multimedia Development Fund (AMDF) for its publishing activities.

This book has been published with the help of a grant from the Canadian Federation for the Humanities and Social Sciences, through the Awards to Scholarly Publications Program, using funds provided by the Social Sciences and Humanities Research Council of Canada.

For more photographs, colour slides, and other items from the Miriam Green Ellis Collection, please visit the web exhibit hosted by the Bruce Peel Special Collections Library: www.library.ualberta.ca/specialcollections.

*For my sisters, Louise and Agnes*

# CONTENTS

    IX   *Preface: "Brains should be used if available"*
   XIX  *Acknowledgements*
   XXI  *Introduction: Miriam Green Ellis, A Passionate Spirit*
LXXIII  *Abbreviations*

### TRAVELLER AND STORYTELLER
    3  Down North (1922)
  73  Alone (undated)
  91  A War Bride's Return (undated)

### ON THE AGGIE BEAT
121  The Women Grain Growers of Saskatchewan (1915)
125  World's Best Wheat from Bush Land (1929)
129  From Aberdeen to Alberta (1930)
133  The Tragedy of the Regina Plains (1931)
141  Men on Relief Go Back to Land (1933)

CHAMPION OF WOMEN AND THE WEST
151 My Car "Finnigan" and I (1920)
161 Sun Dance at Hobbema (1923)
169 Their Second Honeymoon (1928)
177 Banff Fine Arts School (1941)

183 Notes
197 Works Cited
207 Index

# PREFACE

*"Brains should be used if available"*

I DISCOVERED MIRIAM GREEN ELLIS (1879–1964) serendipitously about five years ago when I was collecting information about Oblate missionary Émile Grouard. I happened on the photograph she'd taken of Bishop Grouard in the Edmonton train station in June 1922, when both were departing for the North; Grouard to Fort Chipewyan and Ellis to Aklavik. Finding out that an Alberta newspaper woman had journeyed to Aklavik by train and river steamer in 1922 fired my imagination. This accidental discovery led me to the twenty-one boxes of the Miriam Green Ellis Collection, bequeathed by the writer to the University of Alberta's Special Collections Library—published articles in magazines and newspapers, typescripts, speeches, clippings, keepsakes, photo albums, and coloured glass slides. The more I rummaged and probed in this archive, the more intrigued and, yes, hooked I became. As well as inviting a move beyond conventional disciplinary boundaries to explore writing embedded in the day-to-day challenges of travel reporting and the practical considerations of copy deadline and readership, the exercise continues to show me what unanticipated directions await in the archives.

When I contacted British Columbia–based historian Marjory Lang, author of *Women Who Made the News: Female Journalists in Canada, 1880-1945*, she wrote almost immediately to say how excited she was "to hear that someone is doing more work on this fantastic woman" (Lang, email). Her adjective prompted me to tabulate what made Miriam Green Ellis (MGE) "fantastic." Following the newspaper and manuscript trail she left behind discloses the way we were as westerners and Canadians in the early decades of the twentieth century. Her composed pictures of prairie life offer vivid, idiosyncratic impressions, reflections of a past and a culture that continue to inform our understanding. The fact that she struck out for Aklavik on her own—that is, without the endorsement of her editor Frank Oliver of the *Edmonton Bulletin*—testifies to her curiosity about changing conditions and modes of transport, her interest in the unknown territory with its pioneering oil industry, and her eagerness to see for herself. Remarkably too, the trip illustrates her entrepreneurial spirit; she took a financial risk her publisher was unwilling to take, and parlayed it into a not-inconsiderable advance in her career, both through the sales of articles and lectures and through the publicity that established her in a much wider sphere. Here was a person who made her own way when the industry was unwilling to create this kind of space for a woman. Her lifelong commitment to the Canadian Women's Press Club (CWPC) reveals remarkable professional and personal loyalties, connecting her to the tradition of pioneering women journalists: Kathleen "Kit" Coleman, co-founder and first president of the CWPC; Nellie McClung, suffragist, social activist, politician, and fiction writer; Violet McNaughton, founder of the Saskatchewan Women Grain Growers; and E. Cora Hind, whom Ellis succeeded as Western Canada's premier agricultural journalist. Her tribute to these forerunners and contemporaries, delivered as a talk, *Pathfinders*, at the 1956 CWPC Triennial in Edmonton, indicates the breadth of this network of

*Should Auld Acquaintance Be Forgot.* "A Recipe for Remembrance." To Jane Stewart from the Edmonton Women's Press Club. 10 June 1922. [BPSC]

press women and MGE's zest and sense of belonging. These qualities of independence, loyalty, and pluck only intensify her appeal.

It remains a mystery why the MGE Collection has sat relatively undisturbed for four decades, with the exception of the scholarship of Susan Jackel, Lisa LaFramboise, Marjory Lang, and Kay Rex. MGE's experience as a cub reporter on dailies in Prince Albert, Regina, and Edmonton, and her a quarter century's affiliation with the Montreal-based weekly *Family Herald and Weekly Star* as its western editor, affirm her lasting appeal. She brings a varied and always highly coloured perspective to her writing. Respecting the freedom of the press and identifying the place of the individual in local society, she combines the best features of both metropolitan dailies and rural weeklies, as Paul Voisey describes them in *High River and the Times*. Though not included in the contingent of now-forgotten newspaperwomen whom Jean Marie Lutes studies in *Front-Page Girls: Women Journalists in American Culture and Fiction, 1880–1930*, MGE resembles her American counterparts, whose "bodies, circulated through the pages of the papers that employed them, became emblems of publicity," being "identified with and through the process of making public their images and their words" (Lutes 6).

Miriam's avant-garde, trademark appearance, tramping confidently in cattle show rings in breeches and tweed jackets—shocking for some in the twenties and thirties—solidifies a strong link with E. Cora Hind (1861–1942), her foremother as Western Canadian agricultural journalist. Hind also sported high-laced boots and breeches, along with a gold-mounted cane, a Stetson hat, and a buckskin coat presented by the Calgary Exhibition and Stampede Board and embroidered by the Fisher River First Nation. Ellis delighted in regaling interviewers with tales of the impact she and Hind created in Toronto high society by wearing breeches to the Royal Winter Fair: "'It made a sensation. The kids followed us around as they did the pied piper'" (qtd. in "Woman Reporter" 12). Products of Ontario childhoods and schooling, with lasting influences from grandparents and rural communities, known for speaking their minds, for keeping abreast of agricultural experiments and advances, and for loving the West passionately, the women also shared an aversion to sugar-coating. As Hind replied to a critic who thought her loyalty was blind, "'very early in my newspaper career I learned that the West was big enough and strong enough to have the truth told about it on all occasions'" (qtd. in Haig 73). Both Hind, whose forty-year career for the *Manitoba Free Press* was nearing its conclusion, and Ellis, whose career was being established, attended the sixth CWPC Triennial in Calgary in 1932. Ellis gave the keynote speech for that occasion, titled "Special Fields."[1] Hind, for her part, was eager at that sixth triennial to "display her beloved West to some of her eastern confreres who, she felt, were not sufficiently appreciative of its charms" (Haig 121). When at the E.P. (Prince of Wales) Ranch, as Hind was leading a procession to a corral where a handsome bull was feeding, one Toronto colleague observed, "'I have always wanted to see a buffalo!'" Hind greeted the remark with "complete silence" and "an incredulous gaze" (122). As the keynote speaker, Ellis's address did not disappoint, outlining with relish and personal reminiscences the perquisites and responsibilities of the woman journalist.

Unlike "writers who never leave home except to go to the Archives and write over again the things that were done by our grandfathers" and those who "are terribly clever on deeply technical things," in her keynote address Ellis aligns herself with the "common folk [who] dig out the pith and translate it into common language." While being able to explain the *how* of a process was primarily important in the training of a reporter, she maintains, "a good power of observation may come next, and brains should be used if available."[2] Using these brains to "develop women's place in public life" should be a first duty of the "virile pen." In the aftermath of the Persons Case (the 1929 legal battle wherein five Canadian women sought to have Canadian women declared "persons" under the law, and thus eligible to be appointed to the Senate), with the "pathetic" tally of only two female Members of Parliament and one female senator, MGE argues that "putting up a memorial for these five women who made the challenge is not good enough." Her argument is advocacy, undisguised and hard-hitting: "I have still to be convinced that there are not a few broader, better-informed minds among women than SOME of the men representatives we have at present." Her defence of agriculture as "Canada's biggest industry" and "the biggest new source of wealth" requires that "the agricultural reporter [be] interested and passably intelligent in the farmers' problems in producing wheat." Intelligence and information are a recursive loop: "We must also keep in touch with dozens of scientists all over the world who are trying to breed rust-resistant wheat; working on smuts and other diseases of grains; experimenting on the best varieties to grow in certain sections; and developing new varieties that have stronger straw, or have a bigger yield, or are resistant to root rots or a dozen other things to which wheat is liable." The grain farmer's concerns surpass a parent's worries: "Bringing up a family free of measles and whooping cough, and fairly resistant to sin, has nothing on the farmer who brings through his crop of grain. It may be hailed; it may be frozen; it may be drouthed; it may be rusted; it may be grasshoppered; it may be cut-wormed; it may be saw-flyed; it may be blown out of the earth entirely, or someone else's field may be blown over and piled up on top of it." Ellis closes her sweeping gazetteer coverage of the rich diversity of the "over two hundred thousand farms" in her "own parish" with a word of advice about "the thousands of banquets [that the agricultural journalist] attends each year" and a quip plugging fresh food: "I have acquired a bias about canned peas that I am afraid will never be lived down. It is a pity too, with the surplus of peas there are in the country just now."

    This engaging speaker, with her taste for irony and lucidity of phrase, a contributor to the public sphere for over four decades, is affiliated with a tradition of women writers, yet she follows her own path. The modernist sphere of first-wave feminism, where the work of this single, independent woman resides, differs from the earlier portraits of Canada supplied by female visitors, travellers, pioneer settlers, and adventurers who were wives and mothers. To be sure, these early records are assuming a new importance in our understanding of identity and diversity. Mary Alice Downie and Barbara Robertson's nationwide collage of twenty-nine excerpts spanning three centuries until 1914 chronicles different personal journeys testifying to the writers' "skill, tenacity and…willing[ness] to turn their hand to a multitude of tasks" (Errington 27). Dwellers, as opposed to seasonal visitors, have a special, rooted, and inimitable focus on their surroundings. Those inhabitants, moreover, who write professionally for publication and dissemination in newspapers capture a sense of place and time with deliberation and purposiveness. The call to probe the writing and influence of early Canadian women journalists has sounded, and with good reason. Theirs is work of conviction transmitting information and opinion with vigour. Long before the age of fanzines they enjoyed loyal readerships; with resourcefulness, they secured positions in the often grimy world of smoke-filled newsrooms. They dared to personalize, exercise moral authority, and display knowledgeable command. Their social activism took many forms and tones, from cajoling and subtly ironic to testy and acerbic.

Two recent studies of Canadian press women have spurred my undertaking. After her lively reading of the magazine and newspaper articles of Agnes Maule Machar (1837–1927), Sara Jeanette Duncan (1861–1922), E. Pauline Johnson (1861–1913), Kathleen Blake Coleman (1856–1915), Flora MacDonald Denison (1867–1913), and Nellie L. McClung (1873–1951) as "well-known public figures whose pungent analyses of their society found a ready audience," Janice Fiamengo admits to surprise "that so few scholars seemed to be interested in them" (5, 214). She indulges the hope that "future criticism…will take the form of a multifaceted, historically grounded inquiry that pays attention to details of language and considers the manifold relationships between writers, texts, their audiences, and the social and institutional contexts of literature" (216).

More focussed on the commercial realities of press women's "expanding participation in the paid workplace" than their social gospel, Marjory Lang notes that women were employed by Canadian periodicals "primarily as magnets to attract female subscribers"; she sees the editors of the woman's page as "active moulders of a culture of women" (4, 10). In the post–World War II era, Lang laments that the noble ideals expressed in the Canadian Women's Press Club's constitution, "to improve and maintain the status of journalism as a profession for women and to provide counsel and promote understanding and assistance among press women" (CWPC, "Constitution" 1), dwindled to contentment with "such coy nicknames as 'newsies,' 'paper dolls,' and 'news hens'" (Lang 285).

Ellis never considered herself a paper doll. Unlike Kit Coleman's, her fame did not involve the woman's page: Ellis strode boldly in another direction. With the exception of the trusted forecasts of wheat crop yields by the renowned E. Cora Hind, the field of agricultural reporting was male territory. Nevertheless, in the generation following Hind's heyday in the teens and early twenties, Ellis assumed the mantle of the Canadian West's premier agricultural journalist. Acclaim, however, did not arrive quickly or rest easily on either woman. Both were fiercely hard workers, and these transplanted Ontarians endured long apprenticeships and faced opposition and disappointment. In an often repeated narrative[3] Hind had to wait twenty years before the *Free Press*, initially rejecting her application in 1882, decided to correct the error by hiring the woman who had set up her own secretarial agency and was producing informed, valuable freelance information for grain growers. Two biographies (Kennethe Haig's *Brave Harvest* and Carlotta Hacker's *E. Cora Hind*), Hind's own post-retirement world travel, which she recorded in *Seeing for Myself: Agricultural Conditions Around the World* and *My Travels and Findings*, and the award of an honorary Doctor of Laws by the University of Manitoba in 1935 testify to and acknowledge Hind's accomplishments. Her lesser-known successor, the affable and tough-minded Miriam Green Ellis, built a career that sheds light on the growth,

*Edmonton friends, at the McClung home. Left to right: Jack McClung; MGE; "Wop" May. The house still stands at 11229 100 Avenue, Edmonton.* [BPSC]

passions, and variety of agricultural journalism; her authority, prestige, and suffragist principles affirm her friendship with such Edmonton allies as Emily Murphy and Nellie McClung. Ellis deserves much more than honourable mention. Miriam Green Ellis's writings demonstrate that she is aware of the struggles of farm families and especially of farm wives, interested in all forms of ritual from the cattle show ring to the Cree Sun Dance, keen to travel to and document conditions in all areas of the Canadian West, particularly northern and remote ones, prescient about the second "Klondyke" of the tar sands, and eager to capture in word and picture the inhabitants of the Land of the Midnight Sun. Through all this, Ellis is most concerned about the people in and behind her notes, a concern that is even more evident in her efforts in fiction.

MGE's journalism is positioned at points of intersection between a primitive economy and high agricultural development, between periods of postwar boom and Depression bust, and reflects suffragist victories and the challenges facing individual pioneer women, as well as the cross-cultural dynamics of Native–White relations. Her writing thus requires an understanding of social and literary contexts at the same time as it invites theorizing about what constitutes the public sphere. Georgina Taylor's *H.D. and the Public Sphere of Modernist Women Writers* argues convincingly that Jürgen Habermas's theory of the lifeworld as a sphere set apart from the political or social is "erroneous" (198) because it concentrates on bourgeois men and does not include all those who have the critical capacity to participate. This extension of the public sphere and its participants deepens our perception of MGE's value. Here was an independent woman, a truly public figure, who remained protectively private, likeably consistent—and, on occasion, inconsistent. Her unerring ability to get to the emotional heart of an encounter, to champion the land and its cultivators, and to express admiration and sympathy, along with her quickness to detect condescension, made Ellis a wonderfully attractive subject. With typewriter and camera always in her travel kit, at times toting a rifle, she staked out Western Canada as her territory. In our age of digitally native information, we might be inclined to regard newspapers, a little pityingly, as belonging to the legacy media business. However, Ellis does not present quaint curios but multifaceted visual and textual portraits of lived realities. This introductory sampling of her textual and pictorial language will, I hope, convince others to join in the exploration of this fantastic woman.

# ACKNOWLEDGEMENTS

IN COMPILING THIS EDITION, I have accumulated many debts of gratitude. In the first place, I want to thank Miriam Green Ellis for willing her papers to the University of Alberta and thus allowing me to come to know her. When talking about such an engaging subject, I find it impossible to be rigorously impersonal, and so I have used the authorial first-person singular. I sometimes refer to my subject as "Ellis" or "Miriam" or "MGE." Since I've immersed myself in her work, recognizing her turns of phrase and ebullience as well as her insistence on order and protocol, I believe she would approve of the formal though mysteriously retained married name, the personal affiliation, and the professionally concise acronym.

Librarians have been indispensable resources. Susan Mavor, head of Special Collections in the Doris Lewis Rare Book Room of the Dana Porter Library at the University of Waterloo, gave me access to the Women's Press Club of Toronto archives. Staff at Library and Archives Canada and at the John M. Cuelenaere Public Library in Prince Albert provided more valuable snippets of information. At the Glenbow Museum, Douglas E. Cass and Adria Lund assisted my inquiries about the Banff School, as did Dr. Henry R. Glyde of the Department of

Physics and Astronomy at the University of Delaware. The eager high school students staffing the Prince Albert Historical Museum set a new standard for on-the-spot service. Prince Albert residents whom I approached about the elusive Miriam and George supplied generous and prompt assistance: Dr. William O. Cooke, director of Education for the Saskatchewan Rivers School Division; Randy Emmerson, principal of Prince Albert Collegiate Institute; and Barry Glass, managing editor of the *Prince Albert Daily Herald*. Karen Gledhill, principal of Lisgar Collegiate Institute, retrieved useful background material about George's teaching career.

On the local front, the experience of working with research assistants Carmyn Effa and Beth Gripping has been a real delight; as we pored over photos and documents together, their enthusiasm buoyed and intensified my own interest in Miriam. Colleagues in our Bruce Peel Special Collections Library, Robert Desmarais, Carol Irwin, and Jeff Papineau, have been wonderfully supportive and accommodating, as always. Karen Simonson, reference archivist at the Provincial Archives of Alberta, has been a great help in uncovering documents and suggesting further routes of inquiry. The encouragement and patience of colleagues at the University of Alberta Press, including director Linda Cameron, editors Peter Midgley and Mary Lou Roy, and designer Alan Brownoff, make collaboration a sheer pleasure. The anonymous assessors offered generously elucidating suggestions. I am also very grateful to the Killam Research Fund at the University of Alberta for supporting this project.

A NOTE ON EDITING PRACTICE

In transcribing MGE's typescripts, I have silently corrected some typos.

A NOTE ON ILLUSTRATIONS

Unless otherwise noted, all illustrations are from the Miriam Green Ellis Collection in the Bruce Peel Special Collections Library at the University of Alberta. All photos are used with permission.

# INTRODUCTION

Miriam Green Ellis: A Passionate Spirit

*I spent most of my youthful years in a farm home. I'll just describe it, as I imagine that most of you were brought up in similar houses. Perhaps some of you were born in marble halls, but if so, I don't believe I have met you....*

*If the minister and his wife came unexpectedly for dinner, we set the table. As soon as we saw them coming up the lane, I hustled out to catch a chicken. They had hardly finished the photograph album before my mother had the chicken cooked and served.*

*So a home includes things as well as people; it means horehound candy in grandfather's desk; it means pigs getting out of their pens and having to be chased back; it means mother's new set of dishes that must not be broken; it means the mouse-coloured mare that for some reason was called Dexter. She was the only beast on the place that was considered sufficiently elegant to be hitched to the phaeton.*

(ELLIS, "Western Homes I Have Seen," February 1943)

*Writing for a newspaper is different than writing an essay, or writing a speech, or writing a magazine article or a book or a letter. In a speech or a magazine story, the climax comes at the end. In a newspaper story, the climax comes in the first sentence, or, if it is a big story, it comes in a seven-column line across the top of the page. Newspaper stories are written so that the meat of the story comes into the first sentence. After that it is elaboration. But it is never well just to read the headings and think you know what has happened, for there are often extenuating circumstances. The head may read "Miriam Green Ellis kills best friend." Reading down, you may find that I slipped and fell on her and of course that was the end.*

(ELLIS, "University of Manitoba 4th Year English Class," March 1934)

*I resent the smug manner with which some pseudo-farmers and politicians refer to themselves as "dirt farmers." To me those are fighting words. That is supposed to be a slam at someone, but what other kind of farmer is there than the one who works in the dirt? The better use he makes of that dirt, the better farmer he is, the more he has to contribute to the food supplies of his neighbours in town.*

(ELLIS, "Aggie Stag Banquet," 1948)

ON THE OCCASION of Miriam Green Ellis's retirement, at the age of 73, as western editor of the Montreal paper the *Family Herald and Weekly Star*, a post she had held for over 25 years, Canadian Women's Press Club past-president Kennethe Haig hailed her colleague as "that incredible Canadian" (Cram 7). The celebration took place in Winnipeg

CWPC Golden Jubilee, Toronto, 1954. Left to right, standing: Kate Aitken; MGE; Madeleine Levason; seated: Joan Duggan; Charlotte Whitton, Her Worship, Mayor of Ottawa; Margaret Aitken, MP; Eve Henderson. [University of Waterloo Library, Women's Press Club of Toronto fonds]

in early January 1953. Ellis had signed on formally in 1913 as a member of the CWPC, which, making history as well as news, claims "the longest continuous existence of any professional women journalists' organization in the world" (Jackel 53), and she renewed affiliation as a "continuous, active member" (CWPC, *Triennial Report*) until her death in 1964. But she was much more than an affiliate. Ellis was president of the Edmonton Branch of the CWPC in 1919 and served in many subsequent roles for this branch; she arranged the first CWPC regional conference in Edmonton in 1920 and served several terms as vice-president of the regional CWPC, area director for Manitoba, and chair of the Beneficiary Fund and Memorial Awards board. Her characteristically informal history of the CWPC, *Pathfinders*, was delivered as a talk at the triennial in Edmonton in 1956.

Ellis was more than an organizer, however. The vast scope of her published and always personally coloured articles covers topics ranging from stock prices, farm fairs, prize-winning wheat, farmer-entrepreneurs, and city folk going back to the land during the Depression, to learning to drive and change a tire, camping in the Rockies, and visiting the fledgling Banff School of Fine Arts. In addition to crisscrossing Western Canada countless times on her "aggie" beat, she extended her field to Atlantic Canada, reporting on ox-pulls, haymaking, cod and lobster fisheries, and coal mining in Nova Scotia, Cape Breton, and Prince Edward Island. She ventured as far as Honolulu where, being welcomed as "the Dean of Canada's newspaper women," she sent back copy about Hawaiian cattle ranches, sugar-cane harvests, floral industries, and the active Kilauea and Mauna Loa volcanoes on the Big Island.

The largely unmined Ellis Collection, willed by the writer to the University of Alberta, contains holograph manuscripts and typewritten manuscripts, three short stories, and the typescript of her journey from Edmonton to Aklavik, Northwest Territories, in June and July 1922, entitled "Down North," along with 237 photographs, at least half of which were transferred through the technology of the day to coloured glass slides to illustrate her "Journey to the Land of the Midnight Sun" lectures across Canada and the U.S. Watercolour artists with fine sable brushes welcomed the calotype technique of painting and glazing paper-based photographs, which allowed them precision in detailing facial and costume features (Henisch and Henisch 53). The coloured slides of Ellis's magic lantern shows captured "real life" (Humphries 24) with such vividness that the *Toronto Telegram* reporter who attended her lecture to the University Women's Club called it "a fairy tale evening": as "scene after scene of the pathway to the Land of the Midnight Sun flashed before her audience," along with "the picturesque and varied peoples she met," Ellis's depiction of "Canada's backyard" was "a revelation…to those who have thought of the north as a great barren plain" ("Cornelia"). Photographs of and keepsakes from friends (Emily Murphy, Nellie McClung, Gertrude "Peggy" Balmer, E. Cora Hind, and Violet McNaughton among them) add to this archival trove's enlivened sense of the West in the early twentieth century, of a woman making her mark in a male-dominated field, and of the sustaining bonds among press women.

Poring over the contents of the Ellis Collection prompted me to reflect on the suitability of calling these boxes an archive. A donation intended to preserve and, I suggest, re-create and illumine, the archive exists within traditional and spectral frames of reference. It allows the viewer to handle and see aspects of a life. In fulfilling this traditional role for a nostalgic return "to a most archaic place," as Jacques Derrida observed, the archive also challenges with the question of response—what Derrida called "the question of the future itself,...of a responsibility for tomorrow" which "we will only know in times to come" (36). As the half-century mark for Ellis's donation nears, is it now time to start formulating a response? Moreover, the diverse, omnifarious nature of this collection, "made from selected and consciously chosen documentation from the past and also from the mad fragments that no one intended to preserve and just ended up there" (Steedman 68), could be another clue in coming to know the writer and her times. The full and fragmentary pieces of this collection have taught me many things about Miriam. A daring woman of determination and wry humour, a diarist, a writer of non-fiction and fiction, a promoter of rural life and agricultural communities, and a champion of press women who exemplifies their motto, "Every Stroke Upward" (Rex 1), this incredible Canadian is also a person of mystery. Despite the accessible tenor and subjects of her widely circulated publications and their marks of a strong personality, Ellis herself is less and less fathomable. Elusiveness is actually not the problem; it is, rather, the thread that connects the work of over four decades of the woman who, as she remarked in "Down North," wanted "to get in behind the curtain," but chose not to lift the veil on her own life. Ironically, despite Ellis's wide

# ANNOUNCING

## Miriam Green Ellis
### IN A LECTURE
### ON HER
### UNIQUE TRIP TO

# The Land *of the* Midnight Sun

CANADA'S NORTHLAND, with its mysterious lure, its wonderful scenery and its potential resources, is the last of the unknown lands. The lecturer takes her audience down the MacKenzie River to the very delta where it empties itself into the Arctic Ocean. Along the route one sees the various tribes of Indians and last of all the Eskimo, who live in and around the MacKenzie Delta.

MRS. ELLIS is a well-known newspaper woman of Edmonton, Alberta, and so was naturally adapted to catch the features of the trip, which she took last year. As vice-president of the Canadian Women's Press Club, she became well known to the women of her craft throughout Canada, and her stories of the North have appeared in newspapers across the Dominion, and in various magazines, English and American.

*Nearly one hundred beautiful slides illustrate this unusual story of far away lands and people.*

Brochure for MGE's *"Land of the Midnight Sun"* lecture. [BPSC]

## From the Press

Not in months has a Toronto Woman's Club provided such a fairy tale evening as that of the University Women's Club last night. Dark went the lights and for almost two hours they sat entranced as they took a magic journey to Canada's Land of the midnight sun. . . . . . Mrs. Ellis used her eyes well and her delicious sense of humor and keen love of real human beings made her lecture a joy.
—*Toronto Telegram*

Twenty-five hundred miles up to the MacKenzie River and twenty-five hundred miles back. The end of the journey brought Mrs. Ellis to the little Eskimo village of Aklavik, half way up the delta where the river empties itself into the Arctic Ocean. —*Toronto Star*

To hear Mrs. Ellis is to more fully realize the almost incomprehensible size of Canada and the limitless possibilities of her agriculture, mineral and forest wealth.
—*Hamilton Spectator*

If she ever has the opportunity to take a trip to the North Pole, Mrs. Ellis says she expects to see a wild rose growing alongside the pole. —*Edmonton Journal*

This courageous newspaper woman of the West told an entrancing story of her trip down the MacKenzie River last summer, a trip which lasted two months, and revealed much of almost unknown areas of the Dominion.
—*Toronto Globe*

# "The Land of the Midnight Sun"

recognition—a farmer at Fort Smith recognizes her from the Edmonton Exhibition and a Californian student at the Banff School remembers her from the International Stock Show at Chicago thirteen years earlier—she remains a figure of considerable secretiveness.

Although the now unfashionable divide between public and private lives might seem off-putting and curious, however much it enables a certain resourcefulness in seeing the woman in her work, such reticence about one's private or domestic existence actually characterized several of MGE's press women predecessors and contemporaries. As Barbara Freeman concludes in her biography of Kathleen Blake Coleman, the inaugural CWPC president who was arguably best known for her chatty "Woman's Kingdom" page of the *Daily Mail* from the 1890s and beyond, Kit was a distant and enigmatic figure: "With just about every private and public domestic issue she touched upon, she played the expert/mother role but rarely became involved herself" (Freeman, *Kit's Kingdom* 169). Twenty years after Coleman's death, an unsigned tribute in the Hamilton *Herald* attested, "Singularly close to her large public, Kit was yet private and withdrawn. She hated publicity as to her own affairs" (172). In the praise Carlotta Hacker quotes from the *Calgary Albertan*, crop forecast expert E. Cora Hind was "bold enough to shoulder her way into the ranks of men": she "got along extremely well with men,…concentrating on the job in hand" (62, 50). According to Grant Dexter, *Free Press* correspondent in Ottawa for over twenty years, "Men of all ranks trusted [Cora] implicitly. She went to their homes, got to know their wives and families. She heard the departmental gossip; became familiar with the clashes of temperament, the rivalries, the weaknesses, the hopes and disappointments" (qtd. in Haig 59). Though Hind expressed a love of cooking and knitting, she left no record of her own private, emotional, intimate connections. And so, if MGE belongs to a reticent past sorority, how do I understand her publicness and trace a path through her archive?

The more I considered the feasibility of resurrecting a figure about whom so little has been written (with the exception of excerpts from the

1922 diary introduced by Lisa LaFramboise, and slight mention in studies by Grant MacEwan, Kay Rex, and Marjory Lang) and about whom so many unanswered or unanswerable questions persist, the less comfortable I became with the role of revisionist or discoverer. On the contrary, it seems important to let Ellis's work speak for her in establishing a place in literary studies for the press woman. She is not a mere hack, bereft of the trimmings of non-linear narration, extended metaphorical allusions, or récherché diction, but rather emerges as an individualistic communicator, able to capture and hold attention, tell a story, sketch distinctive characters, and stir emotions. To illustrate her range and provide such a speaking platform, this collection includes both published and previously unpublished material. After a necessarily brief biographical sketch, I plan to get in behind the curtain of Ellis's once widely circulated copy to concentrate on the hidden art of her unpublished work: "Down North" and the two short stories, "Alone" and "A War Bride's Return." This introduction to Ellis's voice serves as the prelude to samples from her "aggie" beat along with articles championing women and the West. In all selections it is revealing as well to listen for the harmonies and dissonances with women writers and travellers of her time.

> On winter nights we gathered round a cherry table and read. Grandfather had made that cherry table himself. There was a big kerosene lamp, and I was no sooner engrossed in Bleak House, or whatever I happened to be reading at the time, than I was sent down to the cellar for a dish of apples, and they had to be shined before they were brought in, too.
>
> (ELLIS, "Western Homes I Have Seen," February 1943)

✺ Miriam Green was born in Richville, New York, of Canadian parents who returned to Canada and the paternal farmstead near Athens, Ontario, where this only child went to elementary school. Monitored by a double set of adult instructors, parents and grandparents, Miriam's childhood appears to have been exacting: the freedom of the farm also involved an obedient performance of chores and an acknowledgement of pioneer ingenuity. She later attended Bishop Strachan School in Toronto and graduated from the Toronto Conservatory of Music with the ATCM (Associate of the Toronto Conservatory of Music).

The Green family's move to Edmonton in 1904 was followed by her marriage to George Edward Ellis in All Saints Anglican in June 1905. A graduate of Athens High School and Queen's University, George Ellis was appointed by Minister of Education Alexander C. Rutherford in March 1906 as "Inspector of Schools for the Province of Alberta, at a salary of $1700 per annum" (Order in Council). The newlyweds were clearly relatively comfortable and compatible (she was 26; he was 31) from the outset. In addition to their shared background in small-town eastern Ontario (Ellisville, his birthplace, was a hamlet close to Athens), Miriam and George likely agreed on many of the observations and recommendations in George Ellis's annual reports about the state of schools in the Edmonton area. Although an admittedly indirect perspective on Miriam, about whose activities at the time little is known, the more available views of George indicate some of the possible topics of conversation for this couple. In 1906, he was recommending bonuses for teachers in outlying districts and suggesting that "the secret of success...lies in keeping these schools open the full year; otherwise the children soon forget what they have learned" (Ellis 53). He supported the building of "stables to accommodate the horses driven or ridden by the pupils," "bored wells" to provide good water, "the beautification of the school grounds or buildings," the provision of "a copy of the curriculum" for each teacher, and the holding of conventions "occasionally for a day, say, in the outlying parts of the inspectorate whence teachers seldom get to the central convention" (54, 55). Inspector Ellis was especially concerned about teaching based on and reflecting surrounding conditions, lamenting that "many teachers [of Nature Study] are always wanting to

*Prince Albert High School Girls' Hockey Team.* [Prince Albert Historical Museum]

teach a book instead of nature itself" (54). However, he reserved the least pessimistic forecast for "the establishment of a University in the near future," as a result of which "there will be no need for anyone to hesitate coming to this country, for we will then have all the educational facilities that even a connoisseur could wish for, as well as a land teeming with wealth for the agriculturalist and the manufacturer" (55). Seated next to Minister Rutherford, he attended the inaugural University of Alberta convocation in the Strathcona Oddfellows' Hall in 1908, where he heard President Henry Marshall Tory call for "the uplifting of the whole people," as "our art, our science, our literature, our history, our institutions of government, our religious life, all are so interwoven with the fibre of our own life that in the rounding out of a full-orbed manhood none of these can be neglected" (Tory 15–16). George Ellis's own words, however, were not as hortatory or celebratory. With an increasingly critical tone, his reports continued to point to neglect, noting, in his 1907 report, "the irregularity of attendance" (Ellis 39), insisting that "even a well-equipped school which is filthy should not get the inspection grant," and in 1908 judging that the work of "'permit' teachers" with "little or no training" was "necessarily defective" (Ellis 41). Ellis resigned his position in 1909 to pursue graduate work, accompanied by Miriam, likely in Chicago.

Miriam next appears in the archival record coaching hockey in Prince Albert, Saskatchewan. In 1912, she started and managed the girls' hockey team of the Prince Albert Collegiate Institute, where George was principal. Ladies' hockey was very popular in Saskatchewan, with Regina boasting its first ladies' team as early as 1896; the Prince Albert Tumblers were in action in 1907 (Zeman 252–53). Based on reports in the *Prince Albert Daily Herald*, Miriam also acquired a considerable reputation as a curler. She began writing for this local paper, though the lack of bylines makes her contributions impossible to identify. Equally difficult to trace is the fault line in the marriage.

The outbreak of war in August 1914 affected the couple, as it did millions of others. It drew attention to the importance of the field that was to become Miriam's livelihood and the suffragist principles that propelled farm organizations. With grain and livestock production of key importance, the war "greatly enhanced the value of the Canadian grain belt in international economy" (Wood 290), prompting generous responses in manpower and farm yields from the West. While "for the most part uncomplainingly" accepting conscription, Manitoba grain growers pledged the returns of one acre of grain "to the needs of the

Empire"; the Saskatchewan Co-operative Elevator Company agreed to mill a "patriotic acre," and the Alberta Grain Growers contributed products along with "twelve thousand dollars to various funds in 1916" (290–91). War conditions also hastened the arrival of the enfranchisement of women, granted in all three Prairie provinces in 1916, largely through the initiatives of farm women. Separate organizations of farm women were formed, first in Saskatchewan in 1914, and then by the United Farm Women of Alberta in 1915 and the Manitoba Farm Women in 1916, all supporting public health and education in rural communities, the need for obstetrical nurses, and the temperance cause. The war "changed the status of women in journalism," too, bringing them new opportunities and professional responsibilities ushering in "an era in which the CWPC's power and prestige steadily advanced" (Oliver 12).

On February 18, 1915, George enlisted as a major in the 53rd Battalion of the Canadian Expeditionary Force; his Attestation Paper lists Miriam as his wife. According to his personnel record, he was "struck off the strength of the Canadian Expeditionary Force with effect from 28th August 1916," and "dismissed for misconduct" ("Record" 166). "Misconduct" is a curiously unexplained term; based on his inspector's reports, speculations might include insubordination or disobedience. He returned to Eastern Ontario, to the Leeds County area of his birth. From 1922 to 1938, he taught mathematics and geography at Lisgar Collegiate Institute in Ottawa, where he was a member of the Lisgar Curling Team (city and district champions), advisory business manager for the student yearbook *Vox Lycei*, and honorary president of the Skiing Club and the Glee Club. Meanwhile, Miriam lived in Edmonton and, later, Winnipeg. No record of a divorce exists.

Miriam's independent career is somewhat easier to chart. For the Toronto-based monthly *Woman's Century*, she reported on the 1915 Regina meeting of the Women Grain Growers, a "splendid organization, which stands above all for cooperation," and their mounting campaign for suffrage ("Women Grain Growers" 431). For a short time she was a

"Finnigan, Jr. and 'The Toad.'" [BPSC]

staffer at the *Regina Leader-Post* before joining Frank Oliver's *Edmonton Bulletin*, reporting on the legislature, various churches, sports, and—what became her primary beat—agriculture.

Early Alberta newspapers, like those in other prairie provinces, "showed an active interest in agriculture," ensuring it "occupied a fair amount of space" (Rasmussen 231). With a morning edition suitable for "the Canadian business man" and an evening edition for "the Canadian working man," as part of a paper "the farmer reads semi-weekly," the *Edmonton Bulletin* advertised itself as "the only 24-hour Canadian News Service west of Winnipeg" (13). Miriam's year as Edmonton president of the CWPC, characterized not only by her preparation of "Bohemian refreshments" for the "soiree[s]" ("John Hunt Is Honor Guest") but also by an engagement with a larger community, was certainly covered in the *Bulletin*. Speakers and invited guests for the year included Father Drummond of the Jesuit College, legendary Winnipeg press woman

MGE at "Toad Hall," also known as "Limberlost," north of Prince Albert, Saskatchewan. [BPSC]

E. Cora Hind (whom Ellis introduced as doing "the work of three men for half a man's salary" ["Press Club Entertains" n. pag.]), dean of agriculture E.A. Howes, acting president of the University of Alberta William Kerr, aesthetic dancer Ruth St. Denis, Premier Charles Stewart, and mountaineer Mary Jobe.

Newspaper articles, correspondence, and typescripts provide some details, but curious gaps or omissions, her distinctive leitmotif, remain. Reporting on all sorts of conventions and often appearing in breeches, Miriam always signed her writing Miriam Green Ellis, yet no obituary or memoir of Miriam mentions George or the childless marriage. In speaking to the University Women's Club in Saskatoon in 1945, she borrowed a description from her "favorite book, *Winnie the Pooh*" to compare herself to Rabbit's relations: "I am the last little relation following the procession and sometimes getting lost" ("Watching Other People Farm"). Whether this is an ironic retrospective or tongue-in-cheek candour from a recognizable though discreet personality, who never *seemed* lost, is arguable. Her labels "The Toad," for herself pictured at the wheel of her car, and "Toad Hall," for her cabin north of Prince Albert, suggest the equally strong influence of Kenneth Grahame's flamboyant and impulsive trouble-maker.

> *Everyone interested in trip of far North. Just one regret—it is over, instead of just beginning.*
>
> (ELLIS, Diary 174; 28 July 1922)

※ The major adventure that helped to shape MGE's career was the trip to Aklavik. At the opening of the typescript "Down North," she admits to the tempting lure of a pamphlet about a trip to "the land of the midnight sun" on Premier Greenfield's desk in early spring 1922. Likely a feature in the *Edmonton Bulletin* had caught her attention earlier; in fact, from March to June, the paper ran pieces of steadily mounting and excited information about the Athabasca route north. The article on "Fast Arctic Steamer Service Via Waterways" announced the Alberta and Arctic Transportation Company's plan to provide "a new chapter in the history of the north" with "greatly improved and faster service" on a route that is "fully 350 miles shorter than that via Peace river" (2). The paper promised that "just as soon as the ice goes out on the Great Slave" their steamer would "make a run to Fort McPherson and Clavic [*sic*] on the delta of the Mackenzie, taking freight and passengers to all posts en route,…with the added feature of a good railroad service to the Clearwater at Waterways" (2), and in conjunction with the Alberta and Great Waterways Railway would load passengers from Waterways. The "innovation" at Fort Smith was a "high-powered Winston passenger auto" to meet the steamer from Waterways, covering a distance of sixteen miles in three-quarters of an hour. Between Waterways and Fort Fitzgerald, the ninety-six-foot barge *Slave River* under Captain Con Myers operated on the Athabasca River, while the steamer *Distributor*, piloted by Captain J.P. Bucey, "rated as one of the best 'white water' captains on Canada's inland waters," with years of experience on Hudson's Bay Company steamers on the Skeena River in British Columbia, would ply the Mackenzie River north of Fort Smith. Here was an itinerary designed to attract the venturesome contemporary explorer: "Should the gold find on the Nahanni River develop into anything large, the Alberta and Arctic line will operate a regular service for freight and passengers between Fort Simpson and the mouth of the Nahanni." By April 10, the paper mentioned "the warehouse site on the Waterways river front [being] cleared of timber" and the observation that "everyone appeared to be full of life and looking forward to a busy year" ("River Navigation"). By April 20 topographical survey engineers were "in the field so that when 'something happens' there will be no confusion, and the gold prospectors, oil drillers, and others will be certain of correct map information about the true location of their claims"; as the report boasted in conclusion, "Big things are looked for in the north in the near future, and it is apparent that the government is of the same opinion" ("Wireless Equipped Surveyors"). Along with regular notices of the ice breaking up and channels opening on Lake Athabasca, and reports of "heavy" passenger lists for the regular Monday departures ("Another Heavy Passenger List"), the *Bulletin* carried information about the work of surveyor Guy Houghton Blanchet, whom Miriam mentions in her account of June 24 in "Down North"; he provided "the first authentic maps of the Slave and Athabasca rivers and Great Slave Lake,...[to be] hung in the chart rooms of various vessels of the Alberta and Arctic Transportation Company" ("New River and Lake Maps"). For the day of Miriam's departure, June 19, the news was also positive: "Northern River Steamers Are Making Fast Time Due to Good Stage of Water." Fares were not mentioned, but the cost must have been manageable for an independent woman journalist who had been earning a salary for over three years.

Moreover, Ellis did not travel alone; she was one of at least fourteen passengers, including her uncle and aunt from Pennsylvania, John and Ethel Carley (who may have shared some of the fare). Although in "Down North" Miriam vowed to keep "a regular diary of this trip," she actually produced three distinct texts: the promised diary, 249 small pages (3.5" x 6") of mainly typed daily diary entries, which are really shorthand notes to self, an index of names, and demographic information relating to the 1922 journey; the typescript travelogue "Down North" published for the first time in this collection; and a series of newspaper articles based on segments of the trip. Together they testify to Ellis's purposiveness, curiosity, and determination. Uncle John handily devised "a typewriter table that is as neat as a pocket in a shirt—just the very thing," while Aunt Ethel proofread Miriam's "Eskimo stories" (Ellis, Diary 22, 121; 24 June). As a diarist and a traveller meeting different adventures each day, Ellis faced the time-consuming task of converting her diary entries into fuller notes. On July 15 she conceded, "worked on my notes for some time during the day. Wish I had done them as I was going along, instead of writing them in diary form, but I did not know till I had them

*Lacombe airstrip. Left to right: "Wop" May, MGE, unidentified man. Wilfrid Reid "Wop" May, World War I flying ace and holder of the Distinguished Flying Cross, started Canada's first flying club, the Edmonton and Northern Alberta Aero Club.* [BPSC]

what I wanted to write about" (121). On eventful days she had to work at "trying to get up the courage to start some writing" (165; 23 July). A few personal connections do not find their way into "Down North"; only in the diary do we discover that Mrs. McClung sent her a telegram on the second day (7; 20 June), that "the sweet peas Nellie brought to the station" (8; 20 June) are still doing nicely in the coffee can, and that "Wop" (World War I flying ace Wilfrid Reid) May met her "at the station" on her return (174; 28 July). From this trio of texts, I have decided to reproduce "Down North" because it seems to me the most accessible and integrated writing about the journey, the product of reflection, amplifying the blueprint of the daily jottings but not carving up the text into 1,000-word copy.

As a non-fictional travel narrative, "Down North" conforms to expectations of joining "pleasure with instruction" and using such autobiographical information as it discloses to order descriptions, interject entertainment, and establish "the traveler's character as an accurate, truthful, and perceptive observer" (Batten 8, 116). It succeeds as both a personal account and information-filled reportage. Ellis's journey from the metropole to the periphery, to borrow Mary Louise Pratt's terminology, is actually very attentive to "the reverse dynamic" (4), that is, to the power of the rural conveyed back to the urban. In "Down North," Ellis emerges for me not as "the 'seeing [wo]man,'" Pratt's "admittedly unfriendly label for the white...subject...whose imperial eyes passively look out and possess" (9), but rather as an engaged, curious citizen, who enacts the drama of departure and return, without overlooking experiences of frustration and disjunction.

Having failed to convince editor Frank Oliver of readers' interest in reports of such a trip, with typical self-possession Ellis granted herself a leave of absence. She travelled by train to Waterways, the terminus of the Alberta and Great Waterways Railway, south of Fort McMurray, and then by river steamer down the Athabasca, driving around the rapids by car at Smith Portage, and proceeding by steamer north on the Mackenzie River to Aklavik. "Down North" is full of candid portraits, textual and photographic, of fellow passengers. With a hint of disbelief, Ellis describes Gladys Patterson, "a girl from Yorkshire, England, going down to marry a chap at Norman" whom "she has not seen...since the war and of course has not heard from him since last Fall some time, but she does not seem to have any doubts in the matter." At the Edmonton train station she meets Bishop Grouard, the Oblate missionary who oversaw the immense vicariate of Athabasca–Mackenzie and brought the first printing press to Athabasca Country: "He has been in the north for half a century and knows every white man and Indian right down to the Arctic....He is well over eighty now but still carries on as active head of his big diocese." Although not photographed, botany professor Roland Holroyd from Pennsylvania State University is initially an instructive source—"it will be interesting getting some first-hand information about the plants and flowers"—but soon proves a disappointment when he refuses or is unable to identify any vegetation. Her frustration with this reclusive passenger is evident when she deems his attempted moustache "a rather anaemic affair" and observes, "After weeks of sober living he has suddenly given way to smoking cigarettes, but he does it very genteelly, using a six-inch amber holder. We have warned him to be careful, as dear knows what would grow there if the wooly down were burned off. Poplar comes where spruce has been burned off, we tell him; maybe feather follows down." Wishing that "our fat friend of the Botany department would part with some of the secrets of his profession," she resorts to William McCalla's *Wild Flowers of Western Canada* (1920) as a more reliable guide. By July 2, as the diary informs us, she is referring to the non-compliant botanist as "Hemroid" (66). Ellis's characterization of her fellow travellers could be tart.

When her sympathies are engaged, however, Ellis's writing can convey an awareness of ethical dilemmas and well-cultivated advocacy. At Fort McPherson the young prisoner Alikomiak, to be tried and eventually hanged for four murders, claims her attention: "The lad looks about sixteen but they say he is nineteen. He says that he did not mean to kill Doak but just shot to wound him and force retaliation." On the return journey up south on the Mackenzie, an Inuit woman named Laura, who was being forced to Edmonton to appear before Justice Murphy and possibly confined as insane for having beaten her husband, claims Ellis's sympathy: "I suggested that perhaps the husband needed beating up," she observes. Tints of admiration colour her portrait of Laura: "All day she sits or stands out on the side deck, rolling cigarettes and smoking. When she gets tired standing, she sits flat down on the floor with her legs straight out in front like a baby. That would be a new one to add to the 'daily dozen' and warranted to strengthen the back." Ellis is happy to report parenthetically that Laura was "found mentally all right and sent back, her worst fault seeming to be that she was an inveterate smoker and also drank when the opportunity offered." Ellis encounters and relates tales of survival, like the Pittsburgh native who suffered gangrene, eventually amputated his own toes with a jackknife, and survived alone for over four months with only twenty-five pounds of flour, which he mixed with snow; the man now does not want to leave the North.

Thanks to Ellis's keen eye, "Down North" is equally adept at documenting topographical conditions. Her text has prescient observations on the tar sands' "regular mountains of asphalt," used at the time for superior road surfaces, predicting that one day they would "mean millions of dollars to the country"; despite the opinion of the "cracker-box orators" on board, "squelching one's enthusiasms" that "it was 'just some fool scratching round in the dirt,'" Ellis maintains her "visions of another Klondyke." She documents Native women's importance in preparing hides, befriends Native families, notes features of dress, childcare, and diet, and records Native delight in taking pictures of the white visitors. As well as entering mission schools and churches, and investigating operating room procedures such as the one at Fort Simpson, she relays endearing exuberance and vulnerability, piloting the boat for thirty miles beyond Fort Chipewyan and taking a daily swim in the Mackenzie, admitting to anxiety about mounting her first horse—"I cannot understand why they put the stirrups up so high"—and revealing the perils of a tenderfoot who suffers blisters on a thirty-seven-mile ride inland to Salt Springs.

A strong-willed personality suffuses every page of "Down North." From the outset, Ellis chafes at her editor's apparent lack of interest in her proposed trip to the North Pole, as the opening episode in early spring illustrates:

> *One day I sat in the Premier's office trying to get a "scoop" on the government policy in connection with the administration of the liquor laws, when I noticed on his desk a pamphlet from a transportation company, on which were the words "To the land of the midnight sun." From where I sat in that big blue room, I could see*

*the North Saskatchewan River, just then throwing off its winter bondage and shoving the great cakes of ice ignominiously on the shore to rot. The trees were showing life and the grass along the banks was getting green. It was the time the woods sent out their loudest call, and I lost all interest in the burning question of liquor laws.*

She also strikes a blow for women in breeches, but not without a shame-faced admission. Having "put on [her] knickers and big boots...with a defiant air," Ellis is "anxious to see what was behind that screen of trees,...to penetrate the leafy foliage." One time only does she accede to the captain's directive "that he could not think of allowing me to leave the boat," but she quickly vows "that it won't happen again." Her oath, along with the polemical comment that such a concession indicates "why women do not deserve equal rights," cements her conviction: "That man is about half as big as I am and I should just have taken him by the collar and thrown him overboard." Her trips ashore have a less pugnacious tone, showing an observant naturalist at work. The discovery of wild orchids, "the most exquisite things I ever saw," reminds her of "fairies' graves." Blue-eyed grass, lupines, tea berries, wild strawberries, and the omnipresent pink, rose, and purple drooping blossoms of the *Hedysarum mackenzii* merit detailed description. So do the "never-ending" sunsets, "liquid light lying on the water," "a bright rich amber, shading to yellow gold." The prospect of a return journey revisiting narrower and shallower rivers, unlike the majesty of the Mackenzie, occasions sadness: "it was like the slow unfurling of a great banner, and now we are rolling it up again till it will be just an uninteresting stick." "Sick of being rushed," Ellis rejoices in the reprieve of having missed the boat, meaning that their return is delayed for a few days.

"Down North, 1922," likely composed in the fall of that year and mined successively thereafter for newspaper articles and magic lantern lectures, is a significant and singular contribution to women's travel accounts dealing with Western Canada and the Arctic. Its distinctive immediacy emerging from Ellis's journalism experience, "Down North" also stands apart from the published records of earlier and contemporary women recreational adventurers or professional travel writers, who were supported by family wealth, industrial sponsors, or employed, attending husbands. The personal voice, occasional humiliation, and encounter with a wide social spectrum separate Ellis's work from the amateur Victorian travelogues of the wives of serving or future Canadian governors general detailing their cross-country visits with the elite of the Dominion, as in the Marchioness of Dufferin and Ava's *My Canadian Journal, 1872-78, Extracts from My Letters Home* (1891) and the Marchioness of Aberdeen's *Through Canada with a Kodak* (1893). Though incomplete (or at least un-concluded), Ellis's account is fuller than the report of the American Elizabeth Taylor, a self-taught botanist and collector for museums who travelled down the Mackenzie in 1892 with the permission of the governor of the Hudson's Bay Company, and published brief essays two and five years later in *Outing* and *Travel*. In addition to Taylor's timidity about Indian fellow travellers, "a rough wild set" about whom she registers feeling "a little troubled in having [her] tent pitched so near" (Taylor, "Lady's Journey" 51), she fulfills the requirement of the travelling lady in recommending such "useful" articles as a checked skirt, blouse, felt hat, silk handkerchiefs, moosehide gloves, and "black cashmere stockings" (Taylor, "Articles" 60). Ellis's individual experience and first-person voice distinguish her work from the stereotypes and condescending tone of the essays and stories of Quebec-born Harriet Campbell, Lady Jephson's *A Canadian Scrapbook* (1897) and the fictional first-person narration of Bess Le Ford in Norfolk-born Frances Herring's portraits of the British Columbia interior, *Canadian Camp Life* (1900). Later records of travel show considerably less travail than Ellis's account. Jean Walker Godsell's description of her 1920 honeymoon trip north as a Hudson's Bay Company factor's wife, in *I Was No Lady* (1959), sketches "God's Wide Open Spaces where men were men and where

*Miss Christina Gordon, near Fort McMurray.* [BPSC]

white women were placed on pedestals since they were few in number and far between" (Godsell 2). Clara (Roger) Vyvyan's 1926 journey by steamer, motor boat, and canoe to Alaska, published thirty-five years later as *Arctic Adventure* (1961), was a carefully planned and guided trip that reflects the aspirations of a well-to-do, middle-aged Englishwoman and her female artist-companion, who read Shakespeare to one another en route.

The journey most comparable to Ellis's is Agnes Deans Cameron's arrival at Fort Rae in 1908, recounted in *The New North* (1909), a text that Ellis's informal history of the CWPC reveals she knew. "That book came back at me like a boomerang," Ellis revealed to an Edmonton audience: "When I went down the Mackenzie in 1922, the natives clammed up on me when I said I wanted to write about them. Seems Cameron had borrowed precious photographs and failed to return them, as promised" (*Pathfinders* 8). Ellis was clearly familiar with the earlier account while she was travelling. Fourteen years after Cameron, she visits one

Advertisement for Agnes Deans Cameron's lectures. [Provincial Archives of Alberta PA 1974 0056/5]

of the residents of Fort McMurray mentioned extensively in *The New North*, Christina Gordon. On July 25 Miriam's diary relates a meeting with this Scottish free trader who gives her visitor "lettuce out of a splendid garden" (169). Changes in situation and attitude separate the two accounts. In 1908 Cameron was proud to introduce the fur trader as "operating in opposition to the great and only Hudson's Bay Company" (84), while by the time of her visit Ellis notes that "the H.B. store has taken over" Gordon's role as postmistress. Admiring Gordon's concern for local bachelors pining for mail, Ellis's diary relates matter-of-factly the practical use to which this sensible and now-aging Scot puts the complementary copies of *The New North*: "She is sort of washed out but was very interested in the fact that Miss Cameron had put her in her book and had lectured about her in London. She had been sent many books from the publishers and when she had the post office had given these to the bachelors who had come for mail and were going away disappointed because none had come" (July 25; 169). Cameron, in contrast, had made Miss Gordon's smiling and helpful disposition the pretext for a moral disquisition: "Our happiness consists not in our havings but in our attitude of mind. The world is divided sharply into two classes. The classes are not the white and the black, the good and the bad, the sheep and the goats, as the orthodox would have us believe. We are all good *and* bad, not black or white, but varying shades of grey. Neither are we sheep or goats, but moral alpacas, all of us—something between a sheep and a goat" (85).

Aside from competing claims about being the first to visit Salt Springs, the most arresting distinctions between these two accounts are their scope and tone. With each of its twenty-four chapters headed by a literary or biblical epigraph, *The New North* is a precisely worded, photo-illustrated narrative of close to 400 pages, tessellated with passages of strenuous didacticism, recounting the journey of Cameron and her niece, an accommodating typist, from Chicago to the North, via stagecoach, scow, steamer, and paddle-wheeler, with a return terminus in Winnipeg. The text directly links "a photographic first to a technology of textual representation—the typewriter" (Roy, *Maps* 212). Not all the photographs were taken by Cameron or Jessie Cameron Brown (her niece and travelling companion), but it is quite possible, as Wendy Roy suggests, "that Underwood either donated the typewriter or helped to fund the trip and was rewarded by having its corporate name prominently displayed" ("Primacy" 73). Although she served as vice-president of the CWPC, Cameron (1863–1912) was not officially a press woman; rather, as a teacher for twenty-five years and the first woman high school principal in Victoria, she had run afoul of the school board trustees and been dismissed. Journalism in Chicago and the trip north, along with its resultant lectures in Canada and the United States, and talks in Britain promoting immigration, provided her livelihood before her untimely death. In the opinion of Anglican missionary Archdeacon Charles Whittaker, *The New North* was "an intricate compound of fact and fiction" (MacLaren and LaFramboise xxix). Ellis's *Down North*, by contrast, was a journalist's account of lived experience over the five weeks of a personally funded journey.

Instead of splitting hairs over truth claims separating the journalist and the educator, a more revealing comparison involves the tone of both accounts. Acutely conscious of her role as instructive authority over curious observer, Cameron is quick to impart anthropological lessons: "Among Mackenzie tribes no Yellow-Knife, Dog-Rib, or Slavi starved while another had meat, no thievish hand despoiled the cache of another. A man's word was his bond, and a promise was kept to the death. Not all the real things of life are taught to the Cree by the Christian. Courage is better than culture, playing the game of more importance than the surface niceties of civilisation, to be a man now of more moment than to hope to be an angel hereafter" (199). Ellis's writing conveys her awe and solemnity in encountering "the great walls of patterned rock which the river forces with a gliding stealth" (91). A sense of reverence in the presence of the supreme authority of the "perpendicular…walls of a great corridor" (91) imparts an understanding of human smallness in the midst of this immensity.

In contrast to Ellis's awestruck directness in the vision of sunset at the Ramparts, the entrance to Fort Good Hope provokes Romantic effusion from Cameron, in which duelling emphases on aloneness and impressive pronouncement frame the scene: "Awed and uplifted, our one wish is to be alone; the vision that is ours for one hour of this Arctic night repays the whole summer's travel. The setting of the picture is that ineffable light, clear yet mellow, which without dawn and without twilight rises from the flowing river to starless heavens, and envelopes the earth as with a garment—the light that never was on sea or land. We could not have chosen a more impressive hour in which to pass the portal into the Arctic World" (206). While the differences in length and aim between a typescript and a published volume might challenge the feasibility of this comparison, what emerges is the palpable contrast in tone between Cameron and Ellis. Although she enjoys the rarity of typing without light well past midnight, Ellis finds herself more often silenced by the beauty around her.

The kinds of promotional tours resulting from both trips also underscore the contrasts. For paying audiences in the thousands across Canada and in Illinois and Minnesota, Cameron organized five detailed lectures with snappy titles, under the general title "Beyond the Beckoning Border," all extracted from her recently released book. Less lavish, Ellis's lectures, entitled "The Land of the Midnight Sun," were "a magic journey"; as the *Toronto Telegram* reported, "she used her eyes well, and her delicious sense of humour and keen love of real human beings made her lecture a joy" ("Cornelia"). Though Cameron and Ellis were both observant travellers, alert to the commercial potential of the stories of their journeys, their accounts communicate vastly different personalities. Cameron is the well-read teacher, presumably accustomed to lecturing, while Ellis is the wide-eyed but canny newspaper woman, aware of the value of personal reflection and human interest.

❋ Ellis's two short stories, another unique offshoot of the journey north, have no parallel in the subsequent work of other women travellers. Both set in Alberta and displaying her first-hand knowledge of the locale, they are not light-hearted or breezily carefree, but freighted with moral dilemmas and populated with disconcerting personalities. These narratives probe Native–non-Native relations with a remarkable willingness to see and articulate both sides of the emotionally fraught issues of identity and belonging. The stories would likely face a real battle for acceptance by today's fiction editors; but it is precisely this fact and the lens Ellis affords on early twentieth-century attitudes that make the stories so valuable and revealing.

A tautly narrated exploration of dissociation, "Alone" follows the thoughts and escape routes of a hunted man wanted for murder ten years earlier. Moving from the Crowsnest Pass to the Nahanni River in the Northwest Territories, the story highlights the man's terror of uncertainty, his realization of betrayal from so many others, and the surprising sympathy his death evokes in the Native girl he has abducted.

An anecdote recorded in Ellis's unpaginated appendix to her diary reveals both the germ of "Alone" and the significant changes she introduced:

> *Poole Field told me of a man whose well-to-do relatives live down near Yorkton. But he started West some years ago, and while tending bar down in the Crowsnest got into trouble and killed a man. It seems that an old man came in and ordered up drinks for the crowd and then said he had no money to pay. The bar keeper ordered him to pay and he said he would not and the other picked an empty bottle out from under the bar and hit him over the head. As it happened, it killed the man. So without waiting to see what happened, he lit out and has just been travelling in the wilds ever since.*

A man named Wilson met up with him once and they travelled together for some time, till they found they were not trusting each other and that both were sleeping with their guns under their pillows and decided to separate. He found gold, had $31,000 one time which he cached. Came into a post now and again to sell his furs but usually steered clear of the police. While travelling in the Dawson whenever they came to a telegraph station, he always made an excuse to meet up with his partner at night somewhere.

One day he stole an Indian girl as she was out with some other girls getting fresh spruce for the camp. She got separated from the others a little and was up on a bough pulling off twigs, when a hand was closed over her mouth and her head thrown back. She was so frightened she fainted and when she came to, she saw this man with a red beard but "white eyes" meaning white man's eyes (blue) bending over her and putting water on her face. He had carried her some distance away from her camp. She was fearfully scared and started to cry, but thought that if she cried it might make him angry and he would kill her. He kept saying something to her, which she could not understand, for she had never been in to a post and never heard any English.

She decided to pretend to be satisfied, and wait her chance. He carried her some distance through the bush and finally laid her down on some boughs. She put her handkerchief over her face and pretended to go to sleep. He petted her some more, had her hair down and patted her face and her arms. Finally when he thought she was asleep, he went down to the river and started to chop trees into the river. She knew indications well enough to know he was building a raft, so she waited until he was well into the job, then ran for the shore. It was a steep outbank and she just slid with all speed, down the bank and into the river, floating downstream till she came to a little island. She swam in behind the island and finally it was suffi-

*ciently shallow so she could land. She hid there till dark, then swam across to the main shore and started toward where her people were. She used all her arts to cover her tracks and finally arrived at where the camp had been, only to find it had moved. However, she was able to follow them up, and got back to her mother five days from the day she had been stolen. Under various names he continued to wander, but no trace has been seen of him for about ten years now.*

(Diary, Appendix)

In the story, through her probing depiction of solitariness and the delusions it induces, Ellis manages to make Carson and the unnamed girl he abducts into figures of sympathy. For the man on the run, fear is an embodied presence: "fear, ingrowing and unceasing, gripped him in its coils, like the devilfish, its victim. As time passed, its clutches grew stronger and stronger, till he wondered how much longer he could withstand the vicious monster."

The domestic and emotional details Ellis introduces to her portrait of this terrifying grip create a poignant sense of estrangement and abjection. With the passage of years, Carson's promise to his childhood sweetheart in England, "'Have your sheets and tablecloths all hemmed, and I will be back for you in two years,'" and his plans for a home "'with no rent to pay to greedy landlords'" fade to impossibility. As he risks journeys to Vancouver and San Francisco, his attempt to track down the double-crossing prospector, his supposed partner, shows the gullibility to which loneliness has reduced him and confirms that his stake and money are both lost. The shocking act of abduction testifies to Carson's desperation and muddled thinking: "he must have her for his own; if her people pursued, as they doubtless would, he would fly with her. He had eluded the police for ten years; he could elude them too."

However, "Alone" is not a rape narrative, nor does it illustrate what we would today call the Stockholm Syndrome. Ellis complicates both victim and perpetrator. Though terrified and unable to communicate, the girl realizes that "this man did not mean to hurt her." As the narrator explains for her, "an Indian maiden could read the tenderness in his eyes, yearning blue eyes so unlike those of the indifferent men of her tribe." Rather than shifting entirely to the perspective of this unnamed girl, the narrative succeeds in conveying the dispelling of her fear as she looks into his eyes and finds his gentleness so appealing in contrast to the young men she has known. This dynamic of melting anxiety contributes to the poignancy of the story, which itself indicates how creatively MGE complicated the account she'd heard on her trip down north. Despite escaping to the far side of the river, the girl screams, runs, and wades into the river to try to stop the raft on which Carson, who has abandoned hope, is careening toward the rapids. Managing to pull his lifeless body to shore, she cradles his head and lies down by his side, physically affirming their undeniable bond.

"A War Bride's Return" may have been prompted by Ellis's silent question about train passenger Gladys Patterson's blithe happiness en route to marry her long-separated fiancé. In her fiction, a sheltered English war bride arrives in Edmonton to start a romantic new life of genteel farming, only to be shocked and horrified by the realization that her beloved Canadian husband, whom she nursed back to health in France, is Native. The bride's immediate revulsion, her change from love to hate, and her refusal to listen to any explanation are strong indictments of prevailing prejudices. The contrast between Rose's professed love and readily "upturned lips" at the Edmonton train station when the couple is reunited and her silent petulance hours later casts doubt on all her declarations. The fiction is a fraught "contact zone," invoking "the space and time where subjects previously separated by geography and history are now co-present, the point at which their trajectories now intersect" (Pratt 8).

A roughly contemporary text involving relations between Native and non-Native in an Alberta setting is Georges Bugnet's (Henri Outremont) *Nipsya*, originally published in French in 1924 and translated in 1929.

Ellis may have known the English translation, but the substantial differences between the two narratives are telling. The point of view in the pastoral romance novel is that of the young Métis maid Nipsya (meaning "the willows"), whose affections sway from a passionate attraction to the radical warrior of her people and fascination with the white flirtatious Hudson's Bay Company factor to acceptance of a faithful, humble man who has been waiting quietly on the sidelines. The conflicts in Nipsya's mind unfold within the Métis community. By contrast, the contact zone of Native and white characters in Ellis's story, along with the omniscient narrator's description of the hero's attempts to understand and placate his bride's revulsion and hatred, supplies the central tension, enlarging the gap between the newlyweds and vocalizing the tacit white aversion that underpins and eventually splits their union.

The subtlety of Ellis's narrative inheres both in the warm relationship between the husband and his mother, who has educated him and kept the subsistence farm going in his absence, and the delayed disclosure about true parentage. John's reaction to the news of his birth parentage is not euphoric; rather, his ambivalent response allows the narrative to reflect back on itself, to reconsider John's upbringing, his attachment to his loyal dog, and his devoted "mother's" locket. Although Ellis works hard to air the views and desires of both sides of this doomed partnership, she spends most time dissecting John's interior dilemma, "torn between his duty to his mother and his love for his wife." Rose constantly questions, extracting protestations of fidelity and explanations about a beloved collie: "'You do love me, do you not?'" and "'Was there another girl, John?'" and "'Who is Flossie? You talked of her all night in your sleep.'" John is "afraid that Rose would not understand" and "shiver[ing] in dread at the outcome," but he makes the effort to see matters from Rose's uninformed and judgmental perspective: "He was not ashamed of it, but how would it seem to an English girl who knew nothing of Indians except such as she had read in Cooper's novels. But, he defended himself again, he could not tell her of himself without seeming to cast a slur on that mother, who had done so much for him." The unnamed mother reads Rose's language perfectly: "'No, she will never understand. I saw the look of horror in her eyes when she saw me.'" For her part Rose recoils in revulsion: "'Don't touch me. I hate you....I wish I might have died before this happened.'" Possibly echoing the situation of separation in her own life, Ellis's principals do not get together, yet the current of sexual tension carries through to the story's suggestive final line, its concluding emphasis on the English girl's safe entrepreneurialism exposing her hypocrisy. The former bride, who is using her stenographer's salary to start her own chicken business in Edmonton, decides "to invest in hens" but "she would not get a cock till later on."

Why would work so vivid in its emotional insights, so attuned to the cadences of speech, and so knowledgeably anchored in an Albertan or Arctic setting remain unpublished? Through all Ellis's work shines the writer's candour, admiration of resourcefulness, and fighting spirit. She was not an observer who kept her distance, but an understanding listener eager to support the underdog. The typescript of her journey to Aklavik provided material for over forty newspaper articles. Fiction, however, may have been a more tentative undertaking for Ellis; she may have been stung by rejection or may have chosen not to consult or prevail on her friend Nellie McClung for a literary contact.

> *I think farming, if successfully accomplished, takes more brains, more diversified ability than any other job I know. As a matter of fact, when the conventions do not get me down, I am rather glad that I am associated with two such important and useful industries as newspapers and farms.*
>   (ELLIS, "Watching Other People Farm," 15 January 1945)

✳ MGE's women friends and colleagues were acutely aware of the lures and liabilities for their sex of the country life ideology, especially prominent in agrarian periodicals at the beginning of the twentieth century. In her address to the annual convention of the Manitoba Home Economics Societies in 1913, reproduced in *The Nor'West Farmer*, Nellie McClung drew a forcefully Horatian distinction, verging on parody, between city and country living: "A lenient, unfaithful nurse," the city is "a waster of time, a destroyer of ambition, a creator of envy, but dazzling gay with tinsel and redolent with perfume, covering poverty with cheap lace and showy ribbons, a hole in her stocking but a rose in her hair!"; by contrast, the "stern nurse" of the country makes her child "work till every muscle aches [but] rewards him with a contented mind, an appetite that makes his life a joy, and though the midday sun may blaze on him with burning heat, at evening time comes a shade, and in the night comes rosy slumber" ("Why Boys and Girls Leave" 1105). Though the country life glimpsed in the agricultural press "was more an object to be sought, an ideal state that was merely possible" (Jones 103), there were real toads in these imaginary gardens and never-ending chores in pursuit of this possibility, particularly for farm women whose muscles also ached and whose slumbers were not always rosy. In *Janey Canuck in the West* (1910), Emily (Ferguson) Murphy summed up the demands on the western farm woman nicely as being "a combination of Mary, Martha, Magdalen, Bridget, and the Queen of Sheba" (74). Women's lot was severe, Nellie McClung recalled in the second volume of her autobiography, *The Stream Runs Fast* (1945). As well as "all their hard work and their strivings to keep clean and make a decent living for themselves and their families," she noted, the women have still "the additional burden of child-bearing"; the situations she saw were not glamorous: "These little houses are places where people have the minimum of comfort. They go in and out, eat and sleep, but everything's done the hard way. The women are tired and overworked and sometimes very cross. They battle against hard water and chapped hands, and chapped hands would lower the morale of an archangel. The houses are cold, the floors full of splinters" (McClung 210). Yet in the midst of these challenges—and, arguably, because of them—

a remarkable solidarity among prairie rural women moved them "to sign temperance petitions, to contribute their mite to women's missionary societies, to agitate for the vote, and to demand recognition of women's right to employment and the value of their domestic labour" (Strong-Boag 403).

The two female farm editors who were the acknowledged experts on conditions in their day, independent women working in the public sphere as highly informed boosters of organized agriculture, operated from cities. Both E. Cora Hind and Miriam Green Ellis were headquartered in Winnipeg, but they made it their business to be out in the field literally and in close association with farm folk and the realities of the private sphere. In many ways E. Cora set the benchmark for Miriam. Cora's insistence on accuracy and detail in on-the-spot coverage, her direct contact with both farmers and agronomists, her particular attentiveness to women's trials, and her loyal service to one newspaper all had a powerful effect on the nature and reach of her younger CWPC colleague's journalism. It is important, I suggest, to have some sense of E. Cora's career to realize the blueprint she supplied. In her *Pathfinders* talk, Miriam recalled driving E. Cora "on our crop-inspection trips," paying tribute to her friend's unmatched hallmark: "Probably the thing for which she was best known all over the world were her crop reports. No one else has ever hit the wheat estimate on the nose so precisely year after year as E. Cora Hind. Chicago and London waited for that report. It was a natural that she should be the first woman to get on a grain boat sailing out of Hudson Bay" (Ellis, *Pathfinders* 12).

When E. Cora was finally hired as agriculture and commercial editor by the *Manitoba Free Press*, she never shied away from speaking her mind and presenting crop conditions as she saw them. Advertising a growing average daily circulation of 25,968 in 1904 as "the largest paper" in Western Canada, with greater numbers than "all the other daily papers in the Canadian Northwest" ("Three Years' Growth" 12), the *Free Press* stood by their crop expert whether her forecasts were high or low. The

1904 crop year was her first big public test. An expert from Chicago announced that rust damage to crops would be severe, and even the premier (who was also the Minister of Agriculture), Redmond Roblin, declared in the *Chicago Inter-Ocean* and repeated in the *Free Press* that "wheat on [his] farm, which ten days ago looked good for 35,000 bushels, yesterday was found not to be worth cutting" (Hind, "R.P. Roblin" 4). E. Cora hit back not only with a positive and proven accurate forecast of yield—"the danger from rust is reported to have been overestimated" (Hind, "Sixty Per Cent" 1)—but with a swinging attack on the premier's role as wheat speculator: "That the Premier and Minister of Agriculture, who is credibly reported to be up to his neck in a 'bull' wheat gamble, should use his public position to further his private ends as a speculator, to the detriment of the Province is—to use the mildest terms—grossly indecent" (Hind, "R.P. Roblin, Wheat Speculator" 4).

Relying on her own investigations in the middle of fields, not from the roadside, along with reports from trusted correspondents and agents along the Canadian Northern Railway line, her forecasts set a new standard for accuracy. In 1905 she estimated 85,000,000 bushels, with the actual crop being 84,506,857; in 1907, her estimate was 71,250,000 against the actual crop of 70,922,584 bushels (Hacker 42). When conditions were not ideal, E. Cora was not afraid to say so. In 1913 with a cool July and fears of black rust, she reported on fields she'd actually investigated, and most of her "Crop Conditions" articles were featured on the front page. Having "motored forty miles around Brandon this afternoon, taking in a circuit north, south, east and west," she noted the late crops with "the worst damaged wheat fields being ploughed down" (Hind, "Crop Conditions," 19 July, 1). One week later, making "a motor run of twenty miles around Souris,…getting into the fields every few miles," she observed "a very lightly stooled crop" with "considerable spotting of red rust on leaves" and estimated—again correctly—"a yield of 15 to 16 bushels of high grade wheat" per acre (26 July, 1). As for "the secret of a good many of the bumper crop stories and the 25 bushel average yields," Cora remarked tartly that such estimates are "made from the thickly stooled headlands...and from a motor travelling 20 miles an hour" (1).

Throughout the war years, when Cora's reports, still regularly featured on the first page, ran alongside lists of Western Canadian casualties, she could be very positive about projected yields. The situation in the spring and summer of 1918 was especially favourable. Predicting "the second best crop in [the] history" of southern Saskatchewan, she observed that "every head is filled to the top and the grain is full, plump and very bright in color" in a district where "the areas of cultivation are enormous," adding the admission "I inspected this whole territory for the first time in 1913 and have been over portions of it every year since, but had not fully grasped the extent of the increase until today" (Hind, "Shaunavon" 1). With the headline as "*Free Press* Crop Expert," Cora filed on "enormous yields" for the Swan River Valley Districts, cautioning against prematurely cutting fields for feed since "some of the men who cut them now wish they had let them alone, for fields that were apparently quite as badly frosted show considerable recovery" (Hind, "Will Be Enormous" 2).

The same forthrightness characterized E. Cora Hind's contributions to the *Free Press* during her post-retirement international tour. Undeterred about sounding alarm bells on over-production, Cora reported that "in every one of the 27 countries visited, with 2 exceptions, they are determined to grow their own wheat," and hence "it would be unwise for the Western Canadian Plains to increase their wheat areas" (*Seeing for Myself* xii, xiii). Always connecting her Winnipeg reality with this global experience, she registered real sorrow at the news of Kipling's death; although she was in Paris, she recalled Kipling's talk in Winnipeg and her conversation with him afterward. His remark, "'My heart goes out to the women on these prairies who are so brave and who are being 'frazzled' out with small daily trials and the doing without things,'" prompts Cora's reflection: "I wondered then, as I wonder now, after these last strenuous five years' drouth how many of our public men as they cross the prairies of the west have given the same thought and sympathy to the 'frazzled' nerves of the prairie women" (Hind, *My Travels and Findings* 31).

From the beginning of her journalism career, represented in this volume in the selection of five published articles from her "aggie" beat, Ellis echoed this sympathy with prairie women. Reporting on the 1915 Women Grain Growers' meeting in Regina, a prelude to the triumphant campaign for women's suffrage across the Prairie provinces the next year (in advance of the federal parliament's extension of suffrage to women two years later), intensified Ellis's admiration of these practical, capable managers. The concerns about the education of their children and desire to have school grounds beautified no doubt reinforced the views she shared with her recently enlisted husband.

When MGE's career became affiliated with the *Family Herald and Weekly Star*, one of a number of farm press periodicals meeting "a widespread and relatively unfluctuating demand" and enjoying "a longevity unknown to consumer and popular-appeal publications" (Kesterton 169), her niche and market appeared to be secure. Despite its title, the paper, which was not sold at newsstands, was published and delivered to subscribers across the country twice monthly, except for the once-a-month issues in July, August, and December. Contributing in the glory days of the paper's circulation, in the boom twenties and even throughout the depressed thirties, MGE knew how to engage her readership with human interest stories and a particular emphasis on pluck from specific locales. Ironically, when the paper folded after a 99-year run (1869–1968), editor Peter Hendry cited their "desperate" but ultimately unsuccessful attempt to bridge "two widely divergent worlds: the old nostalgic image of a countryside now almost completely changed, and the new, dynamic, business-oriented agricultural industry which is rising in its place" (6). The "Voice of the Farm" testimonials that accompanied the final issue on 26 September 1968, from subscribers ranging from Prince

Edward Island to British Columbia and Oregon, vivify a sense of loss. A subscriber from Saskatchewan was prompted to versify:

*We'll miss the color,*
*And the prose.*
*We'll miss the verse,*
*And goodness knows,*
*We'll miss the Family Herald.*

("Voice of the Farm" 4)

From PEI came "deep sorrow" and the recollection that "farm kids 50 years ago were brought up on the good news and pictures in the Family Herald"; an Ontarian wrote that "rural people will feel lost without it," while an Albertan who had enjoyed the paper in Newfoundland and British Columbia lamented the loss of "a national farm magazine,…a force that did make for unity in a way no other publication can hope to achieve" (10).

MGE's knack was her ability to appeal to traditionalists and progressives in her stories' honest stress on resourcefulness that, however, could overcome only so many obstacles. Her interview with the Albertan wheat king returning from the Chicago Exhibition discloses her pride in the determined experiments of this Leicester farmer, who dared to raise prize-winning wheat in Wolf Creek ("World's Best Wheat"). Her reported visit to the multipurpose Jamieson family farm in Alix, Alberta, is another opportunity to extol the united labour of immigrants, this time from Scotland, while acknowledging the instinctive ability of Canadian farm boys ("From Aberdeen"). The sharp contrast of boom and bust separates the boosterism of her articles in the twenties and her reports of the desiccation of the dirty thirties. Ellis's account of the "pulverized" land, exposed to hardpan and overrun with Russian Thistle, her "afternoon's drive south of Regina" to face "such a complete cessation of all effort," and her crisp, sadly declining numbers recall the specificity of E. Cora Hind's forecasts at the same time as they widen the reach of the "tragedy" ("Tragedy" 3). Manitoba-born novelist Patricia Blondal captured such an expansion and suffusion of doom in *A Candle to Light the Sun* (1960), which opens with a meditation on Depression-era Mouse Bluffs, a fictionalization of her own hometown of Souris: "1936. The wind blows the promises thin, the fears in" (10). Ellis's Depression articles intensify the human consequences of the situation depicted by poet Anne Marriott in *The Wind Our Enemy* (1939):

> *They said, "Sure, it'll rain next year!"*
> *When that was dry, "Well, next year anyway.*
> *Then, "Next"—*
> *But still the metal hardness of the sky*
> *Softened only in mockery.*
> *When lightning slashed and twanged*
> *And thunder made the hot head surge with pain*
> *Never a drop fell;*
> *Always hard yellow sun conquered the storm.* (3)

For me, Ellis's reports substantiate and complement the personal recollections of journalist and historian James Gray, in *The Winter Years* (1966), when he recast his enterprising hopes as a young Roaring-Twenties Winnipegger employed at the Grain Exchange, "synonymous with unmitigated affluence," forced to confront the "ego-shattering discovery…[that] there was no alternative to applying for relief" (632, 631). Without being saccharine, Ellis's report on back-to-the-land "colonization schemes" offering "wholesome hope" for "drab lives" and influenced, significantly, by interviews with the potential farmer's wife sketches a more optimistic outlook than the young James Gray, an unemployed husband and father, saw gaping in front of him in 1931: "The Dirty Thirties were almost over before governments recognized that a hard core of unemployment had become a permanent fact of economic life" (636). Alert to the needs of emotional and fiscal well-being, Ellis looks ahead to the promise of a new future on the land.

> *I believe that women writers, by their support of women candidates and by fitting themselves for the positions of authority and confidence, could develop women's place in public life.*
>
> (ELLIS, "Special Fields" 1932)

✳ It may seem a contradiction that the agricultural reporter whom horses and lambs nuzzled immediately and the CWPC stalwart who declaimed with such bravado about women's place in public life at the Triennial in Calgary should feel diffident and "fussed" when facing an audience of "high-brow" women, as she confessed at the opening of "Watching Other People Farm," her 1945 address to the University Women's Club in Saskatoon. However, Ellis regains composure, if in fact she ever lost it, as she rehearses highlights of her years in a "boomerang" fashion, "just lighting here and there and back to here" and refusing to tone down her "slangy" talk with the cheeky retort, "I know lots of other words I could have used." Through the ease of what she fashions as a conversation with her listeners, she reveals a lot of her personality in off-hand remarks. She describes one occasion when she was forced to accompany a salesman to meet a widow who was doing well in the poultry business because "it seemed she used his particular feeds." The writer found herself at the woman's house, with its "nice big reading table, comfortable chairs,... old things that had come from her own home, [and] beautiful furniture that was all friendly with each other and with her." She concludes, "as soon as I saw the woman and her surroundings, I knew that she was the story, not the hens." She sets up this anecdote to illustrate what might be called a proto-feminist principle: "I am always interested when I hear of a woman doing well. I don't know why, really, for why shouldn't they? Women can be just as stupid as men, but they can also be just as smart." The former girls' hockey team manager marvels that artificial ice can mean "hockey in summer." Mild barbs colour her recollections of time wasted at hundreds of conventions listening to "inane remarks" and seeing fidgety men noisily scrape and move their chairs, in contrast to women who "stay put better." She cites the particular example of a Percheron Breeders' convention: "The president made this plea to the members: 'Get your ideas consecrated before you come to the meeting.' I laughed at the time because I thought he had used the wrong word. But in the years since, I have sometimes wondered if he did not have the right idea. A little praying and thoughtful consideration before a convention might save a lot of inane remarks and stupid resolutions, not to mention the amendment to the amendment. Anyway, we report them and fix them up not to sound too silly."

MGE was less sparing with herself, indulging in mildly deprecatory, though unforgettable self-portraits. For the Saskatoon audience, she describes racing to meet the 3:30 a.m. train to Edmonton after a late evening at a conference in Olds. In her speech, she tries without luck to stuff her pyjamas into her stockings and ends up sailing "across the street to the station with mustard-coloured pyjamas flying in the wind." A bi-plane trip to Lac La Ronge, north of Prince Albert, brings up the embarrassing "skirt business" and the difficulties of maintaining "modest pride…as you sort of straddled up from one side to the other on these two rods" of the Model T plane, a difficulty she overcomes by wearing slacks on the return. An intimate or caustic twinge may have entered Miriam's voice as she offered her audience the following pithy remark about animal and human mating practices: "A cattle breeder will study long and earnestly the pedigree of a bull before he buys him to mate to his cows, but humans seem to marry pretty indiscriminately" ("Watching Other People Farm").

Always admiring endurance and accomplishment, and striving to honour promises, Ellis in the same speech concedes to the request of the "good-looking" priest managing the college farm at Muenster,

Saskatchewan, that she not print her "swell" picture of him in overalls and peak cap; instead she opts for the photo he supplies in clerical garb despite the fact that "it had successfully washed out all personality from his face." At Lac La Ronge, she notes, Indians have lived in the area for centuries, pointing to the clay pots in use "before the Hudson's Bay Company came with their *copper* pots and pails" ("Watching Other People Farm").

Although Ellis's writing continuously relates or returns to the West and connection with the land, the concluding selections of this edition focus more directly on her temperament as a self-sufficient woman eager to tell a story, by turns candid and sharp-tongued, intuitive and curious. As much as she admires pioneering fortitude, any passive acceptance of privilege merits her indignation.

In "Watching Other People Farm," Ellis notes that her farewell to George at the barracks in Prince Albert begins her experience as an unaccompanied driver. Obtaining a license in 1915 was apparently of much less importance than being able to change a tire, replace tight fitting rims, rest secure in the presence of a spare valve, and cover the magneto (the electrical generator used in the ignition to provide power to the spark plugs) with "a jacket or pair of trousers." A well-developed "auxiliary vocabulary," she notes, is also a prime asset. The naughtiness of her jalopy sparking off and on during a funeral procession leads Ellis to christen it and every subsequent car "Finnigan"—a reference to the most famous example of American humorist Strickland W. Gillilan's verse, "Finnigin to Flannagan," a tale in Irish brogue of the Great Western Railways roadmaster Mike Finnigin who, having been told to reduce the verbosity of his reports, wired his comments on the next derailment as "off agin, on agin, gone agin—Finnigin." Clearly she was familiar with Gillilan's *Saturday Evening Post* verse, collected in 1914 as *Including Finnigin*. In a postscript twenty-five years later, Miriam reflected on changes in technology, car design, and coiffures: "Today most of us do not know if there are any spark plugs in our cars or not. I used to say that I would never buy a sedan and referred to them with superior scorn as hearses. No, I wanted to feel the pure air floating around me. Today I feel aggrieved if the slightest draft disarranges my hair, or my temper" ("Watching Other People Farm").

Ellis's report of the 1923 Sun Dance at Hobbema conveys an entirely different mood: the curiosity of a non-participant observer. With "regeneration and thanksgiving" as its major purposes, this communal ceremony, known to the Cree as "nipâhkwêsimowin (Thirst Dance)" (Pettipas 57, 56), was a significant milestone. In 1914, an amendment to Section 149 of the *Indian Act* declared such "indigenous forms of activities...subject to the approval of the superintendent general of Indian Affairs" (149). Deputy Superintendent General Duncan Scott had given permission for the performance of the Hobbema ceremonies, which are represented very differently in Ellis's unpublished typescript and in the "sensationalism" (Pettipas 174) of the *Edmonton Journal*'s unattributed account, titled "Sun Dance of the Crees at Hobbema: By Special Permission of the Government Red Men Observe Wierd [*sic*] Ceremony." Member of an invited party of Hudson's Bay Company managers, the *Journal* reporter is ushered into the Sun Dance "hall"; he or she comments on "moist, wet copper bodies," "the flash of white cowrie shells and teeth against dark bodies," and "the inextinguishable crash of the tom-tom" in this "Pagan rite" (3). Ellis, in contrast, takes her own photographs, distinct from those published in the newspaper, and observes from the outside only; yet she captures features of shared human interest. Comparing the lack of awareness of "the significance of the old pagan ceremonial" among the younger generation to Christian children's loss of "the dramatic significance of Lent, Good Friday and Easter," she admits sadness at witnessing what might be "the last Sun Dance ever to be seen in the West" (Ellis, "Sun Dance"). She marvels at the endurance of the dancers and the intricacy of beaded costumes, and hints at future uses of the brightly coloured cottons left behind. She concentrates not on the sweat but on the "ingenuity in the decoration" of the painted faces. Toward the end of the ceremony she realizes that some holy importance attends the gentle and reverent handling of the buffalo head behind a drawn screen.

Ellis's interest in people's stories is an omnipresent feature of her writing. At a campsite outside Banff, she encountered an elderly farm couple taking their first vacation alone in decades; she represents the meeting in vivid dialogue and engages herself in their adventure by helping them to open up their camp beds, following them into town to allay their fears about the road, and advising about the most efficient way to have their new car converted into a sleeper unit. Her visit to the fledgling Banff Fine Arts School is a celebration of "education in its most liquid and attractive form" and co-operation in extending the Carnegie Foundation grant; it is equally a roll call of illustrious faculty and a description of the practicalities of acquiring materials in wartime and accommodating students of different financial means "companionably." Amid the tallies of growth in subject matter—theatre, art, and music—and enrolment, what shines through is Ellis's firm belief in "aesthetic values" enriching a diversity of communities.

> *I think of women as the "shock troops." She tries to get the children soothed down before father gets home. She adjusts the household to meet an onslaught of in-laws. Out in the country she milks the cows and feeds the calves, while father goes to a convention. When funds get low she makes over her wedding dress so her daughter can go to a party. If worse comes to worse, she makes flour sacks into under clothing, taking care to put on a little pretty embroidery.*
>
> ("Canada Has Something," Yorkton, Saskatchewan, 1939)

✸ As an independent professional in the late 1930s, Ellis could observe and comment on patriarchal domesticity, but she did not have a participant's perspective. From what I have gleaned from her writing, she was never called on to soothe children down before father got home, never made over her wedding dress or transformed flour sacks into lingerie. When she addressed the Rotary Ladies in Yorkton in November 1939, Ellis had both praise and critique. Capable managers and domestic mainstays, women, in her speech, incarnate "a tremendous wealth of stability, initiative and energy"; yet she interrupted her trajectory with the qualifier that this wealth "isn't working to capacity." "Women fought hard to get the vote," she noted, "but having it they lay back on their laurels." Her exhortations to public action and commitment underscore the question that has been lurking within and around my reading of MGE. To what kind of public sphere do Canadian women writers of the heyday of the CWPC, specifically those covering agriculture in the West, belong? In what ways does their journalism reflect or contain an understanding of an early twentieth-century Western Canadian public? Do their contributions to widely circulated newspapers actually suggest that "a public is a multicontextual space of circulation, organized not by a place or an institution but by the circulation of discourse" (Warner 118–19)?

The CWPC public to which both E. Cora Hind and Miriam Green Ellis belong was certainly created through the circulation of discourse. Yet these two primary and unparalleled practitioners in the field both fit and disturb the criteria for women writers in a modernist public sphere. They were not generally "involved in academia," nor did they operate under "pre-established critical norms" (G. Taylor 193). In most instances they established their own standards. In the absence of female editors-in-chief, moreover, they made their voices heard "within male-dominated publications" (192). In their dedication to the CWPC, they also experienced what Laura Riding described in *The World and Ourselves* as "a company in operation—or, rather, in the process of being formed,... among whom a general devotion prevails...[and] a thread of common interest is drawn from one to the other" (452). Of course Riding was engaging a specific community. The public democratic exchange she was inviting and envisioning involved mainly literary figures commenting on "world troubles and approach[ing] them with that active certainty which can only come of relating one's sensibilities to the sensibilities of others" (Riding x). The sphere addressed and reflected by Cora and Miriam functioned in a different register, concentrating literally on a ground-level world, aware of its global significance yet resolutely focussed on the people and terrain around them. Although both Cora's "Crop Conditions" articles and Miriam's paper itself have disappeared, their work—so filiated as it is—captures a sensibility about the land as a renewable resource. Now that petro-business and mineral extraction have eclipsed agri-business, it may be timely, not merely nostalgic, to remember the emphases they placed on natural renewal. The spirit of both women continues to renew and enrich graduate student research; the *Winnipeg Free Press* created the Cora Hind Scholarship in Home Economics at the University of Manitoba, while testamentary gifts from MGE established Miriam Green Ellis Bursaries in the Faculty of Agriculture and Food Sciences at the University of Manitoba and in animal and plant sciences at the University of Saskatchewan.

As I consider the Ellis archive, Derrida's question about the future returns as a haunting one. Shifting from heel-hugging skirts to breeches and tailored suits, Ellis's career illustrates the bridge her editor had hoped to fashion linking the appeal of the countryside of one era and the business-oriented agricultural industry of another. She was forthright, bold, and often pugnacious. She did not back down, nor did she readily accommodate conventional expectations, although some of her terminology ("squaw" and "half-breed") bears the imprint of her culture and place. In attempting to compare and locate her in a field of counterparts in the fiction of her time about the challenges of women journalists and writers, I have found no fictional model for Ellis. Her temperamental fighting spirit does not align her with the journalist Aleta Dey, the eponymous heroine of Francis Marion Beynon's largely autobiographical 1919 novel. Pacifist and suffragist, Dey suffers and dies for her principles. She constantly accuses herself of weakness: "Why did I find myself apologetic when I did not agree with the majority? When I was given a mind that questioned everything, why was I not given a spirit that feared nothing?" (Beynon 66). Combining both a questioning attitude and a fearless brio, Ellis never believed that "the wings of [her] soul had been clipped in [her] infancy" (Beynon 66). *Shackles* (1926), Madge Macbeth's portrait of the New Woman who struggles to become a writer, perhaps comes closest, but the novel confines its tensions largely within the marital household and the domestic economy. When Naomi gains her voice and confronts her husband with the injustice of his objections to her writing, she defends women's aspirations with a conviction and directness Ellis would have endorsed:

> *"If you don't get justice," returned Naomi, "it's because you refuse to give it. I am ranging myself on the side of all women whose subjugation to man's dominance is taken for granted, whose toil is unappreciated—unacknowledged, indeed!—and whose capabilities and ambitions are crushed under the burdens men like you place upon them. There you sit, self-absorbed, considering your ease, your rights, your wrongs! Aggrieved because I am not clearing the stones from your path! And carrying out that metaphor, you not only refuse to help me clear, but you actually bring unnecessary material and dump it in my way so that I have extra work to do!"*
>
> (MACBETH 306)

For reasons she never disclosed, Ellis chose not to remain in the marital household and certainly never tolerated being under a male thumb.

While it may seem easy to categorize her as fleeing from the perceived boredom of a music teaching career and a failed marriage into the sorority of press women, I think it is important to see beyond these stereotypes—but it is also necessary to confront the inconsistencies, ironies, and occasional short-sightedness of MGE. She was not clairvoyant: her endorsement of research on reclamation of the tar sands and hope that the country would one day yield gold, silver, iron, and oil existed side by side with her claim that agriculture would continue to be the largest business in the country. The journalist who strode into farmhouses and barns with such genial informality and raced to catch a train in her pyjamas could also be a punctilious upholder of regulations and decorum as chair of CWPC meetings. Boldly claiming and ultimately owning the male turf of the aggie beat, resorting to no coy nicknames, and not isolating herself as a "Lone Scribe" (Lang 22), Ellis experienced the enabling power of a female constituency in the sometimes hostile workplace of the newspaper world, but she also recognized with some regret, in the years following World War II, that the need for the solidarity of a women-only association was waning. In many ways she is a liminal figure, valuing the resolution of CWPC pioneers and exulting in her own mobility. Her conversational style, so distinct from the didactic literariness of Agnes Deans Cameron, nevertheless blends clarity and opacity, as this public personality protects the secrets of a private individual: "In the shadow region between the known and the never-to-be-known" (Frazier 34), Miriam Green Ellis defiantly survives.

# ABBREVIATIONS

BPSC: Bruce Peel Special Collections Library, University of Alberta, Edmonton, Alberta
CWPC: Canadian Women's Press Club
LAC: Library and Archives Canada, Ottawa, Ontario
MGE: Miriam Green Ellis
PAA: Provincial Archives of Alberta, Edmonton, Alberta

# TRAVELLER AND STORYTELLER

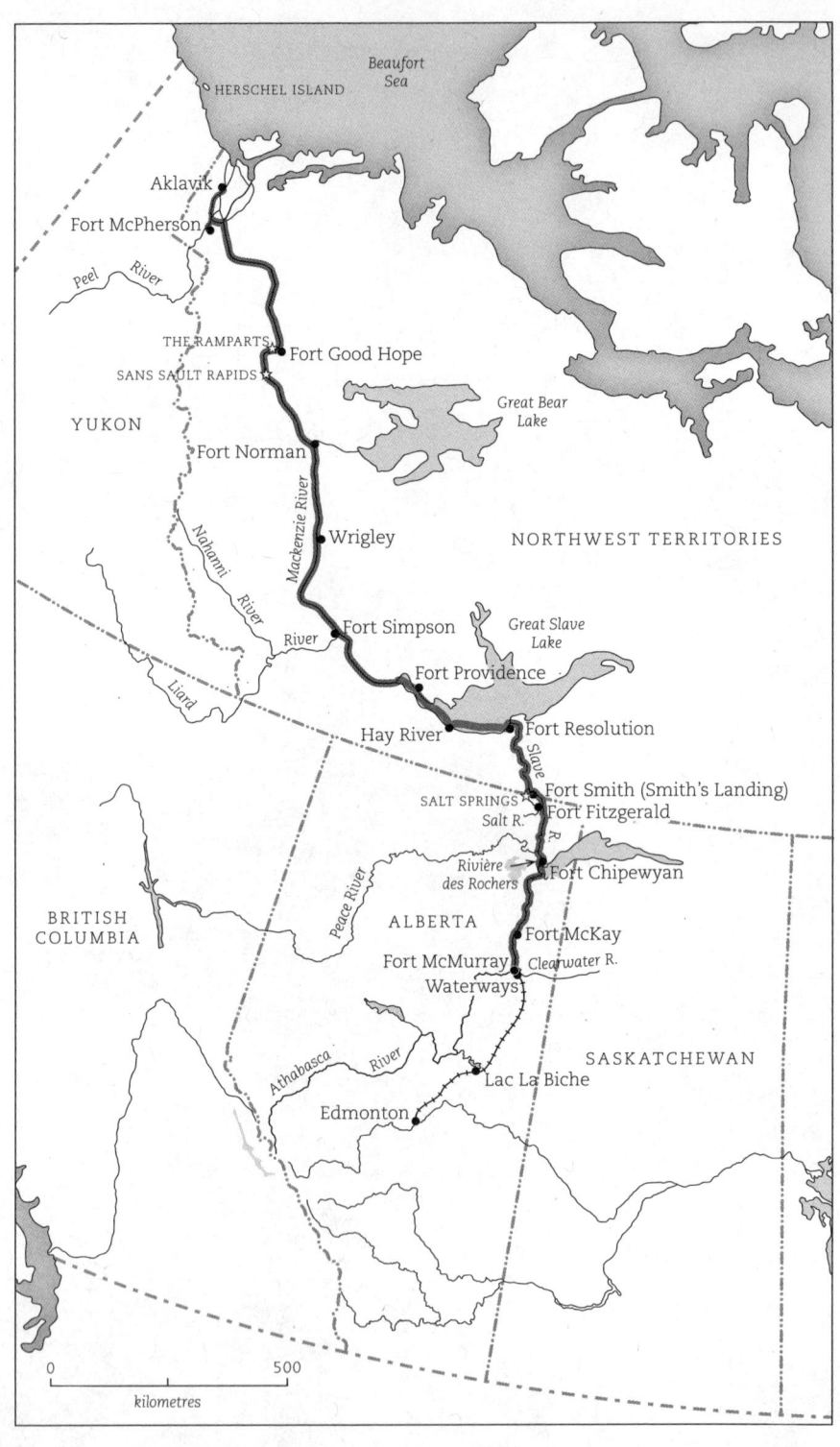

# DOWN NORTH (1922)

SINCE I WAS A SMALL GIRL IN PINAFORES and was taught that the earth was round and flattened a little at each end like an apple, I have wanted to go to the place where it started to flatten. It seemed to me that if one were careful not to slip off the edge, one could probably see the pole in the distance and also see if the firmament wrapped itself around the earth or if it were just a straight canopy. For twenty minutes every morning, as I sat in front of the oven door waiting for my curls to dry, I had plenty of time to speculate whether the earth really did revolve at so many miles a second, whether it really were round, and if so, why the people on the other side did not drop off; worst of all my problems was where the sun went at night and why it got cold in the wintertime.

Years passed, and I still had not solved these intricate problems; finally I accepted them on faith as I did radio and the Book of Revelation. Several times I suggested to my editor[1] that an assignment to the North Pole would be acceptable, but he seemed to prefer an interview with some stuffy celebrity or a story on the cattle market. One day I sat in the premier's office trying to get a "scoop" on the government policy in connection with the administration of the liquor laws, when I noticed on his desk a pamphlet from a transportation company, on which were the words "to the land of the midnight sun." From where I sat in that big blue room, I could see the Saskatchewan River, just then throwing off its winter bondage and shoving the great cakes of ice ignominiously on the shore to rot. The trees were showing life and the grass along the banks was getting green. It was the time when the woods sent out their loudest call, and I lost all interest in the burning question of liquor laws.

I went back to the editor with the subtle suggestion that an up-to-date paper like ours, serving a country just on the edge of the Great North, should have a story on the changes that were being brought about in the life and customs of the Indians by the activities of the traders and missionaries. Quoting from the transportation folder, I told him that here was a river,[2] second in size to the Mississippi and draining a country one-fifth the entire size of Canada, and it should certainly be written up. Seeing I was not making much headway, I hastened to add, that there were a great many other feature stories I could get by the way, such as development work at the Norman Oil Wells,[3] building of the new government offices at Fort Smith,[4] and the rumour of a gold find on the Nahanni River.[5] However, the enthusiasm was all one-sided, so I finally asked him bluntly for two months' leave of absence to take the trip on my own. He admitted that probably the paper would be able to exist eight weeks without me, so as an outlet for my feelings I hurried out and bought a mosquito bar for my head and one for my bed, neither of which I ever used, but which gave me much satisfaction in the buying, for I felt committed to the great adventure.

It was the middle of June when I left Edmonton, my ticket reading "to Aklavik," a place of which I had never heard but which I was told was down in the delta of the Mackenzie, where the Eskimos came to do their shopping. Paragraphs from my diary remind me of incidents, dramatic at the time, but since blurred in the memory of endless days and blazing sun-sets.

JUNE 19—Before my resolution can slip, I am going to make a solemn vow here and now, that I will keep a regular diary of this trip. Each year, I always plan to keep a diary and a personal cash account, and never have carried either past the third day of January. This must be different. Even now my courage is oozing, for the swaying of the train[6] gives me a peculiar feeling in my stomach and my arms are black and blue from coming into unexpected and violent contact with the window. If I complain about its being terribly rough, I am curtly informed, with the contempt that old timers in the north always show to the tenderfoot, that I would appreciate this train better had I gone in during the old days, walking behind a yoke of oxen or maybe cayuses,[7] the one hundred and five miles from Edmonton to Athabaska Landing, and then gone down the river by scow.

"You could choose your stateroom," one said, "either in the bow with the cases of bacon, or in the stern with the kerosene. Then every time you came to a rapids you got out and scrambled along the shore carrying your dunnage[8] and as much more as you could pile on. This road just cuts off three or four hundred miles of misery."

It was certainly a peculiar crowd[9] at the station this morning. My mother said goodbye to me with much the bewildered air of the hen which has been stepmothering a web-footed baby with fond care, only to see it make a break for the first pond and swim away. Instead of the usual well-tailored group with newly shined shoes and correct leather travelling bags with gold initials on the side, practically all the men wore breeches with leather leggings or puttees, khaki shirts and soft old felt hats, and their luggage was in canvas sacks. Most of them had something to do with the fur trade; some were young fellows, going down to work for one of the companies, on two or three year contracts, which meant that they would not be coming back till that time had expired. It seems a long time to be shut away; even letters come only once or twice a year.

I am glad there is a botanist[10] on board; he is lecturer in some American university and will be on our boat, so it will interesting getting some first-hand information about the plants and flowers.

Then there is a girl from Yorkshire,[11] England, going down to marry a chap at Norman. She has not seen him since the war and of course has not heard from him since last fall some time, but she does not seem to have any doubts in the matter.

The train is full to the roof, as everyone who is going down to the far North must come this week to catch the one boat of the year. Seats and aisles are full of bags of all sorts, but the porter seems to take this all as a matter of course.

Even the train crew[12] is a different sort from those aristocratic persons who, with their strikes and contracts, have the fate of nations in their hands. They would need to be, for this train runs on no monotonous schedule, same place, same hour. Usually it jumps the track once or twice and last week it was off three times. Every time it gives a sudden stop, and they are mostly sudden, I expect the worst, and I scarcely know whether to undress or not, but I think I'll take a chance and see if travelling flat will help this nausea.

Bishop Grouard[13] is on board. He has been in the North for half a century and knows every white man and Indian right down to the Arctic. He speaks only a little English, and I had some difficulty talking to him. He is well over eighty now but still carries on as active head of his big diocese.

We stopped at Lac La Biche[14] this evening for half an hour and I walked down to the lake, which lay placidly hidden in among the wooded hills, like an abbey chapel in an old romance. The height of land is just about at Lac La Biche and from there the waters all run north.

*Bishop Grouard at the Edmonton train station.* [BPSC]

LATER—This porter is a character. He bobs around like a piece of black rubber and when anything amuses him he sort of folds up and gurgles. When I asked him how he happened to be on this run, he told me he had been sick last winter and lost his other job, so he took this. He said he had been like the man who had three meals a day, oat-meal, corn-meal, and miss-a-meal, only his had been mostly miss-a-meal.

JUNE 20—I feel fairly cheated that the train is still on the rails. I had the upper berth last night and just as I was getting up there was a lurch and I spilled on the floor. Next time I made it, and by getting right over close to the wall, I managed to stay in. We are six hours late and the boys have nicknamed it the "Arctic Express," but we expect to get to Waterways, the end of steel, tonight some time. At mealtime we stop while the crew eats.

We pass the stations of Chaplin and Pickford. Fame travels far. Chaplin consisted of one boxcar set off beside the track, while at Pickford, a lean-to had been added to the boxcar. We also passed Tweedle, but this only left us in suspense as to whether it were Tweedle-dum or Tweedle-dee. Abbreviations are rather stupid anyway.

JUNE 20—11 P.M. We are on board the boat at last and the adventure seems really begun. It was late in the evening before we finally arrived at Waterways, consisting of a dozen little log stores and houses set in the midst of the woods. A street had been cut out, but the stumps are still standing and there is only a foot path winding down through them, leading off into the woods, along which we walked for half a mile or so with spruce and poplar, tall bracken, and wild roses bordering all the way. The Clearwater[15] is such a tiny river, you could almost throw a stone across, and we go down some eight or ten miles before it joins the Athabaska. It was a wonderful scene as we came out of the forest at the river bank. The sun was just setting and a rose-coloured light settled down on the trees, which rose tier on tier till the colour seemed to blend in and become a part of the sky itself. This glory lasted a few minutes and

*Waterways.* [BPSC]

*Main Street, Fort McMurray.* [BPSC]

*"Going up the Clearwater River."* [BPSC]

then the shadows came, separating out the chains of hills as they rolled away, one above the other, right to the very sunset. It seems as though nature has made a wonderful preparation for such a miniature river.

JUNE 21—The longest day in the year. When I wakened we were on our way and, through the cabin window, I saw a passing panorama of trees and blue sky, with now and then a fleecy cloud. I laid there thinking how quiet and peaceful it was after the train, when my head suddenly hit the top of the bed, and I heard frantic signals to the engine room. I got dressed in a hurry, but by that time we were on our way again; we had just hit a sandbar. The boat swings back and forth across the river like a sail boat tacking to the breeze, for the sandbars are plentiful and the main channel winds in and out among them. The banks have been mercilessly gouged out by the ice at the break-up this spring and all along the shore, great live trees have been toppled into the river, as the ground was cut out beneath them. Some of their roots are still buried in the bank and to these the tree is hanging with a death grip, while the others sway in futile helplessness in the current. The vegetation all along the bank is very luxuriant and for miles and miles we go without seeing a human habitation of any kind.

The big feature of the day was the Tar Sands, regular mountains of asphalt which I am told extend along the Athabaska River for 170 miles. It was a very hot day and in places we could see trickles of liquid tar running down the side of the hills into the river or settling in little pools. One man claimed it was just an oil formation turned wrong side up, and that some day they will be shipping out gasoline from here. At present, however, it is chiefly valuable as a road-surfacing material, and the value of that even is as yet practically negligible on account of the cost of transportation. It has been tried out on the streets of Edmonton and outwears other pavements, but there is the excessive cost of getting it there. Mr. Draper,[16] a man of long experience in the oil business, has built a plant and is experimenting with the sands. There is a possibility that the tar may be extracted and shipped sans sand, the latter to be added again wherever used, but Mr. Draper is of the opinion that as the bitumen and sand are just in the right proportion as they are, it will be foolish to carry on a double process of extracting sand and putting it in again. He prophesies that some day it is going to mean millions of dollars to the country, for the supply is almost limitless.

I had visions of another Klondyke when we came on a lone man digging in the side of the river bank. No one else seemed to share my excitement however, and the captain said it was "just some fool scratching round in the dirt." However, I expect that man had hopes or he would not have been "scratching." It is a little depressing to have people forever squelching one's enthusiasms. There was a white hill, inshore away, and I was amazed to find it was white from an overflow of salt, but my official squelcher said it was nothing to get excited about, for there was salt in dozens of places in this country. However, it does seem a pity that none of it is used.

MIDNIGHT—I am just thoroughly peeved. It has been brewing all day. Talking to the professor person and the manager of the transportation company who is also in the boat, the conversation turned to the modern woman and they conveyed to me quite simply, and both together, what they thought of women who wore knickers and tried to ape men's ways. I told them that for most part their own estimate of "men's ways" was quite correct, and no woman with a particle of sense would copy them; but in some unknown manner, men had stumbled on a much more convenient system of clothes, and as they had no patent on them, women were showing good judgment to wear breeks,[17] when they were more convenient. Tonight after travelling steadily for two days we stopped for the first time to take on wood for the engine. I was anxious to get on shore and see what was behind that screen of trees. All down the river both my eyes and my imagination had been trying to penetrate the leafy foliage but I could get no glimpse. It was like walking along a city street with the doors all shut. So when I found we were to stop I went in and put on my knickers and big boots and came out with a defiant air. My gentlemen friends hastened to explain that of course not many women looked so well in that sort of rig as I did, etc. But their compliments left me cold. However, I was so thrilled with the prospect of discovering shore secrets that I soon forgot about them, till, as I started to get off, the manager told me that he could not think of allowing me to leave the boat. In answer to my very polite inquiry, he said that the mosquitoes would eat me alive, and that there was absolutely nothing to see if I did get off. I persisted, but with the precedent of generations of men who take care of their women folk when it suits them to do so, he absolutely refused. I said I did not mind the mosquitoes, and anyway I was not burning my bridges behind me; if the flies got too bad I could still come back on the boat. But he was afraid I would get lost and they had no one to send with me as they were all going to be busy loading wood and insinuating that they did not want to waste any time sending out a search party for me. I told him that if I were not back on board when he was ready to go, he had my permission (before witnesses) to leave without me. However, I did not go, which is only another instance to prove why women do not deserve equal rights. That man is about half as big as I am and I should just have taken him by the collar and thrown him overboard. However, here is my oath that it won't happen again.

JUNE 22 — When I wakened this morning we had stopped and I hurried out to see what had happened. We were down in the delta of the Athabaska River and there was such a storm on Lake Athabaska that we could not cross. The flat-bottomed boats are not meant for heavy seas, and when there is a storm these shallow lakes work themselves into quite a fury. Sometimes a boat is left absolutely stranded, when a high wind shoves the water away to the other end of the lake, and they just have to sit and wait till the wind changes and the lake comes back to them. From the deck of the boat we could see hundreds of little streams that go to make up the delta; we were in the main channel, which is the only one large enough for the steam boats to get through. We were tied to a little tree on shore, and I thought this was a good time to put into operation, while it was fresh, my resolution to go on shore. Apparently I had worn down the opposition, and after a few remarks that it was so muddy and that I would lose myself in the marsh, I managed to slip my guard and get off. It was certainly muddy — soft, slippery, slimy mud. I spent some hours trying to find nests of wild ducks and geese, for millions of them come in here each year from the South to nest, but only saw a few old mallards flying around. However, I was happy in having carried my point and created a precedent which I intend shall carry me through the rest of the trip. They condoled with me for being mud from my heels to my hat, but I knew it was just the sorrow that the cat has for having swallowed the canary, and anyway I am not worrying about the mud — I have had intimate relations with it before. I found several dead campfires where some other voyageurs had likewise waited for the lake to calm.

I had noticed there was a bathroom on board, and was looking forward just then to a real bath, but found the tub full of ice for the refrigerator. Then the rain came pouring through the roof of my stateroom and the purser fixed some canvas over my head to keep the blankets dry. He nailed the canvas to the roof, leaving a sag in the middle from which the water ran out in a little stream into my water basin. So I got a shower instead of a tub bath. He threatened to charge me extra for having running water in my room.

At one of the Indian encampments we had taken on the Indian agent, Gerald Card,[18] and Dr. Macdonald[19] who is employed by the Department of Indian Affairs at Ottawa to look after the health of the Indians. Both these men have headquarters at Fort Smith, but had come upstream to pay the annual treaty money to the Indians. Dr. Macdonald tells me that he has never had a case of appendicitis among the Indians. Mostly they die of tuberculosis, and last winter a hundred or more died of flu. He could not imagine how the germ came to them, for there is no traffic back and forth to civilization after the river freezes, but in some way it had come.

The Indians who have come under treaty with the Dominion government get $5.00 each every year, the chiefs getting $25 and the headman $15. At Fort McKay a certain family did not come in the first day for their money. They kept the agent hanging around and finally came triumphantly to announce the arrival of a new baby, which was of course another beneficiary. Treaty 8 was made in 1899 with the Indians of Athabaska. These included bands of the Cree tribe, the Beavers, Slavis, Little Red River Indians, Tall Crees, Chipewyans, Yellow Knives, and Dogribs living in the country adjacent to the Athabaska. Nearly 3500 were admitted under this treaty. The reports of this agreement state that there was a marked absence of the old Indian style of oratory and it was only among the Wood Crees that there were any formal speeches made; the Beaver Indians were very taciturn and the Chipewyans confined themselves to asking questions and making brief argument. They all asked for as much or more than had been given to the Indians of the Plains. The greatest difficulty was in assuring them that their hunting and fishing privileges would not be curtailed with the signing of the treaty, and they were also afraid of being taxed, and of enforced military service. In addition to the money to be paid them each year assistance was promised in the way of seed, implements, and cattle for any Indians who wished to farm and ammunition and twine for those who wanted to hunt and fish. While arrangements were made that reserves would be laid out when required, the Indians did not show any enthusiasm for this clause, as they did not want to be confined to reserves.

The report notes that these Indians differed in many respects from those south of Edmonton. They did not use paint or feathers and never clothed themselves in blankets. Also there was little organization among them; the chiefs were chosen on account of being the best hunters, rather than their ability as law-makers as in older sections of Canada. Most of them were professing Christians at that time.

Among the signatories to that treaty were Father A. Lacombe, George Holmes, E. Grouard, OMI, now Bishop Grouard, W.S. White, James Walker, J.A. Arthur Coté, Inspector A.K. Snyder, RNWMP, H.B. Round, Harrison S. Young, J.F. Prudholme, J.W. Martin, Chas Mair, H.A. Conroy, Pierre Deschambeault, J.H. Picard, Richard Secord, and Matt McCauley.

In 1900, eight more bands, including the Cariboo Eaters east of Smith's Landing, were included under this treaty.

In 1921, a new treaty with the more northern Indians was made. This affected the Slave, Dogribs, Loucheux, Hare, and other tribes living along the Mackenzie River. I found that in the records of this treaty, the Indians in addition to their annual money allowance also got a silver medal for the chief, a suitable flag, and a copy of the treaty, and every third year each chief and headman is to receive a suitable piece of clothing. Also the government undertakes to pay salaries to teachers in "such manner as His Majesty may deem advisable." And "once for all to each chief who

*Bishop Grouard arriving at Fort Chipewyan.* [BPSC]

selects reserve, ten axes, 5 handsaws, one grindstone, and the necessary files and whetstones for the use of the band. Each band will receive once and for all, equipment for hunting, fishing and trapping for each family and there shall be distributed annually equipment such as twine for nets, ammunition and traps to the value of $3.00 per head."[20]

It is estimated that there are now about 5,500 persons in the whole Mackenzie district, of whom about 500 are whites, 1,000 half-breeds, and the rest Indians and Eskimos. The Eskimos are not under treaty of any kind.

This afternoon we reached Chipewyan,[21] an important fur-trading post, and Mr. Card and the doctor got off to pay the treaty. Two tribes come here to get their treaty. But each group has to be paid separately. The agent will set up his court and pay the Chipewyans and then go over to the other camp across the bay and pay the Crees. They would not demean themselves by mixing. It was from Chipewyan that Alexander Mackenzie started out in the spring of 1789 to explore the Mackenzie and it was in the mission garden here, 500 miles North of Edmonton, that they grew the sample of wheat which in 1876 took first prize at the U.S. Centennial at Philadelphia. It is the headquarters of both the Roman Catholic and Anglican churches for the Mackenzie diocese. Bishop Lucas has charge of the Anglican missions from here to the Arctic and Bishop Breynat for the Roman Catholics. A tablet in the Anglican church memorialized ten men who had given their lives in the Great War. In spite of the treaty they did not hesitate to volunteer for service.

12:30 MIDNIGHT — We have just wooded up and are started for Fitzgerald, the next post. It is barely dusk and I am writing without a light. I piloted the boat for thirty miles up the Rivière des Rochers[22] after we left Chipewyan. We passed the mouth of the Peace tonight, after which the combined rivers are called the Slave River. Coming down the Rivière des Rochers, we worked our way through dozens of beautiful islands, reminding me of the Thousand Islands in the St. Lawrence.

Instead of the beautiful summer palaces, however, there were only a couple of deserted Indian camps. The Indians were probably over at Chipewyan to get their treaty money. This river flows sometimes one way sometimes the other according as the lake is high or low.

JUNE 23—Arrived at Fitzgerald, we had to pack our stuff, ready to portage across to the other side. There is a series of five rapids, and this sixteen-mile road around is the only highway in the North West Territories. I walked alone down through the wood for two or three miles along the rapids, and the roar was thrilling. I was so anxious to get some photographs that I ventured out on a rock, and then began to wonder what would happen if I slipped off, for the rock was very smooth where it had been worn off by years of resistance to ice and spring floods. I began to think what a satisfaction it would give the manager person to say, "I told you so," and very carefully on my hands and knees worked my way back along the log that made a natural bridge to shore. One place here is called the Rapids of the Drowned, named from some past tragedies when people in canoes tried to run through, and this was not a comforting thought as I crawled back along that slippery log, mosquitoes chewing my neck, and my camera swinging around in my way every minute or two.

I took back a bouquet of blue columbine which made the botany professor enthusiastic. He had stayed on the boat, on account of the mosquitoes.

There was a little herd of cattle but they were kept thin trying to fight the bull dog flies which literally drank quarts of their blood. I was rather amazed when a man came along as I was looking at the cattle, and called me by name. He said he had seen me reporting the live stock shows in Edmonton and Brandon, and had seen me at the stock yards too. Apparently there would be no use in going north to get away from your misdeeds.

Towards evening we came across (in an automobile, if you please)[23] to Fort Smith at the northern end of the rapids and here we are on the boat that is to take us right down to the mouth of the river that is nearly 1,500 miles away. It is nice and comfortable, red carpet on the stateroom, a little shelf across one corner for the wash-basin and a mosquito net on the bunk. It is a much bigger boat than the one we just left which makes regular trips back and forth between Waterways and Fitzgerald. There are the three main fur-trading companies[24] doing business in the country, each with its own steamer into the North and for weeks each had been preparing for this trip, when they take down the provisions for the year, to the far north posts, and bring in the fur their officers have collected.

The supper was delicious, the best buns I ever ate, and the cook, I find, is a graduate of Ann Arbor University.[25] He did not take his degree in domestic science, however, but in medicine. A lot of men came down from the village for supper; in fact while the boat is in port it is like a supper restaurant, especially for men who have been getting their own meals all winter. It is a feast to get fresh pork, beef, and lamb after living on wild meats for a year. After we leave Fort Smith we will only have fresh meat as long as the ice in the refrigerator lasts; then it will be bacon, beans, and fish.

Fort Smith is the capital, so to speak, of the North West Territories. They are really administered directly from Ottawa, but local business is carried on from this point. There is a mining recorder and a small staff who record oil, timber, and mineral claims, and they also operate a little saw mill. Over $100,000 was taken in by the government last year as fees for oil leases.

JUNE 24—We are not sure when we will leave here, as the captain has reported that the ice is not out of the Great Slave Lake yet. It is so hot here that it seems impossible that there is ice anywhere. Great Slave Lake is nearly as large as Lake Huron, but is shallow, and unless a big wind comes to break up the ice, it stays there till it rots.

The only known herd of wild buffalo in the world live west of here. It is estimated there are about 15,000 of them and they are protected by the

MGE *in field of rye at the farm of Mr. Card, Indian agent at Fort Smith.* [BPSC]

government. A party of eighteen in charge of G.H. Blanchette[26] has just gone North to make a survey of the channels in and out of Great Slave Lake and of the Lake itself.

Mrs. Card, wife of the Indian agent, is postmistress at Fort Smith and had just finished sorting out seventy-five sacks of the North when I called. This is really the only full mail the far north gets a year. In the winter, a postman with a dog team will take in mail, but it will only include first class and registered matter.

Not far from the government office, Mrs. Conibear,[27] an English woman, has a store, and carries on independent trading with the big three companies. I am told that she is the only one of the lot who is really making money here. Her husband is an engineer.

The Roman Catholic mission has a beautiful garden here. The Grey Nuns operate a hospital, at which Doctor Macdonald lives. He is the only doctor between Waterways where we started and Fort Norman, where the Imperial Oil Co. has a resident physician. This is a mere matter of 1,125 miles.

Fort Smith, or Smith's Landing as it used to be called, is just at the foot of the rapids, and on the rocks right in the midst of the roaring current, hundreds of pelicans come each year to nest. I could see them with the captain's glasses from the pilot house. It seemed a pretty bare home, not a blade of grass for the little ones to snuggle in.

JUNE 25 — Beautiful day, but intensely hot. About six o'clock we stopped and took on thirty cords of wood. As I wandered in the woods, I heard Canada Birds (white-throated sparrows) calling. The wild roses are in full bloom; few buds are left now.

12:30 MIDNIGHT — Can read easily without artificial light and there is a red glow in the east as though the sun were already rising. I can still hear the Canada Birds from the shore.

JUNE 26 — We came to the mouth of the Slave River this morning and it also has a delta. It seems to be the fashion in this country for rivers to have deltas for they all do it. We started out into the lake, but it was so rough we put back into the delta and waited. Later when we did start again we got stuck on the sand bars and were some eight hours getting off. The mate would take the anchor in the row boat and drop it some distance away, and then they would try and pull the boat off. Sometimes it came and sometimes it did not, and when it did it was likely to ground on another bar in a minute or so. The river channel really extends for miles out into the lake and the boat held to this narrow course north and east till we were almost out of sight of land before we turned west. So it was five in the afternoon instead of four in the morning before we came to Fort Resolution, which is just around the corner from the Slave Delta. The lake was getting rough again and as there was no harbour there, we made a run for some islands out in the lake. The boat rolled and heaved

MGE *with Native woman and children, Fort Resolution.* [BPSC]

as it plowed through the white-capped waves and we were all a bit scared and considerably sea-sick before we got in the shelter of the Burnt Islands. Even there it took two anchors to hold us. Great Slave Lake is about 520 feet above sea level, so we have dropped about 2,000 feet since leaving Edmonton.

This route has been called the back way to the Klondyke since, during the first rush to the gold fields, many came in this way, some never reaching their destination. So many died by the way that, when there promised to be another rush to the Norman Oil Wells, the Dominion government would not allow anyone to start from Edmonton unless he were properly equipped with supplies and experience to see him through. It was at that time that large deposits of lead-zinc were found on the south shore of Great Slave Lake, and a considerable development has been done of late to establish its extent and value. Over on the northeast arm of the lake, at Little Cariboo Island, work is also being done on a large gold bearing quartz ledge.

JUNE 28—We were not able to leave our shelter all day yesterday, not till late afternoon today. The mate rowed me over to the shore this morning, in spite of certain opposition. They were landing some men to cut up driftwood as we are running short of fuel. So while they were chopping, I wandered around. The island had been burnt over at some time and the big scorched trees had been blown down in every direction, making walking difficult, as you had to climb over burnt logs all the time. Down under the pile of debris I noticed a spot of colour and pulled away the brush to see what it was. Imagine the thrill to find some exquisite wild orchids. They were growing out of the moss and were the same in shape and colouring as the big expensive hot house orchids, only they were tiny, just about an inch and a half long. They were in little beds about six or eight inches long and four inches wide, as though they might be fairies' graves. They were the most exquisite things I ever saw. They had a little bulbous root and just one leaf to a flower. I also got another pretty pink flower that looked like some sort of heather. The botany professor is hopeless, as he does not know, or will not tell, the name of a single flower.

It was midnight when we arrived at Hay River, but there was still plenty of light to make a round of the Anglican mission. Canon Vale was anxious to show us the work of the little Indians and Eskimos at this school, and he is immensely proud of the fact that they have a furnace in the school. Storkerson's Eskimo wife[28] and children have been at this school for three years but she finds it difficult to learn the English language. Storkerson was with Stefansson on several of his northern explorations. The children were all in bed and I went around among the cots visiting them. On one little cot was a white bedspread embroidered in red cotton, outline stitch, saying it was from the baby guild of a Montreal church.

Canon Vale told me that the children soon forget their own language after they come to the school. One little four-year-old girl came with her mother of the Loucheux tribe, and readily learned to speak English, after which she acted as interpreter for her mother, but in a few months she had forgotten the Indian dialect altogether.

The garden was just coming up. The ice had just gone out of the lake a few days, and this keeps the air cold and growth backward. However, there is the advantage that in the fall, the lake tempers the climate and there are no early frosts. So they always have lovely gardens. Gardens at all these posts are closely fenced to keep out the dogs.

We are well into the fish-eating country now and the cook got some fish here called connies (an abbreviation of enconnus). They have bodies like a salmon but mouths rather like a whitefish. They grow to thirty or forty pounds, sometimes seventy-five, and I understand that they will bite at a hook, although these were caught in a net.

In the Anglican Church was a brass tablet, to the memory of Private Frank Minchen and a coloured window and lectern had also been installed in his honour. His last gift to the little church before going overseas had been the baptismal font which he had made himself. The chancel choir was also homemade, the seat being of *babiche*,[29] woven things of leather. This village is just at the mouth of the Hay River and about fifty miles up are the Alexandra and Louise Falls. I am told they are very spectacular, regular Niagaras. This trip is much too fast to suit me. I should like to stop at every place and see things at leisure and get to know the people better.

Just a few miles back of Hay River, the Pure Oil Company is boring for oil, and although there are good prospects there is nothing definite yet.

JUNE 29 — Arrived at Fort Providence. I went with Bishop Breynat[30] and the mother provincial who were on board with us from Resolution to see the mission. The Grey Nuns came here in 1867 since when they have established five missions up and down the river.[31] Sister St. Rose showed me her garden with which she was not well pleased as the soil was none too good. However, they grew 3,000 bushels of potatoes last year and these with the 25,000 to 30,000 fish which they put away each fall feed the eighty children and ten sisters in residence. The sun dial at Providence was supposed to have been made by Franklin[32] but this was a myth as the date on it was 1887.

Tonight I watched the most magnificent sunset. The river widened out into a lake, and it was just half past ten when the sun sank below the horizon. After that some heavy clouds rolled up and the water looks like a great pool of black oil.

Ever since we left Great Slave Lake there has been very little current in the river; more like a succession of lakes in fact, but here the current starts and this was what was known in the old days as the "head of the line." When the old York boats were used they had to be towed up from the delta, almost a thousand miles, by man power, and the paths along the banks where the men used to walk with a tow line in hand can still be seen. The river is a majestic thing here, two to three miles across, a vivid contrast to the undecided, shifting little creek in which we started. Along the shore are big dirty cakes of ice kicked out there by the river this spring as it made its first mad rush for the ocean after the break-up.

JUNE 30—There are enough fish in these rivers and lakes to feed a continent. The people here consider whitefish the perfect food because it is the only meat with which one does not become satiated. Just where Great Slave Lake empties into the Mackenzie River, a couple of men were fishing; they had several nets and a fish wheel which kept revolving in the current steadily collecting fish. Every few hours all day and night the men went out to the nets and got whitefish, lake trout, enconnu, grayling or, as they call them, bluefish, pickerel, jackfish, pike, suckers, etc. Farther down near the ocean there are big runs of herring at certain seasons. I never minded baiting my own hook when I went fishing and always took off my own catch, but I cannot say I would care to do it after the fashion of these fishermen. They pulled up the nets till a fish came flouncing to the top, leaned over the side of the canoe, grabbed him firmly behind the gills and took him in their teeth; then their hands were free to strip off the entangling net. They remove the backbone and the great bodies are hung over racks to dry for winter use. A dozen big Huskie dogs ate the entrails so in this automatic fashion the place was kept clean and sanitary. Enough fish are put up for the winter keep of both men and dogs.

Later we had an interesting afternoon at Fort Simpson. I had lunch with Flynn Harris,[33] the Indian agent. It was a bit of a surprise, even in this surprising country, to see a law library in his office, and it turned out that he had been a lawyer. He had been called to the bar in Nova Scotia, in the old North West Territories and, as he said, a lot of other bars as well.

In 1910 the Hon. Frank Oliver, Minister of the Interior, took this trip down the river to investigate the possibilities of agriculture in the far North. As the result of that visit he established a little experimental station at Simpson, and while it has not been seriously developed, it is still being operated in a sort of fashion by the Indian agent. The wheat ripens four years out of five on average and barley matures every year. There was all sorts of garden stuff and Mr. Harris assured me he had grown 900 bushels of potatoes to the acre. They must have been crowding each other considerably. They have a few head of cattle, and a team of horses, the last we shall see. In the mission garden a demure little lilac tree was in bloom just the same as down East. There were wild strawberries under your feet everywhere, luscious big ripe berries.

Simpson is just at the junction of the Liard and the Mackenzie. The Liard starts less than two hundred miles from the Pacific coast and opens early in the spring, forcing the ice out of the Mackenzie from here north, five or six weeks earlier than south of here. Some day when the world needs more wheat I expect there will be farms all along the Liard and the native grasses assure feed for stock.

The Grey Nuns have a little hospital here. There were a lot of business-like dental forceps in the operating room and I asked the little sister what she did with them. Another unnecessary question with the obvious answer that they were for pulling teeth. It was hard to imagine this tiny person, weighing not more than 95 pounds, extracting the well-rooted molars from some of those husky Indians. The equipment for the operating room had been shipwrecked and lost the first time they tried to bring it in.

There were no bad patients, when I was there today. I found that most of their cases, outside of accidents, were T.B. or dropsy. There is no doctor nearer than Dr. Richardson at Fort Norman, 300 miles, and they have really no claim to him as he is employed by the Imperial Oil Co.

Mr. Harris had charge of a little saw mill, and in fact his duties varied all the way from Notary Public to being chairman of the school concert that was put on for our benefit at the mission. It is just a day school, and "schooling," where the little Indian children are not in residence, is decidedly irregular; they just have to catch them for a day now and again as the families journey to and fro. The nun who taught the school knew English; all the rest spoke only French.

I talked with Poole Field[34] and his wife who had just come in from Nahanni country. The Nahanni River is tributary to the Liard and flows south between ranges of the Rocky Mountains. Along its tributaries they had been prospecting for gold and had samples. Their success had instigated a rush to stake claims, and the mining recorder had been doing quite a business.

There was an interesting story in connection with the finding of this gold. It was about the time of the rush into the Klondyke, that an old Indian, chief of Nahanni, came into Fort Liard with some gold-bearing quartz. He would not tell where he had found it, for although he was not specially interested in it himself, he had enough cunning to keep the secret. Failing to get the location, two of the sons of Factor McLeod[35] and another man of the name of Weir started up the Nahanni where they knew the tribe had wintered to see if they could find anything. They never returned and it was generally accepted that they had been killed by the Indians, which naturally deterred others from following their example. Finally another brother started out in search and found the bones of his brothers but no trace of Weir, which led to further speculation. Rumours of gold persisted, however, and in 1916 definite news was brought to Mr. Field, then running a trading post on the other side of the mountains. It was an old pal of Yukon days, Martin Jorgensen[36] by name, who sent the letter by some wandering Indians, and it contained minute directions as to his location. Field that winter sent four dog teams with the supplies across the mountains to the head of the river and in the spring as soon as the ice was out, he was ready. There were six in his party including his wife and her sister and his little daughter. For a boat they built a mooseskin canoe, a style of river craft popular with the Indians. Finally they came to a great falls, which they estimated had a sheer drop of 400 feet, the roar of which could be heard for miles, and here they established their camp.

Following the directions in the letter, they prospected down the Flat River, a tributary, found traces of gold on two or three creeks and finally came to Jorgensen's deserted cabin. Here was another message written on a tree trunk with a burnt ember, giving further instructions how to find him and also the location of the gold-bearing creek.

After many days of travelling, they found his cabin but only charred logs remained and, about sixty yards away, the bones of a man, presumably Jorgensen. The season was getting late, the supplies were getting short even at the main camp, but they decided to stay the winter. They built themselves a winter cabin and went almost entirely on meat rations, to save their other supplies as much as possible. Then they went back to seek the creek that ran in a bed of gold. They found the creek, or at least it seemed to correspond with the one shown in the map, but there was no gold. It was a fearful disappointment, but they felt that Jorgensen was not one to be mistaken in gold and now with his map still in mind they believe there must be another creek running parallel through the mountain ranges; this they are determined to find.

When the supplies got down to one fifty-pound sack of flour and a few cups of sugar they had not worried particularly, but when they found they were reduced to two plugs of tobacco they saw famine staring them in the face so started back up the river and over the mountains to their house at Ross River.

They could find galena;[37] they could find iceland spar; they could even find a little gold, but they did not locate the mother lode.

There are about thirty families of Nahanni Indians from whom the river is named, and they keep very much to themselves, coming into the trading post only when necessary, not even mixing with the other tribes of Indians if any happen to come their way. A man coming into their camp, stops some distance away and fires two shots by way of announcement, and if he is welcome, two shots are fired in return.

Years ago, the Nahannis found what seemed to them great deposits of pure lead. Just as that time they were rather "at-outs" with the Hudson's Bay Company, on account of the price they were being charged for their bullets, so they decided to make their own ammunition. They melted the lead in a frying pan over the campfire, when suddenly it disappeared and, believing that the hot mass had been spirited away, they hastily packed camp and left the place, never to return for they had no desire to displease the great spirit. But the great six-foot seams of galena are still there waiting to be used.

This corner of the earth, hidden in among snow-capped mountains and cut by rushing rivers, has already claimed its tragedies, not the least of which was the peculiar disappearance of Mrs. Field's sister. The women were half-breeds, but had been to convent school when children, and could read and write. Mrs. Field was very charming with her quaint little accent, a great generous nature, and was supremely happy living with her husband and their little girl, hundreds of miles away from human companionship except occasional visits of the Indians. Her sister complained of not being well, and she thought the trip with them would furnish the needed tonic, but the sister's mind, already weakened, became worse and in spite of the closest surveillance she slipped away one day and disappeared as completely as if the earth had swallowed her. They searched for weeks, but never got a trace.

Mrs. Field told me of wonderful trips she and her husband had taken, with dog-team, or canoe, or on snow-shoes, of shooting mountain sheep which stood outlined on the top of a cliff; of following the moose trail; of making camp, carpeting the floor of their tent with spruce boughs; of the wonderful mattresses made by sticking upright in the ground layer on layer of small spruce twigs leaving no bumps and making a delightful springy bed.

There were natural hot springs at their camp, with more farther up the river and in the winter, she said, with snow all round, they had gone swimming in the pools. There was a sulphur deposit on them, and she showed me little ornaments she had modelled from this stuff, which look much like the plasticine things children do at school, only when dry they were quite brittle and broke easily.

I bought a pair of moccasins at Simpson; they are artistically embroidered with porcupine quills dyed in different shades.

I saw much prettier ones on the Indians themselves and discovered that they always wear the prettiest ones themselves. A maiden will spend weeks on a pair of moccasins or a beaded coat for her sweetheart.

When we stopped for wood this evening, I had my daily swim. The water is cold but no worse than the tub I take every morning at home. I did not stay in long as the mosquitoes were bad.

JULY 1ST—We have been travelling pretty well West since we left Great Slave Lake, but this morning we came abruptly on to the mountains and the river swung directly north. We can see the mountains each side of the river; some are snow-capped and some are green to the top, covered with spruce trees.

At the settlements the shores are lined with birch-bark and skin canoes, as the Indians are all in for "treaty." In the fall they go up the rivers and creeks to their favourite trapping grounds and then when the spring comes, they break camp, pack their furs and come down to the post to sell their furs and get their "treaty," which is all in one-dollar bills. They will accept nothing else. According to the size of their family and their fur cargo they plan themselves a boat. If it is to be a skin boat, they build a frame of poles and then cover it with moose-skins. Arrived at their destination, they strip the skins off the boat and sell them too, packing their household effects on the backs of dogs and trek off to their summer fishing resorts.

When Miss Samwell, one of the teachers at the Hay River Mission,[38] joined us at Hay River on her way down to Norman I was so glad that we still had some fresh meat. I could imagine how hungry she would be for a piece of beef after a whole year of fish. She was given the seat next to mine at the table and I was anticipating her pleasure when, to my dismay, she ordered the very fish we had bought at Hay River. I fairly

"Swimming in the great Mackenzie River, Arctic Circle." [BPSC]

"Birch Bark Canoe at Norman." [BPSC]

protested but she said she had become so used to fish that she did not care for meat. So much for my ideas of the necessity of a varied menu.

Being Dominion Day I tried to have a fitting celebration, but could not get any of the men to make a speech and no one suggested that I should.

When we stopped for wood tonight I kept myself busy building smudges for the men who were carrying. The mosquitoes take a special delight in attacking a man when he is helpless with a pile of wood on his shoulders.

I took time for a little exploring trip back in the woods and found a spot that looked almost like a florist's garden. The trees were very high, and there was practically no fallen timber or underbrush. The ground was heavily carpeted with fox tails, giving the appearance at a little distance of a well-rolled lawn. Out of this grew tall rose trees, some of them nearly six feet high, at the top of which were one, or possibly two, perfect roses. The bushes looked as though they had been pruned, rising tall and slender, with this perfect bloom at the top. It was after two when I came back to the boat, but it was daylight all the time and the sun is rising now at 2:30. It is hard to go to bed when there are so many lovely things to see.

JULY 2—FORT NORMAN. In addition to the traders here, there is an Anglican and a Roman Catholic Church and the government has a sub-office for the recording of mines, oil leases, and such like. They had taken a big log house from the Hudson Bay lots and moved it by man power to the top of the hill. Downstairs was the office; upstairs a very complete living apartment with comfortable artistic furniture made of the birch trees with the shining white bark left on. They had made it themselves of course and most of the credit seemed to go to Dr. Richardson, who was down from the oil wells paying a long visit while he looked after a man who had been badly frozen last winter.[39]

This man had a shack out twenty miles or so where he was cutting wood for one of the steamboat companies, and one day last winter he had frozen his feet. Crawling on hands and knees he finally managed to get home but the toes were badly frozen and gangrene set in so that eventually he had to amputate his own toes with his jackknife. He does not know how long he was unconscious after he arrived at the shack, but thinks that it must have been six or seven days. Anyway he was in the shack alone from December 8th to April 19th when the mounted police found him. During that time he lived on twenty-five pounds of flour which he mixed with a little snow, making a sort of dough. He was brought into Norman on a dog sleigh and Dr. Richardson took him in hand. When I talked to him today his worst worry was that the company would send him out of the country when they saw that he was still on crutches and he did not want to go. One might think he had had enough of it, but it seems not. He was born in Pittsburgh, Penn., so he has wandered far from home.

It seems to be the general impression that the Indians are well treated—in fact, that they are being spoiled by the traders who are competing for their furs. We find mostly Slavi Indians down here. I met Bishop Lucas[40] who has been in the country thirty-one years. He assisted in a celebration of Holy Communion at the little Anglican Church and it was quaint to see the squaws in their bright plaid shawls kneeling at the rail.

We can still see snow-capped mountains each side of the river but, between the shore and the mountains, is a great muskeg several miles wide.

In winter they have good sport here shooting ptarmigan—a sort of grouse which turns white, like rabbits, when the snow comes. In summer they are grey like prairie chicken. Picking them off the snowbanks with a twenty-two is a sporting proposition as not a bit of colour shows for target, except the little black beak. There is usually one black tail feather but that is not visible till they start to fly.

Spring, summer, and autumn seem all crowded together here. Although we can still find plenty of wild roses in bloom, the fireweed is also out, and that seems to belong to autumn. For miles we can see its dark cerise blossoms, covering every naked spot where fires have denuded

"*McCleary, Fort Norman; man who was so badly frozen.*" [BPSC]

the land of its trees. They tell us, the autumn tints begin to show about the first of August.

The botany professor is giving encouragement to a moustache, a rather anaemic affair. Also, after weeks of sober living he has suddenly given way to smoking cigarettes, but he does it very genteelly, using a six-inch amber holder. We have warned him to be careful, as dear knows what would grow there if the wooly down were burned off. Poplar comes where spruce has been burned off, we tell him; maybe feather follows down.

They go by sun time at Norman, which is about an hour and a half slower than our watches. The sun dial there was put up by F.V. Seibert[41] of the Department of the Interior. For some reason the old one had thirteen hours on one side and eleven on the other.

We passed the first oil derrick shortly after we left Norman, and then about fifty miles farther down came to the Imperial Company wells. At the Fort Norman Company well, no work was going on, but there were two men in charge—and a horse.[42] This is actually the last horse. They had brought him in to—well, to do the work of a horse—drag machinery around and such like, and part of our cargo was some hay and oats for him. He came running down to the beach, when the boat stopped and seemed interested in the oats, but a few minutes afterwards when his companion was cutting off a chew of tobacco, he left the oats and took the tobacco.

At the leases of the Imperial Oil Company, exploration work has been started in four holes, but only in one have they found any oil. This one is called the Discovery Well, and it was a gusher at this hole that started the excitement here four years ago. They had been cleaning it out and had had another little gusher the day before we arrived. There was black oil all over the rig and the buildings and right down the shore to the river.[43] The well is down about 900 feet and they have had a flow of sixty to seventy barrels a day. But it is known that the flow of oil from this well gradually decreased after the first big gusher, until production

"Two old sports at Fort Norman." [BPSC]

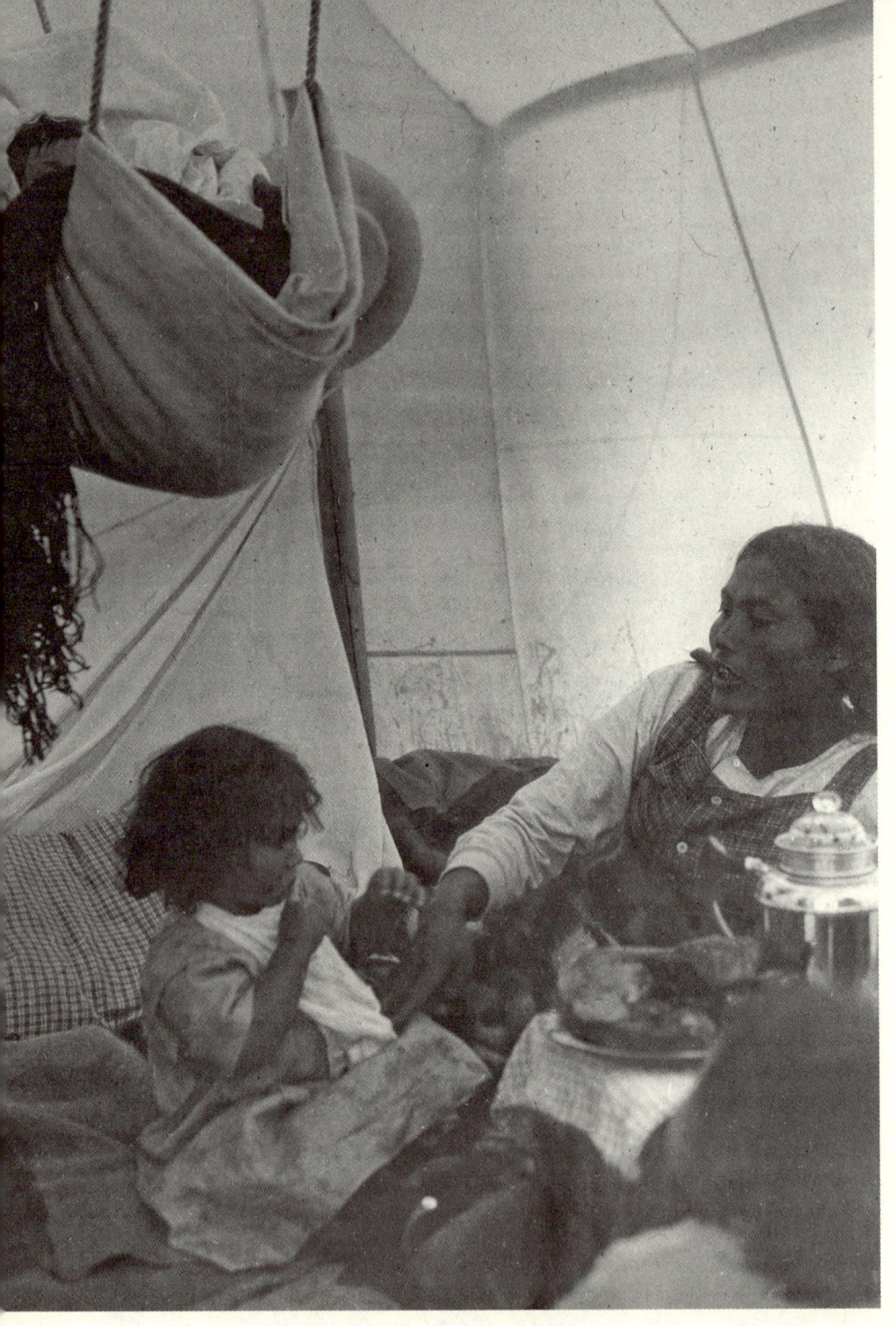

*"Baby two days old in hammock; Indian family—Fort Norman."* [BPSC]

almost ceased. This was attributed to some failure of the oil supply, but it is generally accepted now that the bottom of the hole, which was of shale formation, caved in and effectively prevented the entrance of oil in any quantity. While this work has not demonstrated that any big wells will be "brought in," it does show that oil is there in quantity. None of the wells has been taken to any depth yet. It is so difficult and tedious to get in machinery when wanted, that it takes a long time to accomplish such exploration. They had a little gasoline refinery where the company had refined enough gasoline for their own use in their boats and machinery and the gas was piped into their buildings. But the exploration work of the big company is so slow that most of those who had taken up leases both sides of the river, at the first "scare" have dropped them, unable to do the required work or keep up the dues.

LATER—I closed my diary there and went to bed but was not asleep when I felt the boat pitching around in a most undignified manner and jumped up to find we were going through the Sans Sault Rapids.[44] It was a gorgeous sight. The water was seething beneath us and we were racing down between the rocks like mad. In front, the sun was reluctantly setting, but stretched out to meet us as we came, leaving a long brilliant path up the river. It might have been liquid light lying on the water, only it was more alive, more vivid than light, but not so wicked as fire. High rocky banks ahead reflected the sunset in changing shades of rose to grey and as we hurried past the colors changed again to elusive shades of veiled orchid.

I did not get to bed again, for I could not bear to miss any of it. The rapids and the sunset and everything proved to be only the preparation for the Ramparts,[45] great walls of patterned rock which the river forces with a gliding stealth. For seven miles the shores were perpendicular as the walls of a great corridor, at the end of which is Fort Good Hope,[46] its whitewashed buildings standing out like beacons on the hill on which they are built.

I climbed up a steep narrow flight of steps to the hill top to see the church, the pride of the Roman Catholics. Father Petitot,[47] a young priest of artistic leanings, came out not many years after Father Grouard, and spent his life building and decorating this little church. For the carving he used his jackknife; for nails he made wooden pegs and for paints he used the vegetable and mineral dyes he could find. There are no seats in this highly decorated church but the light burns always in front of the altar, and at the back is a graveyard where two or three priests have been buried and on their graves blossomed wild blue columbine. Wooden crosses marked their graves, jackknives had chiselled their names. There was one fenced-in plot for the Gaudet family, a name which has figured long in the annals of the Hudson's Bay Company in the North West. Apparently of recent installation, were three marble headstones. The centre one was for Mary Dorah Betsy, 1817–1909, nearly five score years, and on her left was Frances M. Terroux de St. Lambert, épouse de Frederic G. Gaudet, 34 yrs., and underneath, Nancy Frances Marie, décédée à l'âge de 3 days. The record, partly French, partly English, told the double tragedy of a home on the Arctic Circle.

JULY 3—That last bit should have been dated July 3 but when there is no darkness and no sleeping time to separate one day from the next one, it is likely to make a continuous record. We got to the woodpile about nine in the evening and I climbed the little mountain to investigate what made the whole place look purple. It was a flower like a wild sweet pea in deep mulberry shade; the ground between the spruce trees was covered with it, while here and there for contrast was a little yellow buttercup growing on a sort of vine. I was fortunate enough to discover the purple flower in McCalla's flower book, and it is called *Hedysarum mackenzii*.[48] It has no tendrils like a prairie pea, but grows upright more like stocks. The flower is a rich rose purple and blends in with the Indian paint brush, which is more of a cerise purple. The hill where there was so much of the *Hedysarum mackenzii* was pure sand. The flowers here are all of more

*Northern Trading Company steamer* Trader. *"Taken at 11:30 P.M. on the Mackenzie below Fort Norman."* [BPSC]

*"Roman Catholic Mission at Fort Good Hope."* [BPSC]

vivid colouring than farther south; even the wild rose when we still find an occasional one, shades toward the cerise rather than the soft pale pink of the prairie.

I dressed in my black dress for dinner, first time I have condescended to wear skirts since the revolution second day out. I stayed up most of the night making a poster for the Fourth of July. Con helped me and did the printing. For material we only had the pictures from stray magazines and it was rather difficult getting a connected thread of thought suitable to the glorious Fourth out of Palmolive and Holeproof hosiery ads, but eventually we got something that I thought quite suitable. As a matter of fact I am quite set up over the thing now that it is finished. It is half past four and we have worked all night without a light and the masterpiece has been hung on the most conspicuous place we could find. There are several Americans on board and perhaps they will get more enthusiastic over the Fourth than the Canadians did over the Dominion's birthday. They will be sure to be pleased at this little courtesy on board a Canadian boat anyway.

JULY 4—When I wakened we had turned up the Peel River—such a dinky little stream after the Mackenzie. This inconsequential little river winds around and turns back on itself and the captain is rubbing the side of his nose and smiling broadly over the prospect that it will be "real steamboating" coming back. Fort McPherson, which for years has been the end of navigation, is about thirty miles up the Peel, then we double back to the Mackenzie and go on down to Aklavik right in the delta of the Mackenzie. I can see the snow-capped mountains from my cabin window. The banks are deeply scarred where they have been gouged out with the ice, and leaving just a shelf of clay sticking out four or five feet above the water. As the frost goes out of this shelf, it drops off and falls with a great splash into the river, often taking trees with it.

I went out on deck, ready to receive the homage of the multitude over my original poster, and was considerably chagrined to find it absolutely ignored. It hung there as unnoticed as last year's calendar. I was just working up a strong case of self-pity when my little cousin came along and said enough nice things about that poster to make me almost forget the others. Anyway I have the satisfaction now that it will go back to the United States to be framed and hung in honour.

LATER—We got into McPherson right after lunch; the people there had just nicely gone to bed when someone heard the boat whistle and they all came out of their houses like bees out of a hive when it is disturbed. There had been a dance the night before—they had started "after the evening had cooled off a little" they said, which was probably near midnight—and had danced through until nearly noon next day. Not having any darkness makes it quite immaterial about when a dance or anything else starts or ends. If they have a hard trip they usually do it at night when it is cooler and sleep in the heat of the day.

The Indians at McPherson are an entirely different tribe from any of the others we have seen. They are called the Loucheux,[49] or "squint-eyed" Indians, and are decidedly of Oriental type of face. They seem more industrious and more intelligent than the other tribes and are heavy-shouldered, larger-built people. Mr. Firth,[50] who was factor for the Hudson's Bay Company for fifty-two years, has retired but lives here still. If more people retired within sight of the farm or factory where they spent their active lives they would be happier. Mrs. Firth is a Loucheux.

A Loucheux mother instead of carrying her baby in a moss bag, as do the Plains Indians, wraps him on her back with her shawl and a brightly beaded and fringed Cariboo belt slung across the shoulders keeps the baby from slipping through.

I met Inspector Wood of the Royal Canadian Mounted Police, his wife and little son here. They came over in their gas boat from Herschel Island, which is their headquarters, to meet the boat and get the annual mail. The Indian girl who came along as nurse maid for the baby was wearing moccasins and pink silk stockings. Everyone wears moccasins although there are some factory-made boots in the store.

*"Drying skins in front of tents at Fort McPherson."* [BPSC]

*Loucheux man and wife at Fort McPherson. "He is blind but watches the boat just the same."* [BPSC]

At one of the tents a couple of women were dressing cariboo skins, and inside, an old man was making a fish net. Most of the people were not making the slightest pretense of working, taking it for granted that a holiday had been declared when the boat came in, but this family seemed not to pay any attention to the excitement around. The one woman was working with a tool that looked like a chopping knife and the other, whose work was in a more advanced stage, was using a tool three or four inches wide, which she held like a dagger.

There were about seven dogs to every tent, all staked, far enough apart so they could not fight with each other. The dogs are better fed and better types than those we have seen along the river; in fact, some are beauties. The Anglican missioner here, James Mordant Crisall, seems to be an energetic person, and I was fearfully curious to know how he got his laundry done. His clerical collar was as properly ironed as though he had just had it delivered from the steam laundry. His fiancée is on her way in to him and they will be married as soon as she arrives. It comes easier to me now to say "coming in" and "going out"; people "come in" or they "go out." Moreover, it is "down North" or "up South" which is a tongue twister for me.

The Loucheux Indians are considered good church goers, and mostly Anglicans. In the graveyard back of the Anglican Church are the graves of four police who froze while making their winter patrol—Inspector Fitzgerald, 43 years old, Constable Taylor, 23 years old, Constable Kinney, 28 years, and Special Constable Carter, 41 years.

At the barracks I saw Alikomiak,[51] the young Eskimo murderer, who has at least three murders in his immediate record. One of these was Sergeant Doak who was killed as he slept in the hut that does for Royal Canadian Mounted Police barracks over on Coronation Gulf. The lad looks about sixteen but they say he is nineteen. He says that he did not mean to kill Doak but just shot to wound him and force retaliation. Alikomiak was tired of being confined to the little barracks for the murder of his uncle. The other two policemen were out on the ice getting seals which form an important part of their diet. He started out to "get" them but they were warned by some Eskimos, and Alikomiak was rounded up again and confined. In the meantime he had shot Otto Binder, Hudson's Bay factor. He had just been brought over from Coronation Gulf by Constable Stevenson. Part of the long trail was by dog team over the ice and then they waited for the river to open to come on to McPherson by boat. He will be taken over to Herschel Island to wait along with three or four other Eskimos his trial for murder.

At the Lamson and Hubbard post there was a beautiful grizzly-bear skin and some good lynx and timber wolf skins. They told me that the timber wolf pelts range all the way from black to pure white. The one I saw was white with a few dark hairs down the back. At all these stores the shelves are very empty; each spring they are sold right out by the time the boat comes. As soon as we arrived everyone was immediately demanding tailor-made cigarettes. They tell me that in a few days after the supplies are received the cigarettes are all gone and for the rest of the year they make their own. In one store there was a camera and a couple of boxes of Lux on the shelves along with some bear traps, and that was about all that was left. In exchange they had great bales of fur ready to be shipped out. It was a good winter for fur it seems, and this is a good place for mink for they grow especially large and beautiful; there are also lynx, wolves and rats. The arctic rat has a silver sheen that is pretty and quite different to the brown rats from the south.

I found arctic bramble or arctic raspberry with a delicate flower and lovely perfume, the pink wintergreen, yellow buttercup, chrysanthemum not yet in bloom. I wish I knew more about flowers or that our fat friend of the botany department would part with some of the secrets of his profession. There was another little flower here like the pink wintergreen only the flower does not open like a ball, but rather closes in like a little sack. There was also a purple headed flower with leaves arranged like on a nettle, but it is not nettle. It opens like a lilac and is a new one to the professor.

*"Alikomiak, Eskimo murderer, at Fort McPherson."* [BPSC]

*"Loucheux child wearing cariboo skin coat, Fort McPherson."* [BPSC]

JULY 5—3 A.M. If those Americans had had an ounce of romance or imagination they would have realized what a thrilling way they were celebrating their national holiday but they were as stolid as the proverbial Englishman. We left McPherson about seven o'clock, wiggled around the corners of little Peel River and came out again in the broad Mackenzie but we had scarcely more than turned our bow to the North than the big river disintegrated into the numberless little streams that go to form the delta. From here to the Arctic Ocean it is over eighty miles, just a network of rivers, backwashes, and sloughs. A couple of nights ago we stopped a few minutes beside a campfire to put off sacks of mail and some other things for Segre's survey party. Mr. Segre,[52] who has done much work in this north country, is now making a traverse of the Mackenzie from the Sans Sault Rapids to the mouth. As the season is short, the party will probably stay in all winter to get an early start next spring. No channel for large boats has yet been found right through to the Arctic Ocean but there must be one some place for a whale came one hundred miles up the river in 1870. He must have found at least a six-foot channel somewhere. Two years ago a steamboat made its way half way down the delta, and we are going to make a try at it this year. Even if Segre does find and mark a steamboat route through to the ocean, it is doubtful if it will be of any great use, as the channels change each year with the shifting sands, the ice and currents.

But that is not telling about the great adventure of seeing the "midnight sun," from Canada's back porch, on a night sacred to firecrackers and sky rockets. We have had no darkness for over a week but there was always a time each night when the sun sank below the horizon. Tonight we got sufficiently over the edge of the world that he never got out of sight. At midnight and at one we were going directly north and going directly into the sun. It seemed just on a level with our eyes as we stood gazing and wondering. The captain kept pulling his cap lower and lower over his eyes, to protect them against the glare, so he could see the channel, but so brilliantly did the sun's rays come across space to us that it was impossible to look long. The sun travelled along the horizon toward the east and then started up for another day.

I watched fascinated but all the time felt that I was doing something a little indelicate, that maybe the old sun had this special place way up here at the top of the world where he came each night to tidy his mind and maybe catch his forty winks before the new day, and here were we poor mortals intruding on his little bit of privacy. I was almost lost in a reverent thoughtfulness, when I was abruptly recalled by hearing the captain swear, quite a considerable swear too. The sun was so straight in his eyes he could not "read the water" and there were no channel maps to guide him. When I looked up, half amused and half resentful at having my reveries thus rudely shattered, the old boy hastened to cover up his last remark with the suggestion "that this would be a great place to hire n------s at fifteen cents from sun-up to sun-down with their bread and milk thrown in." The captain had learned his trade on the Mississippi.

The banks are flattening out, but they are still covered with small timber; although it is small in size, the largest spruce would not be more than twelve inches at the butt. The shores are four to six feet high above the river as it is now but there is every evidence that the spring floods go well over the top. Then as they retire they leave the bank cut in regular steps.

I am fairly exhausted for sleep but it is hardly worth while going to bed now as we will be at Aklavik soon. We took photographs on the deck tonight. Fancy, twelve, one, two, three o'clock in the morning and still able to take snapshots. Also fancy, three hundred miles north of the Arctic Circle and being too warm for comfort even at midnight.

It seems impossible to tell even in a diary how wonderful this night has been. The river has washed the corners off so many sandbars and islands that it is quite clay-coloured, but tonight, the whole picture was idealized by the glow of the never-ending sunset, which left the water, as far as the eye could see, a bright rich amber, shading to yellow gold. One long shaft of a cloud split the great orb in two for a while but the sun soon threw aside this futile veil and we "saw ablaze in the deathless days, the splendid sunset burn."[53]

All is so quiet, so serene and still behind that screen of trees which so jealously guards its shore secrets, the miracle of birth in thousands of lairs and nests is no doubt taking place. There are not only the caribou, the fox, the wolves, the mink, and so on which live here all the time, but thousands of wild ducks and Canada geese come right out to the Arctic coast each year to hatch their young. They fly five thousand miles to fulfil their destinies. The herring drive up the river in shoals from the ocean; the shores are covered with luxuriant vegetation, brilliant flowers punctuating the deep green of the leaves; everywhere evidence of the life that is here, just as two thousand miles farther south. Once upon a time something is supposed to have happened that shifted the earth off its perpendicular axis. I wonder what would happen to this part of the world if it got another tilt. Then, the International Boundary would be the land of the midnight sun and this country would have a chance at filling the world's dinner basket. But would the Eskimo keep to their present location on the rim of the ocean, or would they, when the world sagged, scramble for the top again? Moreover, would the world still demand wheat or would it accustom itself to fish?

The Mackenzie is such a mighty river that any prophecy seems possible of fulfillment. It carries down so much water that for miles after one is out in the Arctic Ocean one may put down a pail and get a drink. If there is an east wind one may find fresh water almost to Herschel Island. The delta is eighty to ninety miles long and where it empties into the ocean it is about eighty miles wide.

JULY 5 — We came to Aklavik early this morning. It is half-way down the delta and is the shopping headquarters for the Mackenzie Delta Eskimos.[54] There are several tribes of the natives. West there are the Alaska Eskimos and farther east there are Kogmolloycs, then the Copper Eskimos; on Victoria Island are what Stefansson calls the Blonde

"Mrs. Stefansson and 'Old Mary,' Aklavik." [BPSC]

"Eskimo women and children, Aklavik." [BPSC]

Eskimos; around in Hudson Bay are others and so on east along the northern shore. The Delta Eskimos live mostly in and around the delta and it was a fearful shock to me to find they were such big upstanding people. Taken on average I think they are larger than Americans, certainly larger than the average of people that walk the streets of New York. I had always thought of them as little hunch-backed people that crawled in and out of beehive looking places on the ice. They had regular tents, but in the winter they live either in their ice houses or in cabins if they are inshore. They only stay at Aklavik long enough to sell their furs and buy their supplies. The coming of the trader has changed life for the Eskimos as well as for the Indians. They used to live absolutely on what the country provided them, little interested in the wonderful white foxes which they now trap and sell to buy guns, fishing tackle, tea, coffee, tobacco, butter, flour, and so on. They have been trying to learn to like salt, but can't. They have also been trying to preserve meat in salt as do the white people, but they do not care much for this either. When their trading is finished they move on to their fishing places. The Mackenzie Eskimos live mostly on fish. Further inland they get cariboo at certain seasons or, if they go back to the hills a little, they can get moose, rabbits, ptarmigan, something like a pinnated grouse that turns white in the winter time, or perhaps a mountain sheep, but the staple diet, winter and summer, is fish. They trap for beaver, lynx and the various foxes, silver, cross, red, blue, and white, and arctic rats. The white fox fur is the basis of barter, as was the beaver with the Indians. Just now the value of a white fox pelt is about thirty dollars. An Eskimo is a shrewd trader and is seldom poor; always he has a few best furs in reserve. He is not tempted with some glittering bauble that he does not need or want, but if you have something he really wants, he will make a generous bargain for it.

The natives put their meat and whale oil into a sack made of the skin of a seal and hang it up to ripen, eating it as they want it. When they are travelling the sack is towed behind the boats. In its prime, they say, it smells like ripe limberger, and I do not doubt that this is true, as some of the trinkets I bought today including some fish hooks and knives smelled just that way or worse. I soaked them in Lux and hot water for an hour, scrubbing them all the time before I dared put them in my bags. I got a little sack made of the skin of an unborn deer and will have it de-smelled and fixed up for Mary P's wedding present. It is decorated with the tiny hoofs, which are not much larger than your finger nail. Where they used to make their knives and tools of stone, bone, or sometimes copper,[55] they now make use of any steel they can get. One of the tools I got today was merely six inches off the barrel of a gun, and this was fitted into a wooden handle, which was a work of art. They use it for dressing hides. The handle is carved so that the second and third fingers fit firmly into a sort of notch and there is no chance of its slipping. Their fish hooks are not barbed like ours are but are merely bent pieces of steel firmly attached to the head of a minnow made of bone. This minnow is a marvelous bit of workmanship. In the head are cut tiny round holes in which are inlaid black eyes. This bait is on the end of a short line and the Eskimo sits over a hole in the ice bobbing it up and down and when a fish bites, it has to be landed at once, the hook being smooth.

A Swede, Pete Stransberg, has started a fox farm at Aklavik. He caught a number of little ones and will breed them to get the valuable cross. This may be easier and perhaps more sure than watching traps.

None of the men wear labrets[56] in their lips or cheeks now and the fashion of tattooing the women's chins seems to have gone out. They wear a wedding ring instead. All the older women had the green and black tattooed stripes from the lip to the bottom of the chin but none of the younger ones.

One young woman had her baby in the back of her dress with a belt around to keep it from slipping through. All the Eskimo women wear a sort of mother hubbard dress and this little mother had just tucked her baby in the back and there it slept, quite snug and out of the way. It was certainly an easy way to carry it, but I wondered it did not smother.

Bishop Lucas was there paying his annual diocesan visit to the mission and was very proud of the fact that the new church at the rim of the Arctic was so nearly completed. He has been in the country for thirty-one years and Archdeacon Whittaker who is now in Eastern Canada was in for forty-one years. Their wives are sisters and Mrs. Whittaker was at Herschel Island for twenty-three years. All her babies were born there. I asked about the vegetation, for the grasses and flowers grew luxuriantly. They told me that potatoes cannot be grown, or at least have not been grown yet, and they had tried lettuce and radishes with little success but they were inclined to think it was not more the fault of the cultivation than the climate. They grew kale every year but to do so had fertilized the ground with fish offal. The soil seems rather sour from constant flooding and the frost beneath. Only about a foot on top ever thaws.

In the summer the Eskimos sometimes use mud sleighs with runners about four inches wide which are coated over with mud and let harden. They will then drag along something like a steam boat.

To avoid being caught while on their winter patrol, caches of food have been placed at various points along the coast by the mounted police. At each place there is always wood laid for a fire, for men have been known to perish even after they reach shelter, just because they could not get a fire built before they became too numb to force themselves to do it. Anyone may use these cabins but must leave them as they find them.

Among the fish which they get in the delta are the whitefish, enconnu, ling, which they call lush, koniak—something like a bull head but looks like a Chinese dragon—the crooked back, a short hump-backed whitefish and an odd trout. The herring come up every summer from the Arctic and are a welcome change. Then the Eskimos eat the hair seal and the white whale. Both the oil and the flesh of the seal are included in their menus, and the skin is used for the bottom part of their boots or mukluks, as it is waterproof, but it hardens when they take them off at night. The old story about the women chewing their husbands' boots to make them soft seems to be founded on fact. The whale skin gets so hard that they could not put the boots on in the morning if they were not softened in some way, but I must say, I do not admire "the way." Some of the mukluks are extraordinarily pretty. They come nearly to the knee and the leg part is made of seal skin with an edging and tassels of wolverine fur around the top and sometimes the ankle is ornamented with strips of white fur from the belly of the deer.

They always use wolverine for the edging of their hoods as it does not collect frost from the breath and freeze to the face as would other furs. They do not get the wolverine here but import it from up river, so this particular fur is more valuable here than any place else. The boots and their fur parkas or coats are sewed with sinew and thus sewn practically never wear out, while fur sewn with thread soon cuts and pulls out.

While the family is travelling and a new girl baby[57] threatens to interfere with the business of getting a living, the baby is sometimes left on the ice to freeze or is otherwise put out of the way. To counteract this habit the Dominion government has appropriated a certain amount of money to subsidize Eskimo mothers who might not otherwise bring up their girls. It is not that the Eskimos are not fond of their children but the business of getting food is so precarious at times that another mouth to feed may jeopardize the entire family. For the same reason the old people or those sick beyond recall are sometimes left behind. They understand and raise no protest. The supplies which are sent in by the government to assist those who could not otherwise bring up their families are administered by the mounted police.

It is not that Eskimos are lacking in affection or that they have no sympathy with their helpless ones, but the life of the greater number must not be sacrificed for those who might not survive anyway. That they are willing to help their mates is instanced by a call which came to Mrs. Hoare[58] who is also a nurse as well as a missionary at Aklavik. It was midwinter when some Eskimos came asking her to go with them to a man who was very ill. For two hundred miles she travelled with them

*"Alex Stefansson, Aklavik."* [BPSC]

"The Eskimos taking our picture at Aklavik." [BPSC]

behind a dog team and in vain for the man was already dying. But they had done all their best.

I was amazed when we were leaving Aklavik this evening to see an Eskimo with a camera taking our pictures. He bought the camera from someone and has learned to develop the films himself, and another Eskimo will probably be practicing the gentle art of dentistry, as he bought out the equipment of a dentist who made the trip down this year in the service of the Hudson's Bay Company. It is easier for them to send in a dentist than to bring in their officers who need dental work done. So when the dentist got to the delta, a young Eskimo, who had been watching the process rather carefully, bought the entire outfit.

The Eskimos seem to be naturally adapted to mechanics. They take kindly to a motor boat and as long ago as 1910 a couple of them had an old engine which they succeeded in operating in spite of its antiquity. Mrs. Hoare told me of one who had fixed the mainspring of her watch. Riveting a mainspring would seem to be rather an acute form of mechanics and the sequel of the story is that the watch went.

Tailor-made cigarettes were very much in evidence as soon as the supplies were opened. All year they roll their own and when the boat comes in they make a dive for the ready-mades.

The Anglican Church has a mission here, with a comfortable mission house and a church just building. Both are set a little way back from the shore so they will not be carried off in the spring floods and a hospital is to be added soon.

Mr. and Mrs. Hoare and their baby, Billy Boy, and the Northern Trading Co. official were about the only white people here. But this will shortly be changed as a mounted police headquarters is to be established with a saw mill as a side line. And now that the boats have found their way, the other trading companies will also establish posts here. There is plenty of driftwood for building and fuel.

We almost arrived in time for a party. The Eskimos had a dance last night in what the missioner calls the community hall, which looks much like a woodshed or lean-to at the back of the mission house. Here they have their school, when there are any children for a school, a hospital, when there are patients for a hospital. It also serves for church and dance hall.

At Christmas the Eskimos gather in at Aklavik for their winter sports, although not altogether after the style of the Banff, Lake Placid, or Quebec carnivals. The big feature is the dog races, the trading companies putting up $150 for prize money. They have a little fireworks display, mainly a few firecrackers which amuse the natives, and they finish up with a big feast which is provided by the trading companies. The pièce de résistance at the banquet is fish and seal oil or *Okchuk*.

Aklavik will this year add to its self-esteem by being included in the list of Canadian post offices and His Majesty's mails will go in once a year on the boat and maybe a second time by dog train in winter—nearly two thousand miles down river by dog team.

An Eskimo woman called Laura—since we could not pronounce her Eskimo name—was brought in by the police and is being taken into Edmonton to be committed for insanity. Imagine a woman who has been living along the shore of the Arctic Ocean all her life going into the asylum at Ponoka. The policeman who is accompanying her says that she beat her husband and I suggested that perhaps the husband needed beating up. She fought like a tiger when the boat started to leave Aklavik but that is also rather natural since the poor girl is leaving everything with which she is familiar to go to a place of which she dreads the worst. She seems to understand English a little but does not speak it. Later she quieted down and when the stewardess went in this evening Laura was lying on the floor of her cabin. It took considerable explaining to show her that she was to sleep on the bed. (Laura was tried by Magistrate Murphy in the Women's Court in Edmonton, found mentally all right and sent back, her worst fault seeming to be that she was an inveterate smoker and also drank when the opportunity offered.)

JULY 6 — It made me rather lonely and sad to leave the land of the midnight sun. It was the grand climax to the great drama of life which we have been watching unfold along a river that drains one fifth of the entire area of Canada. Now, each day will be shorter and the river will be less wide, till we are back in the wee river where we started. It was like the slow unfurling of a great banner, and now we are rolling it up again till it will be just an uninteresting stick.

Two thousand miles beyond what we call civilization, and still human beings are living and working, reproducing and dying in much the same old way. The Eskimos have boats and could leave if they wished but they do not wish and white men who have lived in the North usually want to return. Of course there are the long arctic winters, but I imagine that one becomes accustomed to that, same as the tropics to their rainy seasons. They even accept their two months of constant sunlight as a matter of course.

Tonight we will lose the sun for a couple of hours and probably longer as it is cloudy. It was wonderful luck that there were no clouds to interfere last night.

"Midnight Sun taken 12:20 A.M., July 5, 1922." [BPSC]

Laura, the Eskimo woman, wanders around like a lost soul in the outer darkness. I suppose she wonders what it is all about and if she will ever again see the place which till now has been the whole world to her. She probably suspected there was another world where white people came from occasionally, but from what I have seen of the Eskimo people she had no idea what sort of world that was and cared less.

I feel sorry for her. Sometimes a tear wanders down from her hard sunburned cheeks and she looks at one with the eyes of a dumb beast that has been whipped, he knows not why.

Laura's table manners are not perfect. She had to be taught the use of knife and fork and her drinking is very distinct. In fact she has been relegated to second table, but I think she prefers this rather than sitting with people who stare. Her wardrobe consists of half a dozen skirts which she wears all at the same time and an old green sweater. She is the only Eskimo woman I saw with other than the mother hubbard dress, and she may be specially dressed for the occasion out of missionary barrels.

Her black hair is braided down her back and she has no hat. The other women all had hoods attached to their dresses or parkas. She is very definite in her likes and dislikes, will not touch meat, except fish, and is very suspicious of vegetables.

All day she sits or stands out on the side deck, rolling cigarettes and smoking. When she gets tired standing, she sits flat down on the floor with her legs straight out in front like a baby. That would be a new one to add to the "daily dozen" and warranted to strengthen the back.

JULY 9—Strange to say, the return journey is as interesting or more so than the trip in, at least for me. Coming in, I was so busy getting "copy" that I had no time to enjoy things. It takes half as long again to come back against the current.

There was the most wonderful rainbow tonight. It must have taken some of the colour out of the aurora borealis for inside the main bow there were several reflections in more subdued shades of pink and mauve and outside there was part of a second rainbow. The main bow was almost a complete circle, the last segment lost right at the edge of the boat. About half of it was in the sky and the rest came down across the tops of the trees, along the shore and across the water till I could almost touch it.

I picked a lot of late roses tonight. They were low set like the prairie rose and still not the same. There were lovely little tea berries, some blue lupines and other flowers for which I could find no name. I should like to put this botany professor in irons, for if he does not know, he should, and if it is just that he will not tell, he should be fed on bread and water, until he will.

The flowers are mostly deep cerise in colouring but there are a few blue and yellow ones. The red top seems to be the natural grass of the country here. There is a yellow flower that grows on a tough vine along the ground and is tall or short as the condition happens; there is just one flower on each stalk and it is something like a silver feather. The shores here are gravelly and with the dark green of the spruce trees behind remind one of summer resorts farther south.

I learned that at Fort Norman there is a Roman Catholic priest not long out from Germany. He served in the war and still comes to attention when he speaks of "Our Emperor." Almost next door to him is an Imperial Oil company man who fought with the Allies and in talking it over, they find they were in opposite trenches in some of the same engagements.

Today I saw a canoe filled with a pale yellow moss, and found it was the absorbent material with which the Indian women stuff the mossbags in which they carry their babies.[59]

On our way north, we took on an Eskimo pilot at Fort Good Hope to guide us through the delta and we are leaving him off again tonight. It is apparent that he, at least, appreciates the white man's food. His only English word is "more." He ate so much that the captain was afraid he would be ill and gave him a handful of black figs for dessert.

JULY 10—When we stopped for wood tonight I climbed the steep bank and came to a regular lake of moss. At each step I would sink almost to my knees in the soft plushy stuff. And I almost stepped on a partridge which rose with a fearful whir that sent creeps up my spine. I tried to follow her and take a picture, but she was craftily luring me away from her brood which I could see slyly scampering for cover. Several times I was close enough for a snap shot but at those times she was always in the shade, or the other side of a log or something. I followed her for half a mile, but when she had me far enough from her family, she flew away and circled back to them.

I found a flower that seems to belong to the fireweed family, but it has a much larger blossom and there were only one or two on a stem. It grew along a creek. There was also blue-eyed grass and some wild strawberries. The wild sunflowers are shedding their petals and the *Hedysarum* is in profusion everywhere.

JULY 10—Wrigley. Near here is Justice Creek, where they have just had a little gold rush, thirty-odd claims were staked. As the creek has its source in a lake, there is strong doubt, on the part of the cracker box orators of the ship, that it can amount to anything in the way of a real gold mine. The optimistic think there may be little creeks coming down from the hills which have brought the yellow sand.

I found such an exquisite, delicate flower today. I had never seen one before, but some one has, for it was designated in my flower book as the "one flowered wintergreen" or "single beauty."[60] It is like white wax and is star-shaped, with yellow stamens underneath. I also found some bunchberry in flower. It was a little larger than usual, and most of it had red calico spots, which looked a bit overdone, as though some one being bored with plain white ones had gone around and sprinkled red ink here and there. Another case of "painting the lily." I think it must have been some disease in the plant which made the red spots.

JULY 11—We have the lights for the first time in weeks. However, it was plenty light to roam around on shore, when the regular woodpile was sighted. This adventure of looking for new flowers grows on me. Here there was such a lot of pink wintergreen and another yellowish white flower that I thought belonged to the same family. There were quantities of paint brush, fireweed and grass of Parnassus, and the first goldenrod I have seen was just in bud. This was the first I have seen since we turned south again of the regular pea vine such as grows on the prairies. There have been plenty of pea-like flowers, but not on the trailing vine. The seedlings must have spread their wings wide to have come so far, for we are still a thousand miles from the prairies.

The wild strawberries are delicious, dead ripe and luscious, and the wild gooseberries and currants are ripening. It is a good thing my clothes are strong, or they would be torn off my back on these shore explorations. I have to climb through dense underbrush and over or under fallen timbers and occasionally I try to build a little raft to get across the creeks, but usually it happens that I slip off the logs midstream and have to wade. Every once in a while I have to come back to see if the boat is still there. It might not be pleasant to play Robinson Crusoe in these woods with a million mosquitoes to the square inch and not even a man Friday.[61] I think maybe I should take my rifle with me when I go, for if by any chance I did get left I would have a chance to make my living. Tonight dark navy blue clouds in the West and lightning that fairly split the sky in two brought me in early.

JULY 15 — We have been tied up in the river for two days waiting for the storm to subside on Great Slave Lake, but we are going to make a try for it tonight.

We stopped at Resolution for a while and let off a little bull which we had brought up from Providence mission. The bay is so shallow here that the boat had to anchor several rods from shore and the bull was shoved off unceremoniously and had to swim or sink. He swam, while I went ahead in the row boat and towed him. He is the worst little scrub I ever saw and it seems rather a pity that his kind should be reproduced. They have about a dozen cows at the mission here and the poor things were crouching over the smudges trying to get away from the mosquitoes and bull dog flies. The cattle here must have rather a hard time, with the intense cold in the winter and no proper housing and in the summer they cannot eat comfortably on account of the flies. It would not take many bull dogs to take off a pint of blood.

The gardens have advanced as much in two weeks as they would other places in six. With so much daylight and the constant supply of moisture from the frost beneath, they do not get a chance to stop a minute for a long breath.

We are racing to get to Fort Smith before the boat leaves the other end of the portage for Waterways. Personally I am hoping we miss it, for I want a few days to wander around Smith and I am sick of being rushed. However I don't dare mention this as everyone else is fairly tense with the fear that we shall not make connections.

JULY 17—Thank heaven we missed that boat and now I will have three days.

JULY 18—Again thank heaven we missed the boat for when I thought everything was past, the "big adventure" still awaits me. All down these thousands of miles of river banks, I have wanted to get in behind the curtain of trees that formed such an effective screen along the edge, and see the life, birds, beast, flower or human, whatever it were. Here I met a government surveyor whom I knew and he is arranging a trip for me to Salt Springs, supposed to be thirty-seven miles inland. I had heard of them but did not imagine that there would be any such luck as my being the first white woman to see them.[62]

I had to choose between seeing the buffalo, which range west of here, and going to Salt Springs, and it is a horrible strain making a choice when you want to do both things. My surveyor friend is this year exploring the territory over which the buffalo are ranging and a great area will be set aside as a preserve for them. They are the last of the wild buffalo. For years the law has protected them, but accidents will happen, and if an Indian mistook one for a moose or a rabbit or something, one could hardly expect him to leave it lying on the ground, when he found he had shot a buffalo. A ranger who came in today told us he had seen a few of the big humps about twenty-five or thirty miles out and of course I was fearfully keen to see them. But I cannot do both the Buffalo and the Salt Springs in three days, so have decided on the Salt. They will be sure to "stay put" till I arrive and maybe the buffalo would carelessly wander off twenty, fifty miles, in an unknown direction.

It was a real disappointment to give them up. There are about fifteen hundred in the two herds and I am told they are fine beasts, larger and richer coated than their brothers in the parks. Two thousand calves from Wainwright park are to be turned loose here next year.

JULY 22—It was some adventure. Almost I did not have it. After everything had been arranged, I found I had to ride a horse. I had supposed we would walk or paddle, but it was pointed out that we could do neither of these things in the time allowed. I will never forget the expression of contempt on Fred Seibert's face when I said I had never ridden a horse in my life. However I was determined to go if I had to swing from tree top to tree top like Tarzan of the apes.[63] So, shortly after lunch, on the hottest day I ever remember, I took my little bag and my twenty-two and climbed to the top of the hill, where we were to start. It is the longest, sandiest hill I ever knew. Each foot sunk into the sand like deep moss at every step. Arrived at the top, I found that the word had gone forth that a woman tenderfoot was to take her first ride, and all the inhabitants had come out to see me start. I was hot and tired and peevish and decided I just would not give them this free entertainment, so I intimated that I was very hot and did not want to cool off too quickly, so I would walk a little.

I cannot understand why they put the stirrups up so high. I just could not get my foot high enough, till finally someone held the horse while I took my foot in my two hands and lifted it up and finally got on. Once on, I wished I had a Shetland, for I seemed miles high, and I felt sure I should break every bone in my body when I fell, as I had not the least doubt I should as soon as the horse started to move. But I grabbed the pummel of the stock saddle firmly and managed to stick on.

There was Mr. Seibert and his assistant who were investigating the wood buffalo, Mr. Cassels who was making a survey of the Salt Plains, Mr. Maxwell Graham,[64] director of wild life for Canada who had just come in to check up the table manners and bad time habits of the buffalo, and most important of all was Joe, the Indian guide. Joe became interested in me as soon as he saw the pretty automatic Winchester I was carrying.

That first afternoon we had the worst thunderstorm I ever experienced. We could hear the brittle poplars cracking and falling all around us and I expected every minute my horse would bolt and I had visions of myself dragging for miles, one foot in the stirrup. None of the trees happened to hit us and we rode right on. The lightning was so dazzling and the thunder so terrific that even the horse shivered under me. I shivered too, but tried to pretend not to mind. The rain came down in torrents after a little, but that was a relief as it drove to cover the big bull dog flies that had been making life miserable for both man and beast. They lit on those poor horses in swarms and they are well named for when they bite, they literally take a piece out and they are not gentle about it either. Down East we used to call them horse flies, but everywhere in the West they are called bull-dogs.

Having to keep watch that some of the low-hanging branches would not sweep me off my horse distracted my attention. After I had my face scratched a few times, I let the storm take care of itself and watched for the jagged branches in my line of march.

We stopped about six for supper and I was almost afraid to get off for fear I would not be able to get back on, but the thought of doing without supper was worse still, so I got off. Joe went off to look for a spring and we made a fire and cooked bacon and canned sweet potatoes and tomatoes and there was jam for dessert. Without doubt it was the best supper I ever ate. We went another ten miles and made our camp about half-past ten. We made a campfire and dried our clothes and made some hot cocoa with canned milk. But I needed no soothing cocoa to put me asleep.

I was terrified that I would be so stiff in the morning I should not be able to move, but providence looks after fools and drunken men and my fears proved groundless.

They had brought along an air mattress for me and I was delightfully comfortable with my coat rolled up for a pillow. My little tent had a floor cloth that covered the entire space and kept out the dampness, and what was more important, the mosquitoes.

"Salt River ferry." [BPSC]

    Breakfast was almost ready by the time I was dressed next morning and my friends were surprised and relieved that I was able to move. As soon as the dishes were washed, we put up a little lunch and started on the last leg of our journey to the springs. None of the party had ever seen them except Joe, and he was none too sure of his direction.

    I was getting quite expert at mounting my horse by this time, and started off gaily, but before we had gone a half mile we came to the Salt River and found the bottom too soft to hold the horses and we had to take them back to camp and walk. We tried the horses a couple times and one got so badly mired, I was afraid we would not get him out at all. He was a pleased pony when he got his feet on hard ground again.

    But we had to cross the river and as the men did not want me to get wet they scurried along the shore to find something for a raft and discovered the remains of a birch bark canoe about eight feet long with the end torn out of it. In this they ferried me and then Mr. Graham across, one walking each side and holding up the broken bow out of the water. However, they need not have bothered, as we came to other creeks and muskegs, which were just as wet as the river.

We walked for some distance through the woods and then came to great stretches of bare plains. They were as flat as a floor and bare of all vegetation except here and there where the ground was a little higher and on these oases the vegetation was very luxuriant, trees very large, and the flowers of the most brilliant hue. Bleached buffalo skulls were scattered around on the plains and here and there we could see a bear track. All the creeks were carrying a strong solution of salt and when they overflowed in the spring, the salty water covered all these plains and killed all vegetation.

We were just rounding one of these oases when Joe called out that here was the spring. I hurried up to him and saw what looked like the chancel of a great outdoor cathedral. The woods bent around in a great half circle and in the centre, where the altar would have been, was a little clear running stream, tumbling out of the very face of the bank. It is hard to say how far it had been travelling underground, but when it came to the surface it was carrying a saturate solution of salt. It emptied into a shallow basin, the bottom of which was lined feet deep with pure salt crystals. All around the basin, the salt piled high where the sun had evaporated the water. This salt tests practically one hundred per cent pure salt. We boiled a quart of the water out of the spring and, after ten minutes, there was about three-eighths of an inch of salt in the bottom of the pail. Several tons had been sacked and cached near by for missions farther down the river. The Indians come here for their salt and sometimes sell it to the trading companies, getting three dollars a sack. They can paddle up the rivers and creeks to within about a quarter of a mile from this spring.

And I find that this is only one of twelve similar springs on these plains and all in a comparatively small area. There must be a mountain of salt somewhere in the vicinity from which these springs come, for each is carrying its full quota of salt. They drain out into the creeks which cut the plains and then into the Salt River and then into the Slave River and so on to the Arctic Ocean. Even in the Salt River, there was a definite taste of salt and we saw no fish in it. We will know more about it all when Mr. Cassels has completed his survey.

The percentage of pure salt in each of the deposits left on the ground after the water has been evaporated by the sun at different springs varies slightly, but any of it is pure enough for use without further refining.

Imagine the tons of salt wasted there each year since time began and perhaps this wonderful country will some day disgorge gold and lead and silver and iron and oil and wheat in just such prodigal quantities. By that time the commercial geography of the continent will have to be readjusted to accommodate the manufacture of untold natural resources in what is now largely an uncharted and unmapped country. And the rapids and falls in every river lend themselves to the reality of power for this development.

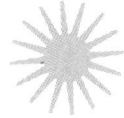

# ALONE (UNDATED)

A FOOTFALL—every nerve in John Carson's body tightened into knots; but it was only a rabbit thumping off into the woods.

He cursed himself for a fool and a coward. But fear, ingrowing and unceasing, gripped him in its coils, like the devilfish, its victim. As time passed, its clutches grew stronger and stronger, till he wondered how much longer he could withstand the vicious monster.

"Oh, God," he said wearily, as though it were an idea many times rehearsed, "why did I bolt like a guilty cur? Anything would have been better than this damnable skulking."

Carson sat on a bit of log, idly feeding the tiny fire he had built under his tea pail. He could hear the gentle swirling of the water in the Rabbit

Kettle—as the Indians called the huge bowl of rock in which the water, hot and oily, slowly circled like an exhausted whirlpool. All around were bright bits of cloth tied to the trees, relics of a recent pilgrimage of the Nahanni Indians. They believed the place sacred to the Great Spirit, who came to this restless steaming pool at the very top of the mountain to cook his rabbits. So they called it Rabbit Kettle.

It was like a crater, full of ever-moving water. From a crack in one side, a little stream spilled out and ran down the mountain. For miles and miles, it travelled south, in the valleys of the Rocky Mountains, till it joined the Nahanni River, then south and west to the Liard. Finally it reached the great Mackenzie, which bore it north again and out into the Arctic Ocean.

It was a queer notion of the Indians, thought Carson, to make these expeditions—many days' travel from their regular routes—to do homage to the god of the Rabbit Kettle, and to seek to propitiate him by gifts. Their best-loved treasures, their trinkets and food, they threw into the unknown depths of the pool. Bright coloured bits of cloth they brought to decorate the trees around, assuring the Great Spirit of their devotion.

So acute had become Carson's hearing that the Indians suspected something uncanny about him, and in the evenings by their campfire, queer, fearsome things were told of the strange white man, who travelled always alone. His red hair and blue eyes set him apart from all others.

Listening and hiding, that was his life, he thought grimly, and wished he had given himself up to the police at the time. No punishment could be worse that what he had endured for ten years, afraid to go in the travelled trails, afraid to meet anyone; often afraid to light a fire; afraid to sleep, in case they should slip in on him, unawares.

Sometimes he wondered if he had really killed the man, but the memory of that ghastly thud as the big body crumpled up on the bar-room floor, left him in little doubt. No, he had not meant to kill him, but small comfort that. His thoughts blinded him so he did not see the great walls of rock from which the setting sun drew out a rainbow of blended colours, not the timbered valleys, which in the distance looked like rich carpets, not the snow-capped mountains that towered above even where he sat.

He saw, rather, the tiny home on the moors where he had spent his boyhood, and the doubting, hopeful look in the eyes of his mother when he left her to take up free land in Canada; and that last evening when he had wandered over the hills with Jennie, who had been his sweetheart since they were children.

"Have your sheets and tablecloths all hemmed, and I will be back for you in two years," he had tried to laugh as he said it, but with rather poor success. She had made no reply.

Her hands were so cold and as she pressed them against his cheek to warm them, she dropped her head on his breast and a hard dry sob seemed to come from the very depths of her being.

"Don't do that, sweetheart," he had said, his arms pressing her so closely; "You make me feel as though you were saying good bye for ever. You will wait for me, won't you darling?" he had added thoughtfully.

"Yes, I will wait," she had said quietly but with little enthusiasm.

"Don't you want me to go, Jennie? You know I would not leave you except to make a home for us," he had pleaded, wishing she would speak or cry or anything rather than that attitude of quiet finality. "We will have 160 acres all our own and as soon as I have built a house and a little stable for the cow and laid by enough money for this trip, I shall be back. You will like having a home of your own, Jennie, with no rent to pay to greedy landlords." All this had been discussed many times before but he felt somehow that he must explain again.

She had pushed him gently but firmly away from her.

"I'll be going home now, John. Goodbye. No, don't come. I think I would rather be alone."

Next morning he had left for Canada, the land of hope and promise.

In the weeks and months that followed, how often had he longed for her comforting presence, her warm arms around his neck. His lonely meals were lonelier as he failed to imagine her across the table from him.

Every two weeks he had a letter from Jennie, rather prim, formal messages, but he treasured them all. He had them right now in a little buckskin wallet in his shirt. He could feel them pressing against his heart. But the last one was ten years old. He wondered where she was, what she thought when she had ceased to hear from him.

A year later he had forsaken his homestead to join the mob that was trekking happily and carelessly into the Crowsnest. It was the boom of '94 and farming seems very tame to the thrilling possibilities of gold, ready-made.

Arrived at the busy little mining town, he had taken a job as bar keeper while he was getting his "outfit" together. One night, a man half drunk and very boisterous swaggered in and ordered drinks for the crowd. There was some argument about paying, and with an oath, the fellow had drawn back a doubled fist. Instinctively Carson had grabbed an empty bottle and had struck the disturber over the head. He could still remember the awful stillness when the man had dropped to the floor; in the excitement that followed he had slipped out.

At first he followed an old trail to an abandoned mine. From that he had forced his way on, sometimes wading for miles up the cold, hurrying mountain streams; sometimes following the hard moose trails, which left no impressions of his tracks.

Every sound was ominous. A deer stepping over a fallen tree sent him to cover like a frightened hare; a squirrel chattering in a nearby tree—and he suspected an enemy giving a call to his comrade. A hoot owl brought out cold sweat on his body; a field mouse rustling in the dead leaves terrified him.

Once that first year he had seen a notice, tacked on a tree trunk, offering a reward of $5,000.00—it was for his capture, dead or alive. He had not seen one lately, but the Mounted Police seldom quit.

He lived on the game which he shot or trapped. He clothed himself in their skins. About the only things he needed of civilization were tobacco, tea, and ammunition, and for these, he went out once a year to one of the smaller trading posts, where there was less likelihood of meeting a Red-coat. He made his purchases quickly and fled back to the sheltering woods. Like everyone else in the country, he paid for what he got with fur, and he always had plenty of it. He asked for no credit. He made no friendships.

Then came the Dawson rush of '98.

One night, crouching behind some underbrush outside the light from their campfire, Carson overheard some men talking of the wonderful gold fields of the Yukon—and how men had grown rich over night.

Gold! If only he had enough to leave these imprisoning mountains. If he could get on a boat for the Orient; if—

Far into the night he sat and wondered, fighting the corroding dread that almost completely possessed him, whipping up his courage to the point of walking into their camp.

For two days he followed them cautiously, contemptuously noting their amateurish efforts to understand the lore of the woods and the significance of stream channels.

It was an incongruous group. He could see them plainly in the firelight.

One man with heavy shoulders and fair hair looked like an Irish policeman. He had thrown himself down with a disgruntled sigh, his head on his pack:

"I wish that I had never started out on this damned trip into a land that God and everyone else has forgotten. We will starve to death before we get anywhere, and no one will know anything about it."

"Grinding out on that old story again, eh?" said a tall swarthy fellow who was cooking something over the fire. "Well, if we depended on you for our meals, we sure would starve to death."

"Oh, quit beefing, fellows," said a slight young lad, the smallest of the group; "if we get into the Yukon before winter sets in, we should consider ourselves lucky.—I think we should find a moose along here somewhere; this looks to me like moose country."

"Oh, yes, IF. Well, I'm tired of your IFs. The old United States would look awful good to me right now and I'd be willing to sell my eternal rights in all the gold mines of the Yukon for just one peep into Mike's bar room down 63rd Street. We don't know where we are, nor where we are going and if we don't starve to death we will freeze like frogs in a few weeks. The winter comes early in this north pole suburb. I don't know why we did not grab off one of those Indians to guide us," he finished with a whine.

"Say, fellows," spoke up a good looking man who had been studying a map, "I think this river must be the Nahanni, and if it is we're perfectly OK."

"Just what I was saying," said the Irishman, "if we only had a guide."

So! Thought Carson from his hiding place, this is my chance. If I am ever going to make a break, here's to it. They need a guide and I need someone on whom to practice talking again. They are from the States and they won't know anything about that old story, he assured himself, as he walked into their camp. His name, he told them, was Fisher.

He guided them as far as Hoole Canyon on the Pelly River about three hundred miles from its junction with the Yukon.

Then in the proximity of settlement, the old fear overcame Carson. He just could not take the chance of meeting the police; but he cringed at the thought of turning back alone. He wondered if he could not persuade "the youngster" to go with him—"Doc," they called him, probably because he looked like a student.

"You fellows will not have any trouble in finding your way from here," he said that night. "I have decided to go back to the Nahanni."

The big Irishman, his name was Loucks, at once broke into vituperative argument.

"You would leave us out in this god-forsaken country to starve to death, would you? Well, out with it, what is your price?"

"Shut up, Loucks," said 'Doc.' "Fisher did not sign any contract to take us into the Yukon and he does not have to come unless he wishes. But," turning to Fisher, "we have you to thank that we have arrived this far, and we would sure like to have you stay. Don't you want some of this glittery stuff?"

A sardonic smile passed over Carson's face. Little did they realize how badly he wanted gold—nor how much he hated to lose his newfound companionship with his fellow men.

"I think I have another pretty good lead, and that is why I have resolved to go back to the Nahanni. I think the chance for gold is just as good, and the competition not so keen. I was prospecting around there this summer when I met up with you. How would you like to go partners on the proposition, Doc? We can always make a living with the traps anyway."

"What makes you think there is gold there?" said Doc.

Then Carson told of a chance encounter with the old chief of the Nahanni Indians, who had told him of a mine up the river. Gold meant little to the Nahannis who seldom went down to the trading posts, but his natural caution prevented the old chief from imparting the location of the mine to Carson, of whom he was suspicious anyway.

"But I know their hunting grounds pretty well, and I think with a good partner, I could locate the place," said Carson looking directly at Doc.

"I had a chunk of the stuff in my hands, nearly as big as a hen's egg, and the chief said there was lots of it," he added craftily. "Besides, there are some hot springs over there, water warm the year round—have your bath every morning, lots of game, a grand place to winter, and we would be right on the spot in the spring."

But Doc had set his heart on the Yukon.

Loucks had said nothing during this conversation, but that night after the others had turned in, he came around to talk further of this gold mine and of the hot springs. Next morning he announced he would go with Fisher; he wasn't so likely to freeze to death anyway.

Fisher would have preferred any of the others, for he had not taken much to this loud mouthed, boasting, cowardly fellow, but beggars (and murderers) could not be choosers. Anyone was better than no one.

Many days of travel and many weeks of prospecting, but they had not found the lost mine. They went up one creek and down another, until in the upper waters of the Nahanni, they found some placer. That fall, they "panned" about $13,000 worth of "dust." But they still greedily longed for the Lost Mine, where according to the Indians the "pay streak" ran rich and deep.

"How be," said Loucks, "if we take some of this money to buy regular equipment, and go right after it next summer."

Carson was afraid that Loucks, who had never become accustomed to finding his way in an unchartered country, might insist on both of them going out to buy the equipment, but rather to his surprise Loucks seemed quite willing to go by himself, said his teeth had been bothering him, and he would like to see a doctor or someone who could use a pair of forceps.

In the evenings when they discussed what they should buy in town, Carson came nearer to liking Loucks than he had ever been. When he got used to things, thought Carson, Loucks would be all right. It was natural that a chap who had never been off the city streets should be timid in the woods.

"Try and get some mules that are not too handy with their hind legs," he said with a laugh. "If you stay close to the river you should not have much trouble in getting them back. You might bring back a few newspapers—and for the love of Pete, don't let anything happen to the tobacco. I could do with a new pipe too."

"Would you like a little box of bonbons too?" asked Loucks with a smirk.

Carson planned the trip for him as well as he could.

"You should be able to get out in a month," he said. "When you come back, the rivers will be frozen over and with the mules you can make pretty good time. You should be back in ten or twelve weeks at the longest."

"Sure, I'll be all right," said Loucks; "but it may take me a little longer than that. You know I cannot get around in these woods as easily as you can. But I suppose you can go on panning out the odd bag of dust. It might come in handy." And his eyes narrowed down to a slit as he looked at Loucks who had got up to put more logs on the fire.

"I guess I may as well get started tomorrow or the next day," he said casually.

"How much of the gold do you think you will need?" said Carson. "Five thousand should buy a pretty good outfit."

"I have been thinking we ought to have that gold in some safe place," said Loucks casually. "If I took it out with me, I could put it in a bank. Then we would be sure of it. Here, some damned Indian is likely to come along and clear us out."

"No, the Indians won't touch it," said Carson.

"Well, I think it would be safer in the bank," persisted Loucks. Carson rather reluctantly agreed; as there seemed no very good argument against, he let the matter drop.

Next day Loucks left camp with all their precious sacks of gold. While Carson waited his return, he made his plans. Of finding the mine, he felt sure. Well, he would take away what he could carry, and some way or other, would get on one of those boats going to Japan or China. There in a strange land he would start life anew. He thrilled at the idea of walking abroad like a man, without thought or fear of someone behind him.

He kept panning more gold each day, and getting everything in readiness to move on as soon as Loucks returned. But weeks lengthened into months, and Loucks did not come.

Suspicion curdled into fear, and finally he bitterly accepted the fact that his partner had double-crossed him.

Filled with rage at the dastardly theft, he forgot his fear, for the time, and followed. He would find the cowardly beast and get his money back.

He cautiously entered Vancouver, but no one seemed to recognize him. Finally he got news of the erstwhile partner—but he had gone on to San Francisco. Savagely, Carson turned the rest of his "dust" into money and followed.

For many weeks he searched, following this clue and that, only to learn eventually that Loucks had been killed one night down in a Chinese dive. But the police reported that no money had been found on him.

Carson decided he would go back and look for the Lost Mine himself. He must have money, must have a lot of it if he were to leave this land where he was always a "marked man." He was still full of bitterness at the perfidy of his partner, but there was some satisfaction, that even for the $5,000 reward, no one had recognized him.

His money all spent, Carson worked his way on the boat back to Vancouver. Then a strange thing happened. Carson supposed that no one on earth knew of his Lost Mine, except old Chief Nahanni, but the night they left Seattle, he met a man by the name of Wilson, who was apparently looking for the same mine and he had a map of the location.

Carson immediately jumped to the conclusion that Loucks had sold out to Wilson, but then he remembered that Loucks did not know the location and so he could not have made a map had he so desired.

"Ever been up in that country?" said Carson, who was still using the name of Fisher.

"No, that is the trouble," said Wilson. "I have knocked around a good deal, but never farther north than I am right now."

"Queer thing, this," said Carson. "I have been prospecting around that river for the best part of a year, looking for a mine that seems to correspond identically with that map you have there."

Wilson was instantly suspicious; so Carson told him of old Chief Nahanni's story and of the partner who had tricked him, and so convinced Wilson that his story was true.

"Mind if I ask where you got that map, if you have never been in the North?" asked Carson.

"I got it from a chap by the name of McHenry," said Wilson. "Ever hear of him? No? Well, he claimed to have happened on the mine when he was making a lone trek into the Yukon. He told me he brought out as much gold as he could carry and had it coined at the mint at Sitka. Anyway he got a pot of money somewhere, for he came back to Arizona loaded with it. He was going back again to properly stake the mine only he met a wealthy widow and fell for her.

"The lady decided that if she were to be married, her husband must live with her. She had a big sheep ranch down there. She said they had all the money they wanted, and she had no desire to be left a widow again. The old boy did not need much encouragement, for he told me he had nearly gone 'flooey' working up there all alone."

Carson shuddered. How well he knew that feeling.

"So he sold me the map. What do you say to going partners in the deal? I have the map and you have the knowledge of the country. If we find it, there should be plenty for two."

Carson did not doubt that it was the same mine as that for which he was looking, but it was strange he had never heard of this chap McHenry.

They spent the winter on the Liard River, but the short, idle days and the long, lonely nights are hard tests to the nerves. They started quarrelling. Suspicion and fear made a poor combination. Sometimes Carson suspected Wilson of spying on him; Wilson may have had something on his conscience too. As the winter wore on, they scarcely slept. So afraid was each of the other. Their guns were always beside them and at the slightest noise in the tent, each would find himself looking into the barrel of the other's gun.

In the quiet light of day, they realized that such a condition could not continue. One or both would unwittingly commit murder. So they decided to separate, each going his lone way to find the mine. It was arranged that if either of them found it, he was not to stake, but simply take out what gold he could carry.

That summer Carson prospected the right fork of the Nahanni; Wilson the left branch. In the winter Carson trapped enough furs to buy him a little outfit and in the spring went across the Divide and down to Ross River trading post to get his supplies.

As the skins were bring counted, it seemed to the ever alert Carson that the trader was watching him covertly. His instinct was for instant flight, but that would certainly arouse suspicion. But he would get out as soon as possible—no use to take a chance now after all these years. He had a feeling that the man was measuring his height, taking note of his red hair and blue eyes and that the tattooed symbol on his right hand had not been overlooked. Uneasily he followed the man into the back of the store, where, as he got such things as he wanted, the man casually, very casually, mentioned that the police were out again looking for an Englishman who had killed a man down at the Crowsnest years ago. They had heard that he was prospecting for gold up on the Nahanni and were on their way in. "The poor chap has probably been punished enough by now, I imagine," he added without looking up, and Carson knew that he was getting a kindly warning.

That night he travelled thirty miles from the post before he dared to stop. His blood curdled with fear, bitterness, despair. All his life he must go on, crawling like a snake from one place to another. And he had been so sure that this summer he would find the mine—that with the gold in his hand he would be free. There was only one other creek that he had to prospect, but now he could not go back.

No one saw him again until the following year, when he walked into one of the Hudson Bay stores over on the Mackenzie River, hundreds of miles from where he had last entered the habitations of men. He hastily bought what he needed and was gone before they realized it was Carson, wanted for murder. And so he existed, always moving on, always alone; years and years of being alone. Day after day and night after night, building his little fire, making tea, eating some dried moose meat. To him, the rugged beauty of the mountains meant only a place to hide; the tumbling streams were only obstructions to his flight; the vivid sunsets merely foretold another night of clutching fear for there was ever the terror of uncertainty.

Small wonder as he sat by the Rabbit Kettle this night, and thought of all those years of slinking solitary isolation, that the monotonous prospect appalled him. Noticing again the gaudy bits of calico which were tied to the trees, he wished for the simple faith of the Indians. If they had done wrong, they brought gifts to the Spirit, and went on their way, content in their atonement. The men paid homage and asked that much game would fall to their guns that year and that their nets would be full; the women, that their children would be kept well and safe from hunger; the maidens and their lovers asked his blessing and went their happy way in each other's arms.

As he looked into the swirling depths of the pool, the fancy came to Carson to offer sacrifice too. Surely luck would not be always against him. He had but one treasure to offer, his only link with the old life. He took from his pocket the little moose-skin sack and fingered the letters tenderly. In one was enclosed a sprig of heather from his native moors, but the flower was now little more than dust. He replaced them in the bag and wistfully, almost hopefully, dropped it into the pool. For many minutes it rode round and round on the surface of the water, as though loath to lose itself from his sight.

With a sigh he turned and followed the little waterfall that escaped from the crack in the Rabbit Kettle down the mountain side. It broadened and grew larger, as though gathering strength to challenge the mountains which barred its way, then wound quietly and mysteriously along the valley. Looking ahead, where mountains rose tier on tier, it seemed impossible for the waters to get past these mighty dams, but with a sharp turn here and a detour there, they accomplished what it was foreordained they should. Carson loved the rivers; to him they were friendly, the only friends he had. He wished he too might have the courage to break through and fulfill the purpose of his life.

Three days later, he saw and heard signs that told him he was near an Indian encampment. Spruce and cottonwood trees lined the river banks, which here and there had been gouged out by the spring floods when they raced through in a tantrum. The roots of the trees hung down naked and ashamed as though trying to get beneath the cover of the water.

That night Carson did not build a fire; the Indians were friendly enough when he met them, but he suspected everyone.

As he lay concealed, he could smell the rabbit stew which the squaws were cooking over the campfire; he could hear the children laughing and playing; in his mind he saw the men sitting around talking. In morbid loneliness, he envied them their carefree, happy life with each other. The accursed isolation rankled in his very soul. Every bird and beast had his mate; he only was alone.

Next morning three of the girls went out to get spruce boughs with which the Indians carpet their tents. The little twigs of the spruce trees stuck in the ground at a slight angle make a wonderful mattress. One of the girls was standing on a dead tree reaching up for the new tender twigs. Her smooth brown arm was upstretched; her black eyes laughed down at the other girls who had not dared as she had; her legs were bare and on her slender feet were gaily embroidered mocassins. She was youth, challenging life and waiting its fulfillment. Without realizing what he meant to do, Carson crept around to within a few feet of the girl and then as she gathered up her load to follow the others back to camp, he jumped out and grabbed her. Before she could scream he had put his hand over her mouth. In sheer terror she fainted and he picked her up in his arms and carried her away with him.

As he felt the warm young body against his, his blood quickened, his arms crushed her closer to him and he pressed his face in her shining black braids. As he held her thus, his instinct claimed her, this lovely maiden just budding into womanhood. He would—he must have her for his own; if her people pursued, as they doubtless would, he would fly with her. He had eluded the police for ten years; he could elude them too.

But her people did not follow; believing that an enemy tribe had stolen one of their daughters, they broke camp in great haste and left the place.

But Carson did not know that and he covered his tracks with the cunning that long practice had taught him. Coming to the spot where he had camped the night before, he laid down his soft warm burden and began bathing her face with water. It was an amazing thing for him to find himself with someone needing his care. Dipping his fingers in cool water from the river, he rubbed her forehead and patted the fresh young cheeks; he stroked her long hair which had fallen loose in the struggle. He was almost sorry when consciousness returned, and he saw that she was terrified of him. He tried to show he would not hurt her, brought her water to drink and offered her some dried meat from his cache, but she would not touch them. Realizing her plight and not knowing where she was, she began to cry. He wished to comfort her, but she screamed when he came near her. So he just sat and watched her. So unhappy was this entrapped thing, he was tempted to take her back to her people.

Finally she stopped crying. She could see that this man was displeased at her tears. If she vexed him, he might kill her.

But a glance at him told her differently. Even an Indian maiden could read the tenderness in his eyes, yearning blue eyes so unlike those of the indifferent Indian men of her tribe. No, this man did not mean to hurt her. She turned her head away and tried to think what she could do.

Believing her asleep or perhaps that she had fainted again, he brought some spruce boughs for a bed, then lifted her so carefully onto it. As he laid her down he smoothed the hair away from her forehead very gently. Never had she felt such kind hands.

He watched her for a time partly to satisfy his starved longing for human society; partly in fear she would run away.

But they must leave this place, he thought. So he went down to the river bank to chop trees for a raft, working where he could watch her, but she did not move. Satisfied she was sleeping soundly, he went a little farther back to get some willows to bind the logs together.

The minute he was out of sight, she crawled on hands and knees to the river, dropped into the water and noiselessly floated down stream. She could hear the roar of rapids ahead, but she did not raise an arm to take a stroke until she was in the shelter of a little island. She rested for a few minutes and then swam rapidly across to the other shore, and hid in the bushes.

Of the man, hungry for human companionship and human relationships, there is little further to record. Once more fate had turned its face from him. He had asked the Great Spirit of the Nahannis for help; a spark of hope kindled when he saw the maiden—maybe the God of the Indians had sent her to comfort him. But she had left him; he was alone again. Was it worth while to fight, fight for a life that bruised him at every turn?

He would let the river decide. For ten years, he had thought of the rivers as his only friends; well, he would test that friendship now.

He put his gun, his axe, his little store of food on the raft he had built for his wedding journey. He heard the roar of the falls below but paid no heed. He was no longer afraid—the river could decide.

He poled the unwieldy craft out into the current and laid down; his eyes grew calm as they had not been for years; he was no longer in hiding. If the river took him back to the habitations of men, well and good; if not, he would still be satisfied, but he would never hide again. The raft scraped over a hidden log here and there; it skirted around the island where the girl had rested a little while before; the trees were passing faster now, the noise of rushing waters grew closer. The thought came to him, that if he guided the raft a little to the south side of the river, he could hold it there against the current, but he would not. The river must take the responsibility, the river that came from the Great Spirit's Rabbit Kettle.

The girl, hiding in the bushes, saw him come and dared not move. She thought he was following her, perhaps had seen her floating down the river.

But the raft slid past; he did not even look her way. She watched him go, wondered at the strange fancy of the white man to lie down instead of steering his raft. Perhaps he slept.

She thrilled at the thought of his warm arms around her. Her heart acknowledged that he had wanted her.

Where was he going?

Suddenly she remembered the falls toward which the raft was racing now; and was it possible that he did not know the rapids were there, that he did not hear them?

She cautiously followed down the shore, and then as she saw the raft caught in the treacherous current, she ran, she screamed, but the figure on the logs never stirred. In the noise around him, he could not have heard her had he tried. She saw the raft stretch out over the watery cliff like a pitched ball which has not yet spent its force; then for a moment, it disappeared from her sight. She waded into the river, she started to swim, and then, back on shore she raced through the tangled underbrush till below the falls, she saw what made her heart freeze with terror. The logs broken and twisted careened prankishly around in the whirlpool. Once she saw the man's head come to the surface, saw him start to swim and then stop. He was thrown this way and that with the whirling water. She took off her encumbering clothes and tried to swim out to him, but she was helpless against the force of the water.

Finally the whirlpool, tired of the listless plaything, tossed him to one side and he was caught in the current.

She ran down the shore and again plunged in. The river was carrying them both down stream, but she finally was close enough to grasp his thick hair in her hands, and turning on her back, she floated and swam until she reached the shore.

Blood was running from his head and his body was bruised and cut. She held her head to his breast but there was no sign of life. She chafed his hands, she bathed his wounds, but the blue eyes never flickered.

His calm face seemed to tell her that he was content. Her own heart told her that but for her, he would still be alive. She remembered his caressing hands, his tender care, and in the soft light of a setting sun, she put her arms around him, drew his head to her breast, and laid down by his side.

In death, he was not alone.

# A WAR BRIDE'S RETURN (UNDATED)

JOHN BEAR WAS ON THE WAY TO THE STATION to meet his fair-haired bride, whom he had left in England, the day of their marriage seven months before. It was still an hour before the train was due, and as he walked westward, along the broad Edmonton street, his steps were slow, his eyes thoughtful. He saw none of the crowds that jostled him on their way to the theatre, saw none of the beauty of that glorious summer evening. Although he was looking right at it, he did not realize the beautiful sunset with its brilliant but soft blending colours of rose and purple. Ordinarily John Bear loved those sunsets, which seem more brilliant in Western Canada than anywhere else, and many a time he had tried to describe them to Rose, who could not believe that in June the nights never got really dark, that the city lights were not put on till close to eleven, and that there was a reflection of the sunset in the sky all night. John had loved the incredulous look of surprise that came when he told her of these things, and the eagerness with which she drank in all his tales of the wonderful rivers that had their origin in the snow-capped mountains, and of the little wild deer and moose that had scampered away from the river's edge as his canoe came round a bend in the stream.

But he was thinking of none of these things now. He wondered how Rose would like it here. It was all so different from the home she had known all her life, the little vicarage with its clinging vines, and the garden where the roses were the chief pride and joy—after his daughter—of the old doctor. What with his roses and his books, he had scarcely time to prepare his sermons, and it was Rose's regular Saturday night duty to urge her father to prepare a new sermon for Sunday. Those books on early English drama were his great hobby, and John remembered how Rose had laughed when he had said that one needed to have a harelip to read those old books, with their s's made like f's. He had fancifully raised his daughter after these two hobbies.

After the last operation on his leg, the doctors had decided that John would never be able to go back into active service again, and arrangements were made for his return to Canada. They said that he would eventually be strong and well again, but that he should live an outdoor life. Even yet, when he was tired, he limped a little, just reminding him of the treachery of the German prisoner pretending faintness, who had shot him in the hip as John turned to get him a drink of water.

All those long days, as he lay in the hospital, his only hope in life was Rose's regular visit. She came every afternoon to relieve the nurse in charge, and as she went about among the cots, straightening out their pillows and writing their letters, there was many a "God Bless You" from the lips of the suffering soldiers who watched her bright face.

With John she had stayed a little longer than with the others, and when he was well enough to leave the hospital, the temptation had been too great and he had accepted her invitation to stay at the rectory till he should go back to Canada. Pain mingled with his joy as he watched her there among the roses, saw her practical management of the little household, her sympathy for the old parishioners who came to tell her all their woes, her loving care of her old father. When she came to his chair and helped him move to make the throbbing leg more comfortable, the pain in his hip was nothing compared to the anguish of renunciation, when he felt that she could be nothing more to him than just a friend, that he would leave her in a few weeks and probably never see her again in his life.

Then one day, as she had stooped to put her arm under his shoulder to help him change his position in that tedious hospital chair, her cheek had touched his, and as she started up in confusion, he had grabbed her hand and that "Oh, Rose" that burst forth from his lips was sheer anguish. He lay back on his chair, with the perspiration standing in great beads on his face. Instantly she was all anxiety. Had she hurt him; was the wound worse; what was wrong?

The tears came to his eyes, as he whispered, "Oh, Rose, I want you so much."

She had stood for a minute, looking out over the garden, at the dear father who was pottering about among the roses, at the old dog who was majestically following him up and down the paths between the bushes, at the vine-clad vicarage, and then, with a wonderfully sweet look in her clear blue eyes, her gaze came back to him.

"Forgive me, Rose. I should not have said that."

"Why should you not have said it, John, if you love me? For I love you too. You do love me, do you not?"

"God knows I do, but I should not have told you. When I came to your home, I thought I was strong enough to hide it all in my heart, and now, heaven help me if I am going to give you pain."

"But, I do not understand, John."

She looked into his eyes that told their own story of pain and longing, and then she said slowly:

"Was there another girl, John? For if there is you must tell me and I will understand."

"Oh no, Rose, it is not that. There has never been any girl but you."

"Then what other reason can there be, John?"

He rallied a little and, with a whimsical smile, he parried, "I have not a cent in the world, not even a job. I am as poor as old Henry who comes to the door every morning for a cup of your tea, and of course I could not marry like that. And dear knows when I will even be able to get around on this bum leg of mine."

Not daring to look into those clear steady eyes, he rambled on:

"It isn't all sunsets and rivers and mountains, out in Alberta, you know, and when I change this uniform for a suit of overalls and settle down on my homestead over there, no neighbours for miles, and just work to do, well, it would be different, you know. I don't believe you can realize just how different it would be."

"It was not your uniform I loved, John, but as you say, it might be different," and she turned and left him.

Of course she knew he had not told her the real reason, and now she had left him. His heart cried out with love for her, and still he knew he had hurt her to the very depths of her being. Why had he come, why had he let her learn to love him? It had been bad enough, when it was he alone that had had to suffer.

As he lay there, almost helpless in body, he felt that this other helplessness was infinitely worse to bear. He would have to go away, go away at once. Oh heaven, was he never to see that dear face again? Why, he thought rebelliously, had they been given this wonderful love, when they might not carry it through to its culmination?

Never would he forget the torment through which he went that night, and when morning came, he had decided that if Rose loved him as he loved her, she had a right to know that barrier that separated them. It would hurt her again, but he could not bear that she should think that he did not trust her or that there was any reason over which he had any control. He would tell her everything in the morning.

But when morning came, and the old doctor came, as he had made the habit of late, bringing a cup of tea for the lad who was so brave through all his pain and for whom he had formed a strong affection, in spite of the fact that the young rascal laughed at his priceless old books, he got no response to his cheery "Good morning." A little startled, he came over to the bed and called.

"It will be c.b.[1] for you if you oversleep like this again, my boy."

But John lay there like one dead, and the doctor hastily put down the cup of tea, and felt his heart. It was feebly beating, but he could get no response when he spoke.

He went to the door and called Rose, little realizing the stab he was giving her when he said, "Rose, I am afraid John is dying."

But he did not die, although for a while they thought he would, and the old vicar had a special tremor in his voice as he read the prayers for those grievously sick. Rose begged the doctor that she might take care of him there in her own home, and realizing her skill from her voluntary training, he intervened with the colonel to let him stay. This was a little easier than it might otherwise have been, as the military hospitals were full almost to overflowing and the vicarage had helped house many of their soldiers since the beginning of the war. For weeks John never knew her, did not know the tenderness with which she watched for every strengthening of his heart beat.

Incessantly he had called her name. It tore her heart to hear his cry: "Oh, Rose, I want you so, Rose, darling, I love you. Rose. Rose." But never did he say aught that would give her a clue to any reason why they might not marry, and after much thinking, Rose came to believe that he had been over-sensitive of the fact that he had no home for her and no money on which to make their start. But she was willing to wait till he was ready, she told herself, and she had always been poor. Why should he think she would mind that? If he ever got well again, she would tell him so. But would he ever get well?

Slowly John came back to consciousness, and Rose. With his weakness of body he seemed also to lose his strength of purpose. If they two loved each other, what else mattered? Why had God put the love into their hearts, if it was wrong? Love was all that mattered, and his poor weak arms reached out in longing for her. Then one day, as she came near his bedside, he caught her in his arms and kissed her. Rose, believing he had lost his fooling notions, whatever they had been, gave her lips unreservedly to his kisses, and nestled into his arms.

After that, if he had any notion of trying to tell her again of the barrier between the uniting of his life and hers, he remembered that hurt look, when he had tried to tell her before and the look of trust with which she came to him now, confident that all trouble was past, and he could not tell her. Her love and her dear kisses were too precious; he could not give them up now. Sometimes, when Rose talked of the home they would have "in Canada," his heart smote him, and he suggested once that he would stay in England and make a home for her there. But Rose was full of the wonderful land of the great prairies with their background of immense mountains, of beautiful sunsets, and great distances, and the spirit of love and adventure thrilled her. The thought of being with John, making a home in that new country, was as wine to the sheltered English girl, and she talked only of that. She would raise chickens and make the butter and they would be free and prosperous in no time.

Before John was scarcely out of bed again, the word came that he was going to go back to Canada on the next hospital ship that left the following week. They sat hand in hand and John promised to come back for her when he was better and had found the little home. Rose could not bear to see him go like that, and finally, the day he was to leave, she had persuaded him that they should be married now, and she would then feel that he was her very own, and it would not be so hard to see him go. She would know that he would come back. So they knelt beside him, as he sat in his invalid chair, and the old vicar had made them man and wife, till death did them part.

Then, the old vicar had died of influenza that next winter, and Rose had written him that she would come out to him. A new vicar was coming to their little home; she had nowhere to stay, so she was leaving on the next boat.

CHAPTER TWO

All of this came back to John, as he walked up Jasper Avenue that evening, to meet the train which brought back to him his bride of an hour. For the thousandth time he asked himself why he had not told Rose he was of Indian blood. He was not ashamed of it, but how would it seem to an English girl who knew nothing of Indians except such as she had read in Cooper's novels? But, he defended himself again, he could not tell her of himself without seeming to cast a slur on that mother who had done so much for him. What would Rose say when she saw that dark-skinned mother? Well, he would soon know, he thought grimly. He would have to tell her that night, and John shivered in dread at the outcome.

Just then the train came steaming in, and John forgot everything else in looking for that fair-haired girl who had won his heart so completely, and in the joy of having her in his arms again. Nothing else seemed to matter. Quite unconscious of the crowds around him, he folded her close against his breast, and met her upturned lips.

John had decided that her first taste of life in Canada would be pleasant at any rate, so he had planned that they would spend their honeymoon in Edmonton, and took her to the palatial hotel overlooking the Saskatchewan. That night, in their great happiness at being together again, John could not bear to mar the hour with any crude unpleasantness, so he put it off till the next day. And when another day came, and she gently told him of the last hours of her dear father who had passed out in the faith that his only daughter would be safely cared for by a loving husband, he could but comfort her. Thus several days passed, and John reviled himself for being so weak, but he had not the courage to disturb their great happiness. It was so wonderful, being thus together. He thought of trying to find work in town, but when he suggested it, Rose was all against the idea. She wanted to go to the country where they would have their own home, and besides, the doctor had warned her that John must live outdoors. It would not be altogether theirs, he warned, for his mother had an actual claim to his home whenever she cared to come. Rose agreed to this. It was so fine of John to want his mother with him. But John decided in his own mind to ask the colonel, who lived in Edmonton, if there was not a place for him in the regular army. They had told him he was a good soldier. He hated war and all that therein was. But the longer he thought of it, the less was he able to tell Rose that he, in whom she had such confidence for truth and honesty, was of Indian blood. If she could only live in the country a while, till she understood that there were many people of that mixed parentage, it would be easier for her.

Next morning, he found a rather subdued Rose, and wondering in his heart if she had found out anything, he tried to find the cause for this change. Rose would not let him touch her, and for the first time she said nothing about going out to the farm. Every day she had been prattling about the chickens she would have, the cow that they must get at once so John could have lots of cream and milk, and of how she would sell the butter so they could afford to build a fireplace in the little home, but today she said nothing and just looked at him with reproachful eyes.

Finally John could bear it no longer and said, "Rose, I know I have wronged you, but it was just because I loved you so that—"

"You love me," said Rose cuttingly, "then you might tell me how many others you love too."

"You know I love no one but you, Rose, and never have. There has been no other woman in my life. What do you mean?"

"Then who is Flossie," said Rose, wishing to believe and still incredulous. "You talked of her all night in your sleep."

In his relief John laughed out loud. "Yes, I admit it, there was another girl, Rose. Next to my mother, Flossie was my best friend for years." But seeing the hard look come to his little bride's eyes again, he went on, "Flossie was the love of my childhood; she had yellow hair, a little darker than yours, Rose. Flossie was a big collie dog, and it has always seemed to me that she was the most beautiful dog that ever lived. Out in the country there were lots of dogs, but they were all mean common little curs. Flossie was so different, with her wonderful dignity and her beautiful pointed nose. She is the first thing I remember, and as long as she lived, she hardly ever left my side. I often wondered where she came from, but mother never seemed able to tell me. When I get troubled, I always remember the amazing fidelity of that dog, and it has comforted me over lots of rough spots when I thought that everything was at its worst."

"Who is the girl in the locket that you wear, and what is the coat of arms on it?" said Rose, determined to have it all over at once.

John fingered the locket a minute and then said, "I don't know who she is, Rose. When I went away to the war, my mother gave it to me, and told me never to part with the locket or the picture. Mother is not one to talk much, and as it seemed to pain her, I did not press the matter, but wore it as she wanted. It seemed she had had it a long time, and I guess it was the one treasure she had to give me when I went away. I found out since that it is a McDougall coat of arms, but that is all I know of it."

Rose's apology was very sweet, but it did not make it any easier to tell her why the thought of Flossie had come to him when, in his dream, he thought that Rose had left him because she found out he was Indian. Yes, he must stay in town. He could not take Rose out to his mother. His heart would not let him say anything about that mother who had done so much for him, but at the same time, he was afraid that Rose would not understand. And torn between his duty to his mother and his love for his wife, John wavered.

That day his old colonel came to call on them and said many pleasant things about John's record in the war. "I could always have confidence that whatever he undertook to do, or felt was his duty, John would carry it through to the bitter end, no matter at what discomfort or danger to himself," said Colonel Thompson. "Many a private in the regiment has John to thank for escaping c.b., for I could never make him tell anything where it involved a hardship or punishment on anyone else." Looking severely at his old subaltern who was standing embarrassed and protesting before his senior officer, and turning to the little bride whose eyes were shining at this praise of her husband, he went on. "This medal that I wear really belongs there," pointing to John, "for if it had not been for him, the medal would just have gone to my next of kin. I would not have been here to wear it. I am not wishing him any hard luck, but I hope that if he ever gets in a hole, that I will be around to pay off some of the debts I owe him. But I believe that now he has you here, he is not going to ask any odds of me at all."

When the colonel had gone, she plied John with questions as to what he had done for the colonel, but not a thing could she get. It was nothing at all, according to John. A little piqued, she said, "You are as bad about keeping things to yourself as the Indians about whom you used to tell me."

John looked up startled.

"I am—"

Just then came a knock at the door and the bellboy brought a telegram. "River in flood. Mother missing. House in danger. Alex McKay."

"Oh John, what does it mean?" said Rose looking over his shoulder. "Where could your mother be missing? Who is Alex McKay?"

"Alex is the chief of the reserve, and he is not the kind to send this unless it was serious. What can have happened to mother? She knows the river and certainly would not go on it when it was rising. I heard yesterday they were afraid of the bridges here and were arranging to weigh them down with heavy cars, but it has never come anywhere near our house before. There was more snow in the mountains this year than

I ever remember, and then the spring rains have been bad too, but why is mother missing?"

John could not think that anything could have really happened to his mother, who knew the river all her life. But he was plainly troubled and immediately began to plan for getting out to the farm. A train would leave the West at midnight, and he could get to within forty miles of the farm. He would get a horse and would be able to get there in the morning sometime. Rose would stay at the hotel and he would come back as soon as he could.

"No, I want to go with you, John. I may just as well go now as any time. I can ride too, and there is no use in your saying anything, for I am going. We can have the trunks come out on the train Friday." John tried to argue, but Rose was determined.

Leaving the train at three in the morning, Rose waited at the dingy little station, tired and rather frightened, while John went to try to find some horses. There were two dirty-looking half-breeds hanging around, without any special purpose. The younger of the two, who wore a beaded waistcoat and a big hat with a beaded band around it, cast several covert looks at Rose, which did not serve to increase comfort. The older man had a black shirt with slouchy trousers, and tied around his waist was a bright-coloured scarf. He was wearing moccasins. Rose recalled the stories she had read of Indian attacks on white people and watched them closely, scarcely daring to move. She hoped there were no half-breeds near her home; she did not like their looks.

John came back finally with two saddled ponies, one a buckskin and the other a spotted one. She did not think they were big enough to go such a distance, but did not say anything. John was explaining that he could not get a sidesaddle in the place, and that she would have to ride in the stock saddle. It was a good thing she had worn a kilted skirt.

Rose soon found out that riding over these rough trails on rougher ponies was a far different thing than what she was used to, and after ten miles would have been glad to rest. But as she had insisted on coming, she would be game. She would not complain. Many a time she thought she would fall off, but pride kept her holding on. After a mile she noticed they were being followed by a couple of men on horses, much like those they were riding, and later, to her consternation, she found they were the same two men who had been around the station that morning. When she told John about them, he just said curtly that they were friends of his. Rose could scarcely understand this, but she was so tired and sore that she could think of little else than herself. When John said it was just five miles more, Rose thought she would never be able to sit in the saddle another minute, and when they finally arrived at a little shack that John pointed out, she was almost unconscious of the fact that this was the home to which she had looked forward with so much pride.

Just a little hovel, and so tired was she that she did not notice that it was scrupulously clean inside, nor that the little semi-circle of trees, in which the house was set, made it seem like a little rustic park. Had Rose been less tired, the beauty of the scene would have impressed her for she was very susceptible to the beauties spread out by nature, even wild nature like this, which was so different from the planned beauties of old England. Just below the house, the river was rushing madly in a dirty brown torrent, and carrying with it trees, old logs, bits of planks, every sort of backwash that can accumulate on the banks of a river during a year of busy changes in the natural world. The great Saskatchewan, of which John had spoken so much, did not appeal to Rose's tired senses as anything but a mad thing, and even as she watched, she shuddered and turned sick, for floating down the rushing stream she could see a living thing.

"Oh look, John, what is it?"

John looked and seeing the yellow pallor of her face, was smitten with contrition that she should be so tired. One look at the thing in the river told his practised eyes that it was a dog, too much spent to battle the current to the shore.

"Just a dog, dear," he replied, realizing she was near collapse. "And there goes somebody's barn," watching a pile of logs go galloping past.

"Thank heaven we are safe, but this is only the second day of the flood. It may get us yet."

Then the grim, worried expression that had been on his face ever since he had received the telegram the day before returned, and he jumped off his horse; as he turned to help Rose, she fell in his arms. Her determination had kept her up till now, but tired muscles and exhausted nerves would not serve her any longer.

He carried her into the house and laid her down on a bed in one corner of the room. He knew she was exhausted, and left her while he went to see if there was any sign of his mother. He looked in the barn, but there was nothing there but the old sow, who set up a lusty squeal when she saw him, and he rightly guessed that she had not been fed for some time. The horses were gone. Outside there was nothing to be seen but the goat he had bought in Calgary from a government man, who in order to get the people of that country interested in the raising of milch goats had given John one of the kids at a great bargain. The goat was looking with much interest at the river, so John went to drive it back, afraid that with the flooding river, the banks might give way at any time and take the goat with them.

He was just wondering where he should go to look for his mother, and what he could do about Rose. She had looked so pale he was afraid she might be ill, but he must find his mother. Just then, the other two riders came up and he told them shortly what he had found; they started off without further ado down the river. John went back to Rose, but she was still unconscious. He did what he could for her, and was fairly beside himself with misery. Rose was ill; she lay like a dead thing there; and there was the awful uncertainty about his mother.

Presently he heard someone coming and looking out, saw the breeds returning, one leading John's two horses, and the other supporting his mother while he walked alongside. John rushed out to meet his mother, and found out that one of the horses had gone down to the river to drink, lost his footing, and been carried downstream. The mother had seen what had happened and, without a thought for her own safety, or of anything except that she must save John's horse for him, pushed out the canoe and paddled after him. John could imagine how the river must have carried her, and how often she must have been in danger of her life in that perilous trip, not only from the rushing current, that none but a paddler as strong as his mother could have battled against for a minute, but the river was practically full of trees and debris of all sorts that pushed and jammed in its headlong rush. He grew cold with the very thought. It was many miles down the river before she had been able to come up with the terrified horse, and it was not till he was fairly exhausted that she had dared come near him. Then it had been all she could do to get him to shore without drowning both him and herself. But here they were. The other must have broken loose and followed down the river bank through the brush when he heard the cry of his mate. Both the horse and herself had been so exhausted that they had not been able to start back till this morning, and it had been a long walk of many miles through the heavy underbrush, with many stops to rest. She had found the other horse about five miles down stream whinering plaintively.

There was never much show of affection between John and his mother, and she barely told him the outline of the story, which he did not find it hard with his experience to fill in, but John very tenderly lifted her off her horse and whispered, "You should not have risked your own life for the horses, Mother."

He supported her back to the house, forgetting for the moment that Rose was there. But as he came to the door, he said, "Rose is here, mother; the trip was too much for her and she is ill."

Rose was just returning to consciousness, and as she heard these words, she opened her eyes, and saw John supporting a woman, at the sight of whom Rose could hardly believe her senses. Surely it was some trick of her fancy, probably she was still dreaming, and those awful men who had been at the station the morning before, or was it a week ago, and who had followed them on the awful ride afterwards, had become mixed up in her mind with John's mother.

It was a hideous dream, she thought. To her straining eyes the woman, with her straight black hair, hanging bedraggled around her face and shoulders, her face dark brown and seamed with many lines, moccasins on her feet, and an old plaid shawl around her shoulders: she was a squaw, and John had called her mother. It must be some trick of her fancy.

But seeing that Rose had returned to consciousness, he was leading the woman towards her bed and was saying, "Rose, this is my mother; she might have been drowned, but thank heaven—"

Rose had fallen back on the bed, unconscious again.

## CHAPTER THREE

John took his mother to the other bed, and there insisted on making her lie down, although she protested she would be all right as soon as she rested. She told John to go and look after Rose. When he had rubbed camphor on her head and neck, he started to build a fire. He would make some tea. In the relief at having his mother back safe and sound, he was almost happy again. He could not think that Rose was really ill. He had forgotten that the rushing river outside might carry away his very home that night. He began to realize the strain under which he had been the past twenty-four hours, for he was still far from strong, although his friends scarcely knew him for the boy who had come back some months before.

When he brought her the tea, his mother drank it and then, taking his hand, she said:

"You should have told Rose I was a Métis, but since you have not perhaps it is better to leave it so. Before she wakes up again, I must leave here, and if she asks you, you can tell her it was a woman off the reserve."

John started to protest, but she had faced too many crises in life to flinch at this one, so she went on calmly.

"No, she will never understand. I saw the look of horror in her eyes when she saw me. I will go back to Edmonton, and she will never need to know. But tonight do up a little tea and bacon for me, and meet me at the

Hermitage. I have something to tell you you must know, and I will tell you tonight."

"Mother, my house is yours as long as I live, and I have told my wife so. I will not let you go. I am the same blood as you and if Rose loves me, she will love you too. It may take her a little while to get used to things, but whatever happens, this is your farm as much as mine. In fact it is all yours, for if it had not been for what you have done, I would have had no farm."

"Anyway, I am going, John."

Neither of them realized that Rose had come back and was lying quietly listening to this. So this was John's mother after all, and she was married to a half-breed, the same as those men at the station. Maybe one of them was his father. How dared John marry her without telling her of this taint in his blood? She hated him for bringing her to this state. As she lay there, every joint in her body ached, but her mind was clear. So they would try to hoodwink her, would they? Well, his mother would not need to go away, for she would go herself. But she must think it out. So she kept her eyes closed, never moving. Indeed it was agony to think of moving those tortured muscles.

The two half-breeds came to the door just then and curtly announced "River rise like hell."

John went to the door. "Better take the horses and the pig out of the barn and put them back up on the hill. Take my axe there and make a little corral for the pig. Feed her too. I guess she has not had anything since yesterday. My wife is sick, but I'll come and help you as soon as she comes around. I can't leave just now."

The two men slouched away and John turned to his mother who had got up and come behind him. "It looks as though the barn might go, but I don't believe there is any danger for the house. However, when Rose is better, I think I'll take a little sleep, for we will have to watch tonight. Jack and Alex have to go on out to the Junction, with some letters for the agent. Give them some tea before they go, mother."

As his mother went out, he turned back to where Rose was lying so pale and started to chafe her hands. But she jerked her hand away.

"Don't touch me. I hate you. You thought you would make a squaw of me too, did you? Well, if it wouldn't be too much trouble, you can take me over to the station, and I'll wait there till the train goes."

John was like one dazed. He tried to say something, tried to explain, but she only spoke once, and then to say, "If you don't want to drive me, I can walk. It does not make much difference if I die on the road or not. I wish I might have died before this happened."

"Wait till tomorrow, Rose, and if you still want to go, I will take you. The train does not go till Thursday anyway. Let me explain, Rose, dear. I know I should have told you, but I loved you so."

"Yes, you must have loved me, when you let me marry an Indian. You will please go away, where I can't see you, till you are ready to take me to the station."

"But Rose, the river is rising, and I can't leave tonight."

"Of course I would not expect you would consider me before these dirty old barns. Well, I will be able to walk after a little, if you will be good enough to show me the direction."

"Rose, I have not enough money to buy your ticket back to England. You will have to wait till I can borrow some, somewhere."

"I don't want your money. I want to get away from here, and never see you again."

John went out to the river bank, and his thoughts seemed to be rushing madly past him, like the river, full of hideous things and seeming to get nowhere. Surely Rose did not mean it. She could not leave him like that. As he stood there pondering, Jack and Alex came to say that they would look in as they came back next day to see if he were all right. As they went to get their horses, Rose appeared at the door.

"If these men are going to the junction, I will go along with them. It will save you going," she said coldly.

He could not plead with her there, before these men he had known since he was a boy. He begged her to wait till tomorrow, and he would take her, but she was very determined to leave and leave then. So with fumbling hands John helped hitch his horse to the wagon, telling the men they might as well all drive over and give their own horses a rest. They could get them the next day on their way back.

Rose never looked back as she drove away, sitting on a bundle of hay in the bottom of the big lumber wagon, like a veritable squaw.

CHAPTER FOUR

When John turned back to the house, desolation reigned in his heart, and he staggered as he went. He must lie down for a while and think what he would do. But for hours he lay there, his mind almost a blank. He scarcely knew what had happened. After a while, however, it came to his consciousness that he had not seen his mother since she had gone out with some tea for the boys. He dragged himself to his feet, went to the door, and called, but there was no answer. He was so exhausted he could hardly stand, but he wandered on looking and falling. She had said she would go away. Well, she would not need to now, he thought grimly. But he must find her. She had said she would wait at the Hermitage that night. He would feel better when he had something to eat, so he made himself tea, so strong it was black, and ate some bread and bacon. The tea revived him, and he started down the river to the little log hut that had served as a shelter at the old ferry.

His mother was waiting for him, and he said quietly, "She has gone, mother. There will be just you and I now. Come on home, mother."

"No, John, she will come back, and I must not be there. Sit down and I will tell you something that will make it all right."

John could not imagine what his mother knew about Rose that would bring her back to him, but she was not a woman to talk much, so he sat down. At first he was thinking little of what she said, but soon the significance of what she was telling him sunk into his consciousness.

Her father had been a white man. He was a trapper and often came to the Cree tents to bargain for furs. He had singled out the chief's little daughter and, much against her father's will, she had gone away with him on one of his trapping expeditions. Later she had wandered back to her tribe with her baby in her arms. Her life and that of the baby daughter had not been an easy one after that, and when she had grown old enough she had gone to the home of the old factor to work in the kitchen. One day the son came home from college, and from then, she lost all interest in the young bucks who came around. The white blood in her called to this boy, but she would not go with him as her mother had done. The factor's old wife had sent her to the mission school, and she had learned to read and had learned something of their idea of morals and the lonely hard life of her own mother, who had left all for her love to her everlasting regret and misery. All had combined to keep her safe.

Then one day he had gone away, gone back to visit the home of his father in Scotland, and when he returned he brought a young wife with him and a beautiful collie dog. She had been just such a girl as Rose, fair and blue-eyed.

This brought John's thoughts back to the girl who had just left him. Where was she? What was she thinking tonight? If she only knew how miserable he was, she would forgive him, even if she would not come back. What did all this have to do with him anyway? But his mother was talking on in a monotone, repressed voice.

When she heard that John, for that was the boy's name, was bringing a wife back with him, she had gone back to the tribe. But she found that their ways were not her ways any longer, and something was always drawing her back. So she got work at the mission school and, being just a couple of miles from the factor's house, she often saw John and his young bride. It was misery to see him with another woman, but she could not leave. Something held her there. Several of the young Indians would have married her, but she had no heart for them.

She heard from the missioner and his wife that John's wife was very lonely and wanted him to go into town and go into business, but John had spent all but his college days in the wilds, and he would not go. Then she talked of going home to Scotland for a year, and for this the native girl had despised her.

The old factor and his wife had passed away, and one day she had found John drunk beside the trail, his pony grazing nearby and old Colonel, the collie, on guard. He had always been fond of his liquor, but of late he had been drinking a lot and there was a rumour that the H.B. Company was not satisfied with the way things were going since the old factor died.

That summer, the baby was born, and the little wife had died two days afterward in spite of all the missioner and his wife could do.

As she told all this, John's mother had never moved from where she was squatting on the floor of the old hut, but she got up here and went to the door, looked out at the river and finally came back and stood in front of John.

"They sent me over to look after the baby, and the next week John got a letter telling him another man was coming to take that post. He got drunk that night and I did not see him for three days. Then he told me he was going up the river to pan gold. I did not hear of him again. The missioner said he had written to John's uncle in Scotland to see if they would take care of the baby. I had grown to love that baby as my own and I could not bear the thought of separation. I told them I would take care of the baby, but they said he would have to be educated and that, although I was a good girl, I would not be able to bring him up as suited his station in life.

"I told them I would educate the child and bring him up right, that I would work for him, but they did not believe me and went on making arrangements to send him to Scotland. One night I stole away from the post carrying the baby on my back. I knew I would not be welcome with the Crees, so I kept on down the river till I came to the settlement. You were that baby.

"Maybe I did not do right, John, but you were all I had left of my love. I kept you; I could not bear to have you go to strangers who might not want you. We were often hard pressed. But you were never hungry, John. And I saved every cent I could to educate you, for I had told them you would get as good as though you had gone back to Scotland.

"I fastened the dog, but he got away somehow and caught up with us ten days afterwards. Many a time I wished he had not come, for food was scarce on the trail, and he could not forage like an Indian dog. But he was so fond of you that I had not the heart to kill him.

"Perhaps I should have let you go to your own folks, John, but I sent you to school, and I sent you to college, and I did what I could to make you a clean, decent man.

"When you went away to the war, I nearly told you, but I was afraid you might not come back to me if you knew all, and I wanted to think I had a boy, going like all the others, to fight for his country. When you told me you were bringing home a wife, I knew the time must come when I should tell you all. Today when I saw that look in her face, I knew it must come, for I could not bear to see you unhappy. When you tell her this, she will come back, John. I am going down to Athabasca to work in the hotel there. I heard they were looking for a cook."

"Mother," said John reproachfully.

He had scarcely spoken all through this story. It was wonderful to think that he was not an Indian after all. His parents were white; he was of the same race as his college mates, as Rose, and with that thought, his lips set.

As he saw a tear glisten in her eye, he rose and took his mother tenderly in his arms, for she would always be his mother really. The other was little more than a fairy tale to him. This was the woman who had sacrificed her whole life for him. She would see how he could do a little sacrificing for her now.

"We will go home now, mother."

"But I am not your mother."

"You will always be mother to me."

They stood looking at the river for a minute before they started back, and John said suddenly: "Mother, look. I believe the river is going down. If it is, the barn you built with your own hands when I was away will be safe. Let's go back and see."

The barn was safe, and the river showed several inches lower than when he had come at noon that day. As they turned to go in to the house, John said, "Mother, have you ever heard of my father since?"

"That was the man I tried to save today. He came back a few months ago, and was running the saw mill up at the Point."[2]

## CHAPTER FIVE

Nothing but sheer determination kept Rose from screaming as the wagon jolted her aching bones and muscles over those miles of rough trail, but never for an instant did she change her mind as to the course she had taken. She would go back; just how she would manage this, she did not know, but she would work her way; she would do anything rather than stay with those Indians. She was almost past caring when she finally arrived at the Junction. To her great relief, the men had never spoken to her all the way, but now they turned to ask her where she wanted to go.

She roused herself from her stupor to say, "Take me to a hotel."

"No hotel here," they answered briefly.

No hotel. Oh, why had she ever come to this awful land? Why had John not told her there was no hotel? Of course, she admitted to herself, she had not given him much opportunity.

"Is there no place where I can stay?" she asked, almost pitifully.

"Maybe, stay in station."

She would get little sympathy from them apparently. She did not consider them civilized anyway, and was glad to think she had seen the last of them. She finally got out of the wagon, the men never offering to help her, although they must have seen that it caused her agony to try to climb over the side of the wagon.

She found that the nearest "stopping place" was three miles away over on the Fort Trail, and it might as well have been a thousand for all the good it was to her. She was absolutely incapable of going another step. She huddled in a corner of the station, almost stupid, till dusk, and then accepted the suggestion of the younger of the two breeds that she sleep in the wagon. They had spread the hay out on the bottom and spread a couple of rather odorous horse blankets over it. But it was a comfort to stretch her pain-wracked body, even on this poor bed, and after a while she dozed. But every sound of the night wakened her; the mosquitoes were a perpetual torment, and eventually she gave up trying to sleep, the events of the day coming back to her in unending procession. It did not seem possible that only yesterday she had been so happy with John in Edmonton. It seemed years since that telegram had come.

In the morning she was so stiff that she could scarcely move, but move she must. She had had nothing to eat since the sandwiches they had brought to eat on the trail the morning before, but she had no thought of eating. She was feeling very sorry for herself. If she could only die and leave all this misery. She heard her companions of the day before together with the agent of the little station getting breakfast. They had built a fire just the other side of her wagon bed, and when she smelt the bacon sizzling, she forgot her misery in hunger. She was almost grateful to the young breed, when he brought her a rather grimy plate with some bacon and thick slices of bread. After she had eaten it and the sun came out beautifully warm, the smell of the fresh green earth and the wild roses came with a soothing breath to her tired body and nerves. She lay back on her impromptu bed and slept for some hours.

She awakened refreshed and began to think a little of the future. In her fury of the day before, she had just wanted to get away. Now she realized that she had little money, and no home except the one she had just left. Her total asset, with the exception of what money she had left, was a letter of introduction she had brought from a friend of her father's in England to the bishop of Edmonton. He would perhaps be able to help her, and anyway she could work. Her thoughts were interrupted by the breeds, to say they were going back now and would take the wagon. Her heart sank. Much as she had despised and at first feared them, she had felt that they were John's friends and there was a sort of protection while they were around. Now they were going and the last link was broken. In her desperation, she almost asked them to take her with them, but her pride forbade her. Anyway she felt it would just have to be done again, for although she might have accepted John, she shuddered at the thought of that black-shawled woman, his mother.

When they had gone, the station agent, just a young fellow, came over to her and said, "You're John Bear's wife."

She admitted she was.

He looked at her a little accusingly and added, "John Bear is the finest man in this country. I went to school with him and I went to war with him. I was in his company when we went up against the Germans at Ypres. And I was beside him when the dirty devils shot him, and I never saw him do a dirty trick to friend or enemy."

Rose said nothing, and her companion left her to her thoughts, which were poor company to say the least. That night he brought her more tea and bacon, for which she thanked him, and told her that she could sleep on his shakedown in the station house. He would roll up on his blankets under the trees. She was so weary and exhausted that she could do little else but accept, although she knew that he felt she was a bounder. In every action he told her she was not half good enough for John.

Next day the train came, and she went back to Edmonton. She went to the YWCA at the suggestion of the Travellers' Aid, who had greeted the forlorn-looking little figure that stepped off the train. From there she went to see the bishop, but he would not be home for a week. In the meantime she tentatively inquired of the matron at the Y what work she might get. The matron, who was practical in every curve of her little body, asked what she could do. Well, she could teach children, and she thought she could take a position as governess. The matron explained that there were few people in this country who had governesses, and since the war, she knew of no one who indulged in this luxury. It was hard for a woman to get a position now, she explained, as everything possible was being kept for the returned soldiers.

Rose had plenty of time to think that week, and when the bishop finally returned, it was a very subdued Rose who went to see him. She told him everything. He was an Englishman; he would understand and sympathize with her. But while she found him sympathetic, it was sympathy with reserve. He realized her feeling in the matter, but he had known John as a little shaver before he had come into Edmonton to college, and there had never been a finer boy go through. They were all very proud of his war record. It was true he was a half-breed, but since she had married him, she might at least have tried it out. He knew many very fine people who had Indian blood in their veins. His mother might not be very prepossessing in appearance, but no mother could have done more for John than she had. And here Rose had to listen to the story of how that mother had worked and saved to send her boy to school, how she had cooked in the hotel in the daytime and made baskets and beaded moccasins at night, and with it all no neater, cleaner boy had gone to school than John. When she had heard John swear one day, she had immediately decided that she could no longer stay at the hotel, although she needed the money so much, and he had finally got her a position as housekeeper in a private home. This had been exceedingly irksome to her, but knowing there were few homes that would take her and her boy, she had stayed, and bit by bit had saved enough with what John was able to do later for himself to keep him at school and college.

The Bishop waxed eloquent in telling of this half-breed mother. When the war came, John had asked his advice. His mother had sacrificed everything to put him through college, and now that he was able to help her, he felt he should not leave. Still there was the great call, and his mates wanted him to go with the university battalion. What could he do? Spartan that she was, she solved the question herself. She had seen the trouble in his face, and suggested one day that he go out and file on a homestead, as he would probably be wanting to enlist soon. She said nothing of it, but John had known, said the bishop, what it cost her to say those words. He had gone and filed on land not so far from the settlement where he had gone to school as a little fellow.

When he had gone, his mother went out there, and with her own hands had cut down logs and built a house and barn, and got a home ready for John, for he had always said he was going to be a farmer. She had come into town and worked in the winters and gone out to the homestead in the summer. It was her money that had bought the horses and the wagon and the farm implements. The money that had come to her from the War Office, as John's dependant, she had allowed to accumulate, and when John had returned, it made quite a nice little pile to give them a start. Eliza Bear might be a breed, but she was true blue and no boy ever had a better mother.

However, here was Rose and he pitied her from the bottom of his heart, although he would not let too much of this show. No one knew better than he how her English eyes had seen the shack that had been built with such a labour of love. He understood perfectly the revulsion she felt when she saw that dark-skinned woman. Rose had admitted that she must work; she had no one to whom she could turn for assistance, and anyway, her pride would have forbidden that she go back now. No, she would stay here and do anything.

A few days later he told her that he had found a position in the convalescent home for returned soldiers. Her VAD[3] work had given her a little training; she would teach the soldiers to make fancy work and baskets. She had told him she had done this in England. The pay would be small, but she would have her living in the hospital, and the expense would not be large. He advised her to take night classes in stenography at the same time, so that she would be in a position to get work in the civil service or in an office.

Rose found the work very trying, but she had little choice, and often she was glad of the busy days that kept her from thinking what she considered was the awful blunder she had made of her life. The soldiers lying helpless on their cots or learning to walk on the awkward crutches reminded her at every turn of those days in England when she had nursed John. When she saw a soldier trying to keep up his spirits after a fourth or fifth operation, she was reminded of the nights when she had prayed that John might be spared. Well, he had been spared, and for what. Many a night she would have been glad could she have thought she would never have wakened in the morning.

But as time went on, compelling occupation and a healthy body brought her back to a saner view of life, and she began to plan for the future. She went to night school and learned stenography, but this did not appeal to her.

The University Farm was just next to the hospital, and on her hours off in the afternoons, she often wandered over there, watching the sleek cattle grazing on the pastures or the sheep with their lambs. Most of all she watched the work in the poultry barns. The men there got used to her visits, and told her many things about the mating of birds to get the best layers, about culling the flocks to get rid of the boarders, as they called them, and about the best breeds for broilers and those for layers. When the spring came and the incubators brought out hundreds of little downy chicks, she scarcely missed a day to visit the pens where the wee morsels ran and scratched with the instinct that taught them what to do. By the second season, she had decided that she would have a chicken farm, and from then on she saved every penny she could get and read everything she could find on the raising of chickens. The old man in charge of the poultry plant, with whom she was great friends, gave her plenty of hints on the best sort of house, but also warned her that she should go slowly.

However, when she got started, he could send her lots of trade, if she had good stock, for they had many more orders than they could fill both for day-old chicks and for breeding stock. Then she would have her eggs to the good, and broilers too would bring her in lots of money if she had them early.

That year Rose took a position in a lawyer's office, and together with one of the nurses she had come to know in the hospital, rented a tiny house. It was not much of a house, but there was a lilac tree in front and a garden at the back that decided them. There was a little tumbledown barn at the back too, in which Rose saw possibilities. It took all their available funds to get the absolute necessities in the way of furniture, but the joy of having a home again made Rose belittle all such drawbacks. Every evening she spent fixing up and making warm the old shed at the back, and all she could save out of her next month's salary she took over to the old man at the poultry plant to invest in hens. She would not get a cock till later on.

# ON THE AGGIE BEAT

# THE WOMEN GRAIN GROWERS OF SASKATCHEWAN

(WOMAN'S CENTURY, MARCH 1915)

THE SECOND ANNUAL MEETING of the Women Grain Growers has just come to a most successful close. It was held in Regina the second week of February, at the same time that the main sessions were taking place. A good-sized hall had been engaged for the women's meetings, but it still lacked fifteen minutes of the opening time of the first session, when that room was found much too small, and the next morning the sessions were moved to Knox Church. The women who came there—as delegates from the different societies all over the province—had most purposeful faces. That they had come in face of great difficulties many of them did not attempt to deny. But that it was well worth the effort no one would deny, after attending a few of the very fine sessions. Several women carried tiny babies and some of the women had babies not so small, but at what we call the "interesting" stage—interesting certainly for the mother. One young man about a year old vied with the speaker in trying to hold his audience. His smiles were intentionally personal and persistent. It would have been rude not to smile back. But for a mother to hang onto this interesting creature, who changed his position on average three times a second, and take notes of the convention to report to her local, required some management—but that was the thing that impressed one—the delegates' ability to manage things.

The amount of business that was covered by this society under the very able guidance of the president, Mrs. John MacNaughton, of Piche, was remarkable. Their aims are for social betterment, educational uplift, a broader business basis for their work, more aesthetic surroundings, and for rights and privileges as women and human beings.

They considered the matter of a uniform market for Women Grain Growers' butter and eggs. This should mean also a uniform quality, so as to protect both the buyers and the sellers. The farmwomen who are sincerely interested in their work are as ambitious to supply good farm produce as the townswomen are to buy the fresh things.

These Grain Growers' locals serve a great purpose as a social factor. Women will drive fifteen or twenty miles to attend one of these meetings. They are surely worthwhile.

They are keenly interested in the education of their children under proper conditions and with proper surroundings. They are trying to make arrangements for providing nurses in the country districts where women could not afford properly qualified nurses from the cities. They are also making arrangements for travelling libraries, etc. They sent in a resolution this year, asking that the association would try to have the government provide someone to oversee the school playgrounds during the noon hours. Actions and words used by the children, when not under supervision, are not always all they should be, and as the children are so far from home, it is necessary that they take their lunches.

The interest with which these women listened to Dr. Wilson, principal of the Normal School, speak on country school gardens showed that it was a vital matter with them. They realize that a country school surrounded by trees and flowers will have a far different effect on their children than a little square school set up on the bald prairie could possibly have. Dr. Wilson's chief point was that co-operation between teacher and parents was most necessary in this respect as in others. The teacher cannot put up the fence nor plow the garden, but she can help to make the children interested in beautifying their grounds, and the influence of the teacher will do much towards forming the ideals of the community.

The Women Grain Growers were engaged in all matters that interest women. They thoroughly appreciated Miss Cora Hind's address on "Made-in-Canada," and it would be hard for anyone not to enjoy such a practical, concise presentation of this businesswoman's views.

The Women Grain Growers were especially keen on the addresses about equal franchise, women's rights, etc. In fact, it was at the insistent demands of these women's locals that their provincial executive took up the matter of presenting a suffrage petition to Parliament. As a first step they undertook to form a union among all the women's organizations in the province which were working for suffrage. They succeeded in this, passing a resolution to organize a federated board, and this was endorsed by the WCTU[1] and the suffrage societies. The first meeting of this federated board was held in Regina, February 13, and was a successful outcome of the insistent demands of these farm women. Their interests are as wide as they are varied, and only good can come of their splendid organization, which stands above all for co-operation.

*World's Best Wheat from Bush Land.* Published in the Family Herald and Weekly Star, *18 December 1929.* [BPSC]

# WORLD'S BEST WHEAT FROM BUSH LAND

*Jack Canuck Returns from Chicago*

(FAMILY HERALD AND WEEKLY STAR, 18 DECEMBER 1929)

THE TITLE OF "WORLD'S WHEAT KING" carries with it glamour enough, one would think, without the added glamour of romance which twice has given new lustre to the title.

Two years ago, the Peace River country of Alberta saw one of its young farmers, Herman Trelle of Wembley, win the title, thus showing the world that the northern line for the growing of cereals was being pushed further north.

Then this year, with an exhibitor of the same name pushing him close, Joseph H.B. Smith of Wolf Creek, Alberta, is crowned wheat king of the world, while with his oats, he almost wins the double crown, taking second place with his Early Alaska variety, and fourth place with Victory, in another class.

Wolf Creek, Alberta, is 120 miles west of Edmonton, ten miles northeast of the railway town of Edson on the Canadian National Railway.

It wasn't so many years ago, when, if a man said he was going homesteading in the Edson district, his friends sniffed pityingly at the poor bush farmer, doomed forever to a life of drudgery and an eternal battle against nature's heaviest odds.

Now the Edson district houses a crown and its title, that of "world's wheat king," and a quiet, gentlemanly-looking farmer who homesteaded in that district from England, twenty-two years ago, has shown the world that even Alberta's so-called bush land can and does produce wheat that may be adjudged the best that can be grown anywhere.

STRANGE COINCIDENCE

If you happen to be fond of coincidences, the fact that J.H.B. Smith of the Edson district had as his runner-up C. Edson Smith of Montana, former title holder, should give you a thrill.

The wheat king was in Edmonton a day or two after the news of his success reached him over the long-distance telephone from that city. He is tall, quiet, reserved—in bearing far from the type one would imagine as a "poor bush farmer." His black hair and well-trimmed heavy moustache, and his upright and modest bearing give him the touch of the military man.

"Did you expect to win the championship?" he was asked.

"Well, in a way I thought I might. I knew I had pure Reward wheat, and I knew it was good," he answered.

"How does it feel to be a world's champion?"

"Great! I had the feeling I was bound to win if I kept at it long enough," the wheat king replied.

And that apparently is one of the secrets—perseverance, that old virtue we used to write in our copy books, but which, alas, few of us practice as we should.

"I've won over thirty grain prizes at the big Canadian and United States shows during the past thirteen years," Mr. Smith explained, "and I believed I could make the grade in time."

The winner of the title was born in Leicester, England, coming to Western Canada in 1907, two years after Alberta was given its status as a province. He looked around for some time, working here and there, and landing up eventually fifteen years ago at Wolf Creek, a way station ten miles northeast of Edson. The country had not been surveyed then, so the future wheat king "squatted," getting homestead rights when the survey went through. Today he owns 640 acres of land, but only 45 acres is in wheat.

### TWELVE YEARS' WORK

Twelve years ago, Mr. Smith commenced to experiment in the growing of prize wheat. Up to five years ago, he worked with Marquis, but finally gave it up, as his tests led him to believe that it was not suited to bush country.

Then he took up Reward, after taking 17th place with his discarded Marquis at the Chicago exposition in 1924. Meantime his oats were steadily forging ahead, taking 15th place in 1921, 13th in 1922, 12th in 1923, and 2nd in 1924. For three years he did not show, but in 1928 his oats took fourth place at Chicago.

"How do you get your seed?" Mr. Smith was asked.

"I grow it myself," he replied. "I got the first lot of seed from the Dominion experimental farm at Ottawa, and am co-operating with officials there."

"Who helps you prepare your grain for exhibition?"

"My wife and family," proudly replied the wheat king. "I have four children—all boys: Eddie, 15; Ian 14; Joe, 10; and McLeod who is a baby of 18 months."

Mr. Smith's wife was formerly Miss M.J. Stevenson, a Scots girls living in Vancouver.

"What about this 'bush land' we hear of?" the wheat king was queried.

"Oh, it's largely bush land of course," laughed the champion grower, "but it isn't hard to clear. There's a lot of poplar brush, but clearing that isn't difficult. The soil is a sandy clay loam, and when cleared, it yields good crops."

Mr. and Mrs. Smith stayed for a few days in Edmonton on a shopping trip before returning to their farm, where, according to advices, a tremendous mail awaits their homecoming.

The champion is still planning fresh worlds to conquer.

"I'm going after the world's championship at Regina in 1932—showing wheat, oats, and barley," he declared.

# FROM ABERDEEN TO ALBERTA

(FAMILY HERALD AND WEEKLY STAR, 21 MAY 1930)

ONE MORNING LATELY AT LACOMBE, Frank Reed of the Experimental Farm was showing me ten or a dozen colts in the pasture behind the barn. They were yearlings and two-year-olds, several of them cross-bred Shires and Clydesdales. As he told me the breeding of one after the other, I wondered that there was not a thoroughbred in the bunch, for while he is so much of a cattleman that he is elected to office in Angus and Holstein Associations, I know he has an awful hankering for a nice saddle or driving horse.

Suddenly I got a little bunt on the shoulder. I looked around quickly and a soft velvet nose touched my cheek. It was the colt I had been wondering about. A sweet thing with clean dainty legs and a great desire to be petted. I rubbed his neck and patted his nose, and he followed me around the pasture. If I took my hand off him he reminded me of his presence immediately. A half-bred Shire, the same age and about three times as big, strode across to where we were standing, shouldered the little one out of the road, and offered himself for the petting. The little thoroughbred did not shove back but merely walked around to the other side, and the velvet nose was pressed against my face again. After that the two followed me around and left only when the gate was closed between us.

That same afternoon I was standing in a barnyard out at Alix, a few miles away, talking with the owner, Peter Jamieson, when a lamb walked upon my foot and stretched up his little head for petting. I just wondered if this confidence in humans and general well-being were established in all the animals in that Lacombe area, for well do I know that it is a country of good homes, good farms, and good livestock, or if, for the day, I had "it."

Eight years ago, Peter Jamieson sold his factory in Aberdeen and moved to Alberta to farm. For three generations the Peter Jamiesons had been manufacturers of harness polish in Aberdeen, and another Peter was christened to take over the business in turn. But this Peter heard the call of the land, and there is just a suspicion in my mind that his father also had a hankering that way, for ten years before when Peter Junior was riding a velocipede, Peter Senior made a trip to Canada and surreptitiously bought a farm near Alix, Alberta.

But Peter Junior gets most of the blame or credit for migration. His father says "Ter (short for Peter) would not come into the business; he wanted the land," and as a matter of fact Ter went to agricultural college in Scotland and was over in Canada a year before the others. Then Erie, the younger son, was delicate; he came on doctor's orders; and the mother said, "If the boys are going, I'm going too" and of course her daughter Dorothy had to come, since Heaven had ordained that she was to marry Bill Gentleman, a graduate in agriculture of the University of Alberta, and where would she meet Bill but in Canada, for he had left Scotland many years before as emigration companion for some Ayrshires for Ness.

So with his family "walking out on him," what was Peter Senior to do? My tongue is in my cheek as I write this, for, as mentioned, he had bought that Alberta farm ten years before and never said a word about it.

Anyway, there they are at Rodona Farm, Alix, Alberta, Peter Jamieson, proprietor, and the letterhead carrying a sketch of the farmstead says they breed Hampshire sheep, milking Shorthorns, and Yorkshire pigs. They had to give up the foxes when Dorothy left home. She was mistress of the fox department.

Then there are the Rodona bees that furnish a small sideline; Peter Senior looks after them and it's good honey. I know because I tasted it and I taste much honey. I sweeten my applesauce and my baked apples with it; I use it instead of sugar in my cakes, bread, and salad dressing. So I know the Rodona honey is good honey. Peter Jamieson says he has 150,000 bees working on it.

The farm name Rodona prefixes the name of all the stock when registered and it really prefixes the farm itself since the name is on the entrance gate.

Peter Junior looks after the milking Shorthorns and keeps the records. Peter Senior claims the pigs and sheep, and he is also the farm veterinarian.

I looked at them all, everything so comfortable looking and well fed, and presently Erie put his hand through my arm and firmly directed me over to a shed.

"They'll show you all the pigs and cattle, but they forget to show you my part of it." He threw open the door and there was the tractor and the separator. Erie is the mechanic.

"There is the sheep barn over there," he said casually, pointing to a new shiny automobile. I puckered my brow and they all laughed at me. It is the "laughingest" farm family I know. They just seem to enjoy everything. Once explained of course, it was perfectly simple.

Father did not approve of buying an automobile, but he craved a new sheep barn and had the money in his hand to build one. So the boy undertook to build a sheep barn of poplar poles and straw, which they did, and it's a good one built without money and without price, except for nails.

By arrangement the money dedicated to the sheep barn was thus invested in an automobile, which comes under Erie's department.

As stated, Peter Senior claims the pigs and sheep, but we noticed that when Mrs. Jamieson came out to the yard, where we stood admiring the first rain that had fallen there for almost two years, the lambs left their own mothers, and jumped up at her as a happy dog will do.

The Jamiesons knew nothing of farming when they came to Canada except what Ter had learned in his two years at the College at Aberdeen, and that did not count for such a lot on a Canadian farm partly covered with bush.

"I had to learn the things that Canadian boys know instinctively," said Ter. "For instance it was harder for me to learn to drive a wagon with a rack over one of these side hills than to pass an exam."....

# THE TRAGEDY OF THE REGINA PLAINS

(FAMILY HERALD AND WEEKLY STAR, 30 SEPTEMBER 1931)

IDEAL HARVEST WEATHER has been afforded the Western farmers this year, but the thrill of harvest has been offset by the low prices, so low that the harvesters are wondering if it would pay them to take off the grain or leave it standing. There has been little frost during the cutting season in the West, but the threat of insects and weeds for next year is formidable.

Alberta is in the best position so far as this year's crop is concerned; Manitoba comes in the in-between class. The biggest tragedy lies in those bare fields on the Regina plains where many crops of best No. 1 Northern have been grown and which is the area recognized as particularly a grain-growing country. Miles of country are absolutely bare as though nothing had been sown; in many places there is not even a weed, not a green sprig.

But even at that it is infinitely better than it was at the end of July.

The Regina plains have a wonderful power of recovery, as evidenced by the growth after a couple of rains in July. A pittance of three inches of rain has fallen at Regina during the present crop season; there was no snow last winter; high winds kept swirling the soil from one township to the next, so that when seed time came, the land was thoroughly dry, pulverized. Farmers declared they would not put in seed till it rained; but day followed day and no rain and it was past time to sow if a crop were to have any chance of ripening, so with many misgivings, they put in their seed, the wind blowing the soil in their faces as they worked. But some kept their vow; they did not sow and are glad now they did not waste the seed.

Indeed, the face of the whole country north, east, west and south of Regina has changed tremendously since the first of August; naked fields have grown a covering of a sort; thin stands of grain have taken fresh courage and ripened; seed that was blown out or buried has started to grow. It may or may not ripen, but there it is making its valiant effort. Depending on how long the killing frosts keep off and how far mature these mongrel crops, mixtures of grain and weeds, are allowed to become, this feed will be more or less valuable. While it has been balm to the hearts of farmers to see something green on those endless miles of naked prairie, the fodder derived therefrom may be very soft and disappointing for winter feed unless it gets further growth. But the psychological effect of seeing the ground covered is good if nothing else.

The centres of many of the fields have ripened so the grain can be cut or combined and the edges which were covered with drifting soil will be cut for green feed. Of course where the soil drifted two, three, four, and six feet high, the grain could not push through, even had the moisture penetrated.

Ditches beside the highway are drifted full, and gangs of men with drags are busy hauling the dirt back on the fields.

It has been a great year for the Russian thistle, that vulture of arid soils. It thrives in dry years where there is not too much competition from thrifty growing crops and spreads over immense areas. It has a particularly uncanny method of breaking itself loose from its stem and rolling around the fields distributing its seed. The plant develops into a round ball, so it may roll with the slightest wind, and winds have not been slight this year. There are whole fields of nothing else but Russian thistle in this drouth area; and failing all other crops, farmers are harvesting them for winter feed. They make not bad silage.

Many nauseating fires are burning along Saskatchewan roadsides where weed inspectors are burning the Russian thistle before it seeds. But were you ever near a Russian thistle bonfire? The odour is devastating. With the windows of the car closed, this acrid smell still crept in. The very unpleasant odour may come from the salt in the plant or the oil, maybe both; anyway it is terrible.

Farmers do not worry much over being able to eradicate the weed, given a fair amount of rainfall. It does not unduly contest the soil with a thrifty crop; but no crop, and the Russian thistle thrives.

From Regina to Swift Current, where ordinarily there would be scores of threshing machines and combines in early September, I saw two, and they had spit out a pathetic little mound of straw about as big as a table.

Many of these farmers are harvesting to get back their seed; some will not have that, some will have a little more.

In areas such as the Ponteix district, there has been considerable deterioration in the land during the last couple of years. It is said that the surface soil is all blown away right down to hardpan. Considerable land in Southern Saskatchewan was reseeded, but in many cases the farmers did not bother to do so as it was still dry after the first seeding was blown out. Many, indeed, did not have money enough to buy more seed; and there were those who put in no crop at all. They considered it useless to plant seed in soil which had absolutely no moisture and they were probably wise, for 50 per cent of the first germination died. The rainfall in Southern Saskatchewan this year was one-fifth of normal.

The land is dry for feet down, and unless there is a lot of rain this fall, the prospects for a crop next year are poor. Of course, with plentiful rainfall during the growing season, this reserve would not be essential. By July the water holes had all dried up and water was being hauled long distances. Much hardship was entailed; farmers became very nervous, particularly those who had any stock; some stock was sacrificed; stories were told of farmers shooting their animals. However, sufficient rain has fallen in the last six weeks to fill the dugouts again, and renewed pastures are reflected in the increased dairy production.

Ordinarily farmers of Southern Saskatchewan pray for a dry September so the grain may be harvested dry; this year they are praying for rain, as this year's harvest is hardly worth saving, but more moisture in the subsoil would give a measure of promise for next year's crop, when it is hoped the price will be sufficient to make a return on investment.

Around Swift Current a few combines were seen working, hoping for seed and a little better; in one field the combine was threshing out fifteen to seventeen bushels to the acre, a very nice crop for this year. Some of the combines were hauled by tractors, some by a ten-horse hitch, and did I ever see so many white horses in my life! It kept me busy looking for red-haired boys to correspond.

In an afternoon's drive south of Regina, I saw not one combine or threshing machine working; neither were the pathetic rows of granaries, nor indeed were the dozens and hundreds of grain elevators clustering around the village depots. It was hard to realize such a complete cessation of all effort. Saskatchewan automobile licenses are down by 25,000 from last year and a Saturday night in the villages shows a great collection of old relics in the way of buggies and horses drawn up to the curb.

How completely this affects the life of the community may be estimated. The country doctors are working harder than ever but getting small payment, and it costs money to keep driving some hundreds of miles a day. It is not hard to believe the report that one of the lists of relief cases sent into the government by a country storekeeper included his own name.

Taking a line from a little east of Regina, west to Swift Current, sixty miles north of this line and south to the boundary is an area that has had a crop failure for three years in succession. Individual areas have not had a crop for four or five years. This is the thing that has made it so difficult. Each year washed out more and more of the reserve that these farmers had built up. East and west of this block are places which have had a complete failure for one or two years. No place in Western Canada is capable of producing better wheat, and it is essentially a wheat country. Dean A.M. Shaw has referred to it as a hazardous area for stock, so it would appear that the only thing they can do is wait; Regina only asks for fifteen inches of moisture a year.

In 1928 the value of the crop from this devastated area comprising some 45,000 square miles was $174,000,000; in 1929 it was $101,000,000; in 1930 it had shrunk to $45,000,000, and the estimate this year is $9,000,000, or in other words, the income and consequent spending capacity of that area this year will be about 5 per cent what is was in 1928.

Following the Canadian Pacific Railway line south to Stoughton across to Weyburn and Estevan and all the country south of Swift Current, one goes through a world of grief and bare fields, although it has recovered somewhat in the last month. However, this recovery has to do with feed rather than saleable grain. The toughest centres are up around Ponteix and Cadillac in Township 76.

For the whole of Saskatchewan, the estimated gross agricultural revenue for 1921 was $253,000,000, of which $215,636,000 was field crops; in 1928 the gross was $409,000,000, of which $348,536,000 was from field crops; in 1930 the gross had dropped to $175,500,000, of which $120,000,000 was from field crops. So the persistent and continuing value of field crops to the agricultural wealth of Saskatchewan is well sustained. The peak year for farm animals was 1929 when their estimated value was $35,000,000; in 1930 this figure was dropped to $20,700,000, and this year the values will be considerably reduced again with decreased values of different lines.

There has been some liquidation of livestock this year on account of shortage of water earlier in the season and shortage of pasture, as well as a steadily diminishing prospect for winter feed.

During the summer, natural pastures in Northern Saskatchewan have been prospected as never before and wild hay that never saw a mowing machine before was tamed to that extent. Much hay has been cut in the north; some has been shipped in from Manitoba and stock has been shipped from the south to the north; green oat sheaves have been shipped from north to south. Included in provincial relief was more than $100,000 for seed grain advanced by the mortgage companies and guaranteed by the provincial government, in addition to bonuses on seed grain from field-inspected crops. It was thought only reasonable to help them get better seed since they had to buy seed.

For three years, the Saskatchewan government has been giving assistance to its stricken people. As a result of the 1929 crop failure, the government and railways absorbed the costs of transporting fodder. In 1930, help was again given for freight on fodder, but in this case the fodder was bought, and sold to the municipality, the banks lending the money on provincial guarantee, which was just another way round, but put the responsibility for collection back on the municipality. In the past two years, the Saskatchewan government has paid out over a million dollars for these services. Last spring the Dominion government advanced seed where required, and the municipalities gave personal relief. In addition to the assistance given through the Departments of Agriculture and Municipal Affairs, T.M. Mulloy, of the latter bureau, had an employment budget. A million dollars was advanced for gasoline to put in the 1931 crop.

This year, in addition to other assistance in the way of moving fodder and stock, the provincial government has moved some seven hundred families from the south country to the north. Many more have rigged up tarpaulins over their wagons or trucks and have gone prospecting on their own account. Some farms have been abandoned. In other cases these men who are used to the far vision of the prairies did not take kindly to the northern farms where an axe was a necessary adjunct in settlement; some of these have returned. So far as the provincial government assistance in the way of freight on settlers' effects is concerned, this movement will be discontinued at the end of September.

A relief commission has been organized, consisting of Henry Black, ex-mayor of Regina; A.E. Whitmore, Regina; W.A. Mumms, Moose Jaw; W.G. Yule, superintendent of the Royal Bank, Regina; Mrs. Pearl Johnson, Coalville, of the United Farmers of Canada. There has been some criticism of the personnel of the commission in that with the exception of Mrs. Johnson there is no actual farm representation. The manager is M. Daniels, and A.E. Wilson, of Indian Head, is looking after the purchase and handling of grain for seed and feed.

Mr. McMillan, head of the grocery and food divisions, is buying up potatoes by the carload for shipment into these areas where not a potato could grow this year. As a gesture of kindly interest the Women's Institute of British Columbia is sending forward as a gift a carload of fruit and vegetables to the women of Southern Saskatchewan. Other divisions of this relief are the Red Cross Service, looking after the schools to see that they are kept open; the unemployment section is under T.M. Mulloy, and the Department of Agriculture will handle fodder and transfer of stock.

The department is now contracting with farmers in the North to supply the definite demands from the municipalities for fodder. Some municipalities are making their own arrangements. Just now the agents of the Department of Agriculture are out among these various municipalities trying to get a final estimate on fodder requirements. Some stock has been shipped to the north, but it has been found that some owners are reluctant to ship their stock when they do not know into whose hands it may go. So the government and railways are paying freight on stock both ways, and further, the government is contributing 50 cents a head a month toward paying a man to take care of it. This allows the municipality to select whom it pleases to look after the cattle while they are in foreign feeding quarters. The federal government is assisting the province by providing the funds.

In the meantime, Saskatchewan is looking squarely into this agricultural problem for next year. In the first place, rain is required, much rain, that will penetrate three, four, and five feet. There are cutworms by the millions in the south half of the province and even toward the north. There is a potential outbreak of grasshoppers due for next year which promises to be the most serious yet. Seed will have to be provided for next year and financial assistance toward putting in another crop. But there is no thought in the minds of the individual farmer or the Government of Saskatchewan, or indeed of the Dominion, in letting these people lose heart, for there must certainly be an improvement in wheat prices next year. Grain men expect a substantial reduction in world wheat surpluses by the beginning of the next crop year. World conditions must surely be getting better and indeed the price cycle of agricultural products has dropped so low that there is no room on the chart for it to go lower and it will needs turn upward. It is not possible to have a curve if one end of the line goes straight down and stays down, and curves are necessary for charts.

# MEN ON RELIEF
# GO BACK TO LAND

(FAMILY HERALD AND WEEKLY STAR, 7 JUNE 1933)

RURAL REHABILITATION, of which so much is heard these days, is confined by no means to the few hundred families who are going onto the land with government blessing and financial assistance. True, these people are more in the limelight, because in their extremity, they have to submit to careful scrutiny, for the sake of the public which is putting up the money.

It is only a little more than a year since this assisted scheme got under way, first in Saskatchewan, then in Manitoba. Alberta and British Columbia are just starting to take advantage of it. To the end of April this year, 814 families from the four western provinces had been assisted to settle on farms. Of these 250 were in Manitoba; 503 in Saskatchewan; 50 in Alberta; and 11 in British Columbia. But May has been a busy month in back-to-the-land offices and the records at the end of May would show a great increase over these records.

Assisted settlement schemes have been in bad odour in the past and it was some time before governments or private individuals would take the idea seriously.

But apart from these assisted cases, there has been a large flow of people back to the land, in many cases their own land which they have bought back, or taken over from a renter. Many a farm has gone back to the original owner for lack of payments on mortgage or non-payment of taxes; the mortgagee looks for other land with less liabilities. There are the middle-aged or elderly men who, after saving up a little competence, moved into town and bought an apartment house, or a small business, or something which they thought would provide them with a living for the rest of their lives. Some moved to town to send their children to school or university, or to let them have the opportunity take a city job. Many are moving back to the land now, and mostly the children are moving with them. Maybe the boy got married while they were in the city and, in the staff curtailments of the last few years, he now finds himself out of a job. So he takes his wife back to the home farm so they can all work together for a living, and the old mother has the job of teaching the city girl how to keep house on a farm.

Then there are the farmers from the drouth areas, who after several failures went surveying into the North, where drouths are not so persistent and where there are other perquisites such as building and fuel and hay lands. But this did not always mean that their wheat farm in the South was abandoned. More often, part of the family stayed there to keep things going till the cycles moved around to the wet seasons again, while the rest of the family went north to get some sort of place that would carry them in the meantime, and where there was hay land and grazing for the stock. They kept one foot on the wheat farm, so to speak.

What is true for Winnipeg in regard to resettlement on farms is much more evident in the smaller towns and villages where the people are only one step removed from the farm and where everyone naturally knows that Bill Pierce has to rent his farm or at least sell part of it, on account of his wife being sickly, or because he cannot afford to hire help this year. There is another reason that will tend to drive families from the small centres to the farm than from Winnipeg; the average relief for a family of five in Winnipeg is around $40 a month, while in the small towns it is about $14.

The landward movement is also indicated in the number of homesteads which have been taken up in the last four or five years. In Manitoba very little homestead land is available, but in Saskatchewan the records show that in 1928 there were 5,341 homesteads filed on; in 1929, 6,216; in 1930, 4,258; in 1931, 3,106; in 1932, 1,781. Till 1930, these homesteads were free, but with the return of the natural resources to the province, there has been a fee for filing as well as a definite purchase price of $1.00 an acre upwards. Also it is required that the purchasers must have lived at least four years in Saskatchewan. So the records for the past two years indicate exactly how many Saskatchewan people have filed on new homesteads. Some of these are people from the drouth areas, who have taken the opportunity to get cheap land for grazing and hay.

In Alberta, exclusive of the Peace River Area, the homestead returns for the same period are: 1928, 3,743; 1929, 4,949; 1930, 5,500; 1931, 5,776; 1932, 2,447.

While each province in the West may have a different "set-up" in its back-to-the-land movement, all are working on the broad scheme of equal financial responsibility from Dominion and provincial governments and the municipality in which relief is being paid to the applicant.

The colonization branches of the two railways, which have had long experience in these matters, and the soldier settlement[1] officers assist in interviewing applicants and helping to secure suitable farms. The board of trade and the city council are naturally interested parties. The onus of proof that they have a satisfactory proposition is put on the applicant family.

In Manitoba, $600 is made available for the settlement of each family, of which $200 comes from the Dominion government, $200 from the province, and $200 from the municipality, usually Winnipeg, where most of the relief cases are bulked.

It is a requisite that the farm experience of applicants be not too far in the background. They are supposed to have been experienced farmers, and so carefully was the selection made in Manitoba last year, that after seven months operation, only two out of 185 families proved failures, that is, had to give up and come back to town.

The interviewing committee find it most important to have a chat with the wife. In their experience, the wife's suitability and willingness are quite as important as the husband's. Some women are just naturally suited to farming; some do not like it; some are temperamentally not suited to live in lonely places, and believe it or not, some are afraid to go alone with their husbands to farmsteads far away from neighbourly assistance. One such case was investigated. The committee was inclined to criticize this woman living on relief for her determination not to go to the country when her husband wanted to go. But it turned out that the nice kind husband who was anxious to go to the country was out on suspended sentence for wife beating.

So it is very important that husband and wife should be satisfied and have a real urge to start life anew. Those who do it in that frame of mind will sit up nights with the cow when she is sick, pick wild strawberries to trade with the grocer for sugar, and do other disagreeable jobs that are bound to mix in with the agreeable status of a home of one's own.

While the back-to-the-land movement is considered primarily in the light of a relief measure and the cost to the public—$600—is less than it would take to keep a family on relief in the city for two years, it is fondly hoped that a percentage of these assisted families will "stick." If they did, it would be cheaper colonization than many of the schemes that have been used in the past.

As a grub-stake it means that the families are going to be looked after for two years, for $100 is reserved out of the original $600 for the second year. Some do not accept the whole $600, preferring to be in debt as little as possible, but generally speaking it requires about $600 to get the minimum equipment.

At the present time, neither the settler nor the rehabilitation committee is under expense for land—it is given free; there are not taxes or overhead unless one calls the bit of equipment such. And the municipalities into which these people are settled are given a guarantee that they will not become a charge on that community.

Thinking that with a fair chance, many of these families would become permanent farmers, we asked one of the officers, who is also a man of much experience in colonization, if it were quite fair to put these people on farms that had been deserted by previous owners because they could not make a living on them. "Supposing these people do show evidence of desire and ability to farm, will they have a fair chance on that kind of soil?" And his reply was: "Land companies will be more than glad to pick up any such families and settle them on good land. There is plenty of good land lying idle in Western Canada; the companies would be glad to have a good man working it."

But in Manitoba they have almost exhausted these "suitable" farms, that is, farms with buildings where a settler can move right in, and still there are nearly a thousand who want to go. So another scheme is being devised, a scheme recently presented by the Winnipeg Board of Trade to the city council and the provincial government. It is proposed to form a subsidiary trustee company capitalized at $35,000 to rehabilitate another hundred families. This would provide $350 per family with which to build a house and stable. This would allow a much wider range of land selection. Under this scheme, the $350 would be a first charge against the farm and of course the owner of the land would have to agree to such a prior claim. The trustee company would administer the fund and the province and city of Winnipeg or other municipality would subscribe fifty-fifty with the hope that the Dominion government would eventually be converted to the idea and come in on a one-third basis.

It is proposed that in the organization of the trustee company the terms be made sufficiently non-restrictive to permit of enlargement of the capital by not only additional subscription from Dominion or provincial governments or municipalities and also from private capital or from any source.

From the humanitarian standpoint, there is much to be said in favour of getting out into the country. Some of these families have been cooped up in one room for a couple of years, living the precarious life of the unemployed on relief. There was one applicant family over which the Winnipeg committee paused a long time and even after they were gone, felt that they had only sent them out to die. Both the children and parents appeared to be TB, and how could sick people do anything on a farm, and those children should have been kept near a doctor, they felt. However, out on the farm they went and only a few weeks later the committee sent an inspector out to see how they were coming along.

Said the inspector on his return: "I just could not believe that they were the same children. When I drove up, they came running out of the bush from all directions like rabbits; in that short time they had become husky and strong; their eyes were shining and their faces happy."

Twelve per cent of those who have gone out from Winnipeg are on small holdings in and around the city where they will grow potatoes, poultry, and the like. Mostly, however, they are on quarter sections.

Requirements vary with each settler and each settler chooses his own place from those available. Often he is able to get near a relative or a friend, who can assist with the loan of horses or machinery. But the average budget for putting a family on a farm would include: $20 for moving, $30 for building expenses, $100 for a team, $25 for a second-hand harness, $15 for buckets and household utensils, $25 for seed, $15 for tools, $90 for second-hand wagon, mower, rake, plough, harrows, $20 for a cow, and $10 for poultry, which comes to a total of $350. If they do not get horses, they can have more cows and pigs and so on.

In the meantime a ray of wholesome hope has entered some drab lives.

# CHAMPION OF WOMEN
## AND THE WEST

*Jack McClung and MGE in Finnigan, Jr.* [BPSC]

# MY CAR "FINNIGAN" AND I

*A Car Is a Woman's Best Friend and "Finnigan" Has Proved It Many Times*

(GRAIN GROWERS' GUIDE, 7 APRIL 1920)

"I'LL TURN IT AROUND and then you can try your driving." This in the tone of "You have brought this on yourself. Now take the consequences."

I had been half-owner in a second-hand motor car for about two years, but had never driven it. After persistent, if veiled, suggestions that I ought to know how to drive the car, I was one day allowed to try, but by hap or chance, the opportunity came as were going through some very heavy sand roads, and in my nervousness I killed the engine before I had gone out of low gear. In confusion and chagrin I was put out of the driver's seat, never to return till this memorable morning, when, the other partner having to leave town, it became necessary for me to learn to drive.

That day my partner and I drove down to the barracks and, as he turned the car around, its nose back towards town, I heard him make that remark and he was gone without a backward glance. It seemed to me that there were at least a million men standing around; so I threw my head up, slid over to the driver's seat and intended to make that car go or know the reason why. But as not a million men altogether reported overseas in the Canadian army, I judged afterwards I must have been mistaken in the number of men watching.

## DUPLICITY AGAIN

Well, of course, I killed the engine, and then getting out to crank, I found there was "nothing doing." Finally, a young captain came and offered his services, and after he had tried for several minutes I noticed that the little switch that should have turned on the batteries was still on the magneto. I sneaked it over and never told him what was the matter.

I got away then, and I never stopped that whole morning, partly from fear I would not get started again, and partly because I was determined to overcome my fear about driving that car before I let it out of my hands.

My partner was not at all surprised that I had got along all right, but calmly stated that he knew I would be less nervous if I went at it by myself—and he was perfectly right.

I drove that old car for several years after that, and because it was an old car, had the usual number of troubles, but never a serious accident. The new cars are so much better made that, excepting for tire mishaps, few difficulties are encountered in driving over ordinarily good roads. Even tire trouble has lost much of its terror, with the removable rims and wheels. That old car had no less than three very tightly fitted rims to take off before one could get the tire, then the TFRS had all to be put on again, and the new tire blown up with pants and puffs.

## CHANGING TIRES IN THE RAIN

One day as I stood in the drizzling rain, fifteen miles from anywhere, I thought hard thoughts, and said un-nice words. It was in June, and the grass was rank and long; mosquitoes—ye gods! I built a smudge both sides of me before I could do a thing, then found that with the deep ruts in the road I could not get the jack under the axle, so had to start the car and run the front wheels up on a high place in order to get the jack under. Of course I had to move the smudges and after several preliminaries undertook to pry loose those three rims. They had not been off since the year before, and were rusted together like glue. How I bless this day of our Lord and the easily removable rims, when I think of the time I had trying to get that tire off. But when you know there is no help within fifteen miles you don't give up readily, so I finally got the tire off and another inner tube in, and started the remantling of that naked rim. Ultimately I persuaded all the rims back in place and then proceeded to put in the air (by hand, foot, and back). After much perspiration, etc., I got the tire blown up and triumphantly took out the jack, only to see the car gradually settle down on its rim again. (Register nausea.)

The jack was pulled out again from under the back seat and all that performance over again—yes, all of it—for again the tire would not bear the weight of the car. I bethought me to try the valve, so I took off the little cap, spit on my finger and smeared it over the top of the valve in scientific manner—and discovered—the valve was leaking. I turned the little valve cap the other side up, screwed in the valve tighter, but air was still escaping, not nearly so badly, however. I went through all my tool chest, looking in vain for a new valve, so finally blew up the tire as hard as I could and started on. About every three or four miles I had to get out and pump, but—I got to town. After that I always carried spare valves in my pocket.

### SPARE TIRE A GAY DECEIVER

But, as I say, there is very little of that now. You have your spare tire on the back, all blown up, and a change can be made in four or five minutes, with no auxiliary vocabulary at all required.

But that same spare tire can be a gay deceiver too. Maybe your tires are new, and for weeks and months you go along with no punctures or blow-outs. When the little nickle tire tester tells you your tires are getting a little soft, you go to the service station and get them full of free air, knowing there is going to be far less likelihood of tire trouble if they are kept well filled with air. But sometimes you forget to test that spare on the back. It is very disconcerting to go to change tires some very hot day, or worse still, some very cold day, and find that spare soft and flabby.

That old car didn't have its magneto properly covered, so when I drove through a water hole some drops were sure to splash up on the magneto and short circuit the connection, and stop the engine. One night I got out and, wading around in the water to my ankles, cranked that car till my arm and back ached; but it stayed as one dead thing. Finally, as it grew darker and colder, I left the car there (confident no one else could start it), and walked into camp—five miles beyond.

Next morning I walked back in the gay sunshine, and thought I would just give a little twirl before I started to dissect the insides of that car. Behold, she had repented of her evil ways and without further urging started, hitting on every cylinder. After I had this experience a couple of times I held consultation with the garage mechanic, and he suggested making a jacket, or pair of trousers, or some such garment for that magneto.

### HITTING ON ALL FOUR

Another thing that worried me in that old car was spark plugs. My principal driving was back and forth to camp over very bad sand practically all the way. Very often, and always when in a hurry, the engine would show symptoms of bad respiration, hitting as uncertainly as the jazziest ragtime, and the engine would not pull in its usual steady manner. Then I got out my jackknife and scraped the carbon off those spark plugs. If they were very bad, I soaked them in gasoline when I got home.

But in the modern cars there is little of this trouble either. I have driven my present car two years, and have never had a spark plug out.

That old car had short springs too, and I scarcely ever made a round trip without breaking a leaf, or maybe the whole spring, so you may be sure when I was getting a new car I looked for something with a long, well-balanced spring. In the two years I have never broken a spring; in fact, almost any trouble I have had, I have brought on myself.

### HOW AXLES ARE BENT

It was the day we got news that peace was declared. I had not noticed the streets were very slippery till I started to slew around, going down that steep, paved hill. It had rained, and while not exactly frozen, it was still sufficiently glazed to be slippery. As I started down the hill I shoved on the brake, and as the car started to slew, I shoved the brake on hard—the very thing, of course, that I should not have done; but it is an instinctive movement. Anyway, we turned clear around and hit the curb with a sickening thud, and the car gave a tilt that made me wonder where I would land. But we settled back again—it takes an awful jolt to turn a car over. Then I found that my steering apparatus was out of commission. The axle had been bent a little and this was a case for the garage.

When I got my car I hesitated considerably before paying down $20 extra for a bumper. It seemed to me they thought I looked easy, or did not know how to drive. But many a bill of expense that bumper has saved me, and next time I'll get one front and back—it's good insurance. One morning I was going along a very slippery city street, and noticing the drunken manner in which the car ahead of me was slithering around, I slowed down a little, and was only driving about eight or ten miles an hour when my car suddenly started in to the curb and then across the sidewalk. Happily no one was there. Had I hit the building a foot either side I should have broken a huge plate-glass window. But, I didn't. Neither was the radiator harmed—the bumper had justified itself in that one experience. But although the whole thing was repaired for less than $15, it looked like a wrecked car. The glass in one of the headlights was broken; the bumper was in two, hanging down from both sides; the running board and fender were both jammed up a bit where they had hit a lamp-post in passing.

It is against our city by-laws to drive on the sidewalk, so without bothering to take off the broken bumper I started for the garage, going down a back street, as the loose ends of the bumper scraping and rattling along the ground made an infernal row. I saw a man rush out from the walk and throw up his hands, so I stopped. He told me my bumper was broken. I went on, and every man I met tried to tell me the same thing. I felt like mentioning I had suspected as much.

WHEN IT'S GOOD, IT'S VERY GOOD

Ordinarily, a car is a woman's best friend. It takes her off on a picnic, or at any rate for a cooling drive in the midst of a busy day, when her nerves are wrought up to a high tension over something or other; it carries her safely and quickly home at night, if she has been detained until a late hour, when it might not be comfortable to walk alone. It gives her a chance to get away from the crowd and talk quietly to a friend or business associate; in fact, it is a real pal. But now and again it just actually fails her. It is very good usually, but when it's bad, it is horrid. It is like nothing so much as a very naughty pup that comes dragging in some ragged undergarment off the clothesline just when you are entertaining your most aristocratic neighbour.

I was going to a funeral one day. I had been detained in the office till about five minutes after the hour, but did not think much of that, as I took it for granted that funerals were always late, anyway. I ran down the stairs and jumped into the car, turned on the juice, shoved down the starter, but—nothing happened but a sickening whir. I tried again, and finally, it gave a kick. I threw in the gear, but she stopped again. Well, that went on for several times. I would get a few feet farther every time, and finally within a block of the undertaker's I saw them out waiting for me—I had promised to take some of the mourners to the cemetery. Right there we stopped.

That car was plain naughty, for you see it could go if it wanted to. I finally got to the place and they put the brother of the dead man, his father-in-law, and the minister in with me. I still wondered about the car but it had never failed me before and I could not believe it would now. Mr. Undertaker came along with his apologetic manner, which tries to hide the business gleam in his eye under sad eyebrows, and asked me to go to the head of the procession. My natural modesty, and the naughtiness of my car, made me shy at this precedence and I suggested some other place in the line, but I was gently reminded that the minister always went ahead, and suggested again that I would move up. All this time I had been trying to get a spark, and so I used sort of undertaker tones to cover my wrath when I asked him if he could wait till I got my car started. Pretty soon there was a little kick and with the next try, it went, albeit rather chokingly and unwillingly. In my excitement I had probably flooded the carburetor, I thought. Anyway, I moved up in front of the hearse. Finally, they gave me the signal to go on and I went. When I got to the corner I looked back to find the hearse coming along with "measured tread" fully two blocks back.

Well, I waited, and when I got around the next corner I found the hearse out of sight again. I waited, but was still too perturbed about the way the car was acting to realize what was the matter. The hearse finally caught up again, and after some five or six blocks further, Friend Parson said, in a very calm, dispassionate voice, "I think we are going a little fast for a funeral." After that suggestion I brought her down to a walk, and we travelled along quite respectably. Then I heard a motor horn give a couple of honks, so instinctively swerved out to the right. No car passed, as I expected, and I looked around to find the hearse had stopped back at the corner. As I wondered what had happened, the parson stepped in with the calm remark that that was where I should have turned to go to the cemetery. How was I to know? The cemetery was not one of my favourite haunts. I was past the corner and could not turn around there, so I "beat it" around the block and met up with the hearse at the next corner.

FUNERALS BANNED IN FUTURE

We got to the cemetery, had the funeral, and loaded up to come away. Again the same trouble to start. The path in the cemetery was narrow and the hearse and all the other cars were interned there till I got out. Finally, I did get started, and once these funeral persons were out of my car I went back to town at 35 an hour, trying to take out my spite on that car. But the car just enjoyed it—said as much. Never before or since has it acted like that. Would you call it temperament or the natural dislike of a cheery nature at going to funerals? I was certainly chagrined at the exhibition we made of ourselves and I never offered my services at a funeral again.

And that day, as I thought of the "off again, on again, gone again" attitude of that little red car, I christened it "Finnigan," and, although one of my friends tells me a car should be a "she," I tell her that no "she" would ever have acted like that going to a funeral.

*"Women's side of the tent at Hobbema Sun Dance."* [BPSC]

# SUN DANCE AT HOBBEMA (1923)

WHEN THE TREES ARE IN FULL LEAF, then the Cree and their entire households, tents and horses, kettles and babies, journey forth for the great annual festival of the "Sun Dance." It is in penance for their sins; it is a sacrifice to the gods, to propitiate these gods that no undue sickness, or plague, hunger or want shall come near them.

If a squaw falls ill during the winter, she prays to the gods that she may be restored. In return she promises to dance the Sun Dance the next June. Should a brave find his true aim forsaking him, he absolves himself from the evil influence which makes his arm unsteady, or his eye less true, by taking part in the Sun Dance.

But the day of the Sun Dance is almost past. As the Indians die off, there are few among the younger ones to take their places. Few of the young generation of Indians know the significance of the old pagan ceremonial, and take part more as a matter of habit, or else are mere interested spectators—much as Christian children have lost all the dramatic significance of Lent, Good Friday, and Easter. The government also is discouraging the continuance of the ceremony of the Sun Dance, believing it to have a detrimental effect on their efforts to settle the Indians on the land.

As I took the train at Edmonton for the Hobbema Reserve, about eighty miles south, I felt saddened that I was to witness what would, in all probability, be the last Sun Dance ever to be seen in the West. But as a reaction against the sadness, I had to think how I was to get from the station to the place selected for the dance, what means I was going to use to try to see the ceremony, for I understood that white people and especially strangers were not very welcome, and also where I was going to spend the night, for there was not a house except the convent, and the next train to Calgary was about three in the morning.

But I soon found myself on the way to the Sun Dance, and I decided to meet the other difficulties when they arrived. A very courteous Indian was my driver, and from him I tried to get the reason why, the time when, the modus operandi and answers to dozens of other questions, for I must admit my mind was absolutely pure, simple, and undefiled of any slightest suspicion of knowledge as to the rites and customs that are behind the great event. But although he could speak English well, he was, like all Indians, not at all loquacious.

But I found that when the time arrived, the Cree from far and near came together for the great annual ceremony of sacrifice and atonement. For the greater part of three days, the dancers neither ate, drank, nor slept, and their bodies were almost constantly going through the monotonous motions peculiar to the dance. To say it was weird is a commonplace, and my only wonder is that our Natives did not bring us the knowledge of hypnotism, for after staring intently at a tree for three days and two nights, while the weird music goes on continuously and the body gradually becomes more and more fatigued, it is little short of marvellous that all the dancers are not in a state of hypnotic trance.

For the last Sun Dance, about five or six hundred Indians had gathered together on an open field at the Hobbema Reserve, their teepees all ranged along two sides and in the central position, the Sun Dance tent, which is well worth description. It was large enough to hold between two and three hundred people, the Indians on one side and the squaws on the other. In the centre was the sacred tree, the trunk of a large poplar placed in the ground and securely braced. This formed as it were the centre pole and to this were attached all the long roof poles. The sides of the tent were well thatched with young green poplars cut with their leaves on and the roof was partly covered with poplar thatching and tenting. Most of the roof was uncovered, however.

Right around the inside of the big tent, with the exception of a space for the entrance opening, were the stalls for the dancers. These were made by weaving the small poplar trees or branches very closely to form a paling about three and a half feet high. The close weaving means that nothing can be seen through at all. Behind this the dancers stand; the floor inside corresponds to the nave of a church. Directly opposite the opening, there is a break in the paling and here is seen the skull and horns of a buffalo resting on a sort of white couch. I could not get very close, for as I found, one who is not of the elect, and especially a woman, may not go beyond the sacred tree. In front of the buffalo was a square hole about eight inches deep and about two feet long by a little more than one wide. I could not find out the significance of this for the younger men did not know and the older ones did not care to explain.

Hanging from the top of the sacred tree were pieces of brightly coloured prints or cottons, a yard to two yards long and in from of every dancer was a sort of banner of bright cloth, hanging from a stick like a pennant and knotted at the bottom. Towards the end of the ceremony these knots were taken out by the dancers and the banner hung straight. Then after a short sermon from the medicine man, they were knotted up again. After the dance these were all left as a present to the gods. It is whispered that the nuns from the convent on the hill occasionally walk that way, after the dance is all over and the Indians back to their respective homes, and later some of their little orphans appear in bright red or green or blue aprons. The prints are hung, it is said, to propitiate their gods and to keep away sickness. The Cree worship two gods, thunder and the sacred tree.

Every tree and every branch that goes to make up the Sun Dance tent is gathered by the Indians on horseback. They go out two and two, a man and a maid on one horse, and come back with one piece tied to their saddle. It may be a big tree or a little one, but there must be just one to each trip. If any one is found bringing two at a time, he is penalized.

The dancers—there were about forty of them, men and women—were decked in their best and their faces were painted in various ways. The medicine man, who, I found, was chiefly responsible for arranging the dance, and one or two others of the men, were naked from the waist up; their bodies were painted a saffron yellow and decorated in red or blue or green with designs of the moon or horses or possibly just streaks in black across the cheeks. All the dancers had their faces painted in this manner. A few had shown special ingenuity in the decoration. First they had been painted yellow, then the cheeks had been highly rouged, and then in one instance, black spots had been painted all over the face giving the impression of having on a closely dotted veil. Another had dotted just the lower half of the face, and all were decorated in some such manner peculiar to themselves.

With the exception of two or three who were naked, the dancers were decorated with all the beads and quill work, feathers, and such as go to make up their ceremonial attire. Many of these costumes were as beautiful as any you have seen in the museums, and the weight of this solid bead work is hardly to be conceived without actually having it in one's hand. I could not help but think of this when I watched those men and women after three days of constant dancing.

The Indians show plenty of ingenuity in decorating their clothes. Not only the dancers but the drummers and the onlookers were wearing wonderfully decorated clothes. One small girl was wearing a pair of moccasins the entire tops of which were a solid mass of bright blue beads in a pretty design and over them was a pair of puttees also solid to the knees with a blue bead design. Another small boy was wearing a design of elk's teeth hanging from his shoulders to his waist and another had sleeves and front and back done in beautiful porcupine quill work. The dyeing of these quills and the effect of colours produced is marvellous. All of the men had beaded hat bands, and many of the horses wore heavily beaded bridles.

The dance itself is a simple affair. Their feet never move and the movement is altogether at the knees. Their eyes never leave the tree. Each person has a whistle in his mouth which must be blown with every movement, and each one is holding up something, usually a long, brightly dyed feather, in his hand. Then after a few minutes of constant jigging and blowing, the drums give a specially significant blast and all bow towards the tree and disappear from view behind the sort of parapet. Then in a minute, the drums start again and up they come. This started on Thursday in the afternoon and was kept up night and day till Saturday night at six o'clock, when fitting ceremonies brought the last Sun Dance to a close.

It was the afternoon of the last day of the dance that I arrived. Just before noon they had made their gifts. Each person that is dancing gives up, as a part of his penance, a portion of his or her worldly goods. It was told that about forty horses had been offered that day and a lot of clothing, blankets, and money. These go to the outsiders, the visitors from other reserves who happen to be present. The horses and the money, clothes, or whatever it is that is to be given, are brought into the tent, and the ceremony of sacrifice is performed by the medicine man who is also one of the dancers.

As I watched the dance proceed, I noticed that at the far side of the tent were some three or four men seated beside a small fire. This fire they kept going all the time to burn sweetgrass, a sort of incense, which was supposed to give strength to the dancers. Indeed some was put into a small frying pan and, still burning, was passed around to the stalls; the smoke was fanned in with a big feather fan, not ostrich but turkey tails. These same men who were in charge of the fire seemed to be looking after the ceremony generally, in the capacity of acolytes, so to speak. Beside one was a flat, smooth board and on this was a pile of cut tobacco, and in little racks in front of that again were the ceremonial pipes. These the servers filled with tobacco, and now and again took one and gave it to a councillor or a visitor. He placed it in his mouth and the server lighted it. When it was going well, the smoker took it out and pointed it over one shoulder and then the other, and then turned the bowl towards him and went through some other mysterious symbols. He took another puff and passed it on to his neighbour, and then it went to the next and on till it was finished, when the server came and took it away. It was allowed to cool and was filled again by the official in charge of the tobacco; the bowl was held over the little sweetgrass fire, then the mouthpiece and put in the rack again. These pipes were long, the bowls of a dark red stone that the Indians find in the mountains, I am told, and the rest is of wood, all made by hand. These servers were not specially costumed but their hands were all stained yellow.

Then too, I noticed ordinary small pipes being filled and passed among the visitors, but this was apparently an act of courtesy as some other peoples would serve tea.

Being the last hours of the dance, all were getting pretty well played out and sometimes when the drums would start up again after only a second's interval, some did not rise. For three days, they had neither eaten nor drunk nor slept. This goes on without ceasing day and night. The drummers get relief, for as one wearies, another takes his place, but the dancers keep on dancing. I understand that sometimes if one gives out entirely, a friend will step in and take his place for a little. The dancers were of all ages, young girls and youths, pregnant women and old ones. One old body had come up from the Blackfoot Reserve at Calgary to take part in the dance. She must have been over seventy, but she was dancing through to the finish. It seems that she had married a Blackfoot, but she came back to her own tribe for the dance.

It has been mentioned that those taking part in the dance do not drink anything during the entire time. There is an exception, however. If it rains, they may drink what they can catch. In the early days—and this is a true story—a Sun Dance was being held near Edmonton. The weather was very hot and the dancers were almost exhausted. On the morning of the third day, the medicine man, or what is a better translation, the magician, told them that there would be rain that day. The Indians believed, but the white men doubted. Not a cloud was to be seen and no slightest indication of rain in sky or air. Towards noon, a little cloud no bigger than a man's hand appeared in the west, and in an incredibly short space of time, the whole sky was overcast and the rain came down in torrents. The white men still doubted, but they could not help but wonder.

As I watched the ceremony that afternoon, I saw they had in addition to the smokes a large pot of some sort of concoction, which I found to be made of dried saskatoons, meat, choke cherries, and tea. This was specially for the drummers, but it was passed as far as it would go among the onlookers, and small babes in arms were drinking it with relish.

About two hours before the finish, one of the old men got up and gave an oration praying to the tree and telling these thirsty ones that after the dance they could again get a drink of cold water. As he talked on, one of the councillors here and there would say something that sounded like Amen. A little later some stalks of braided grass were passed around, each man getting two, and to the women one of the men passed something which looked like dried leaves. They held their shawls and he dropped in a handful.

At six o'clock, a screen was drawn in front of the buffalo head and the ceremony was not visible to the audience. But after a few minutes, the veil was drawn and one of the braves very gently and reverently laid the head back on its place while the drums played very loud and the chanters mourned their weird dirge. While this was being done, all the men took off their hats and a gangway was cleared right out of the tent. It was mentioned that the buffalo head was placed directly opposite to the opening of the tent; just before this ceremony, the horses and their riders formed themselves up in a circle right around the tent. But at the opening they all drew up so as to leave the space clear right from the buffalo head through to the open. Inside, the people were all formed up on each side, the squaws on one side, the men on the other, and I fully expected some formal procession to come in or go out, but nothing of that sort happened.

Then all got up and at the invitation of the councillor joined in the dance for a few minutes, and all was over. In half an hour, every tent was loaded and the people were all on the way back to their own homes.

# THEIR SECOND HONEYMOON

(FAMILY HERALD AND WEEKLY STAR, 11 JANUARY 1928)

LIFE SEEMS TO TRAVEL pretty much in cycles after all. Forty-odd years ago, a few of the adventurous ones heeding the advice to "go West," headed out of Winnipeg with a pair of oxen and a creaky, whining, grinding Red River cart. In it were all their worldly goods, some blankets, some "grub," a frying pan, and a pot or two. Along the road were natural stopping places, where there was good water and some wood. There the travellers met at night, and around the campfires, swapped yarns, exchanged tea for a little tobacco or salt, and discussed the day's adventures or misadventures.

All who travelled thus had a common interest. If by good chance someone came in from the West, he was eagerly questioned as to the road, or get directions where to branch off to this or that place, had he seen Jim Smith at Edmonton, or was Sandy McPherson still in charge of the store at Prince Albert?

Nowadays the story is the same in a different dress. The sons and grandsons of those early pioneers travel the western plains, minus the oxen. Their motor cars may squeak and rattle, although not quite in the same tone of voice as did the old carts. In much the same way, food and clothing are packed, and away they start—a kingdom within themselves. At night they stop, as did their forebears, where there is good water and wood for the campfire. There they meet the folk travelling in the same manner as themselves, and discuss the thrills of the day, the distance they have come, where they are going and from whence they have come. From those they meet, they inquire of the road ahead and the next stopping place. It is the same old story, only they go in automobiles instead of ox-carts; instead of "stopping places," they say, "motor camps."

Even yet, some of the folk one meets are on their way to find and establish new homes, but for the most part they are tourists—people out on a holiday from "the daily round, the common task."[1]

That the cycle sometimes overtakes itself within the life span was brought home to me one evening as I made camp at the Calgary Auto Park, on my way to investigate at first hand that much-vaunted National Park at Banff. Next door to us were an "oldish" man and his wife. They had put up a stiff new canvas tent beside their car and were endeavouring to get some folding beds inside. After considerable discussion and effort, they had decided that the beds should have been put up first and then arrange the tent over them. I went over to lend a hand and was drawn into the argument.

"Last time 'ma' and me went touring, we didn't have any of these new-fangled beds that double up like a jackknife," the old man said a bit heatedly. "It's as bad as trying to put together old stove pipes that have been lying out in the wood shed all summer."

The car was a six-cylinder, late model; the whole equipment was new, apparently the first time out.

"This is not your first camping experience then?"

"Oh no," answered the old man with a sly look at his wife, "we had a trip once that took three months and we camped outdoors every night."

Still trying to conceal my incredulity, I fell nicely into his little trap.

"Where did you go that time?"

"Winnipeg to Edmonton," was the answer. Then with a broad smile he added: "That was in '84 and we had the orneriest team of oxen a man ever drove; our chariot had wooden axles. The roads those days were not exactly the same brand as they are today either.

"That was our honeymoon. We've never been away since without being cluttered up with the children or when someone was sick. So we decided it was time for another honeymoon and I'm going up town in the morning to buy 'ma' a bouquet of lilies-of-the-valley."

"You're not either," said the old lady vehemently, but quite unconvincingly.

"We don't plan to go back till we feel like it," went on the man; "'Ma' and I both had a hankering to be right out in the woods again, and if we find a place where there is a big spruce tree along side a waterfall, we're going to stay right there till freeze-up."

"I think you can find a hundred places that will do right in Banff Park," I said, "but now that you have started, I believe that you won't stop until you have investigated all the nice spots."

"I would kinda like to see Lake Louise," put in 'ma' who was tenderly dusting off the new car. "I can't believe the water is as blue as it looks in the pictures on the calendars, and I'd like to see the glacier," she added with a faraway look in her eyes as of desires that had been repressed for many years. "But they say the roads up in there are awful dangerous. Maybe we had better not go that far."

I found out that they were a little frightened of the mountain roads, and were planning on an early start to get to Banff while it was yet broad day.

"Who is looking after the farm while you are away?" I asked.

"The youngest boy got married this summer, so we left them the place to themselves," the old man answered.

"I do hope she looks after the little turkeys," the old lady said a bit doubtfully. "She never worked on a farm before, but I told her just how to manage. I had to show her how to make apple dumplings; Jack is awful fond of dumplings."

I offered, if it would be any satisfaction, to drive along right behind them to Banff, and if they got in any trouble, we would do our best to help. We overheard the old man telling his doubtful spouse that if these three women could drive it, he guessed he could. The new car would go any place, he told her.

But I think it gave the old lady a little comfort to know there was someone along side and that evening when we were eating our supper, she brought over a glass of wild strawberry jam, wiping it off on her blue-checkered apron as she gave it to us.

I thought what an ideal trip it would be for a lot of prairie farmers. There is always a little slack time between seed time and harvest, and in two or three days they could be right in the heart of the Rockies. There is always a brother-in-law, or hired man, someone who can keep things running for a couple of weeks.

Men get away to a convention, or take stock to the fair, or in one way or another manage to have a change during the year; but often the wife stays right at home, looking at the same four walls till, in desperation for a little variety in scenery, she insists on new wallpaper. I suspect that house-cleaning is often carried out more with the unrealized desire for a change from the monotony, than for real necessity of cleaning.

And she can take the children with her. The youngsters in those motor parties were receiving a real education. I could imagine the "chesty" manner with which some of them would glibly tell their school mates of the trees that were so big, it took three or four children with arms outstretched to encircle them; or of the milky waters of the marble canyon coming down to mix with the clear waters of the river below; or the hot water that came right out of the rock and the funny smell there was to it; and of the children they had met from British Columbia, or Tennessee, and how many different kinds of motor licenses they had counted.

As to the grown-ups, one could see the great joy they were experiencing in seeing and doing the things of which they had dreamt for years....

## DISTANT FIELDS LOOK GREEN

It was certainly a fine cure for grouches. As I shared the stove in the little cook house with a man who had been farming in Saskatchewan for eight years, I listened to his tale of woe. They had not had a crop for two years, and he was going to keep right on going now till he got some place where he could make a decent living. No, he had not sold his farm; no one would buy a farm; but it could stay right where it was for all he cared....

About a week later, we ran into that same man. He had a different attitude to life entirely since the last time we had been talking to him, and the worried look on his wife's face had quite smoothed away. He was gay, teased "the old girl" about using rouge in her cheeks and was fairly hilarious over the least little joke.

I asked him where he was going from here.

"Well, we like this place about as well as anything we are going to find anywhere, so Jean and I have decided to stay right here and play around for one whole week longer, swim, climb mountains, and maybe before we get through, we'll be playing golf," he added. "Then we are going to hit for home. We had a letter a couple of days ago and they say the wheat will be ready to cut in a couple of weeks and it is the best crop there has been since '15."

In answer to a question he said, "No, we decided to stay right there; just fix things up a bit. Since I've been up here I've been thinking how I could change things around so we would not have to depend altogether on wheat. Wheat is all right, but there are so many things can happen to it. I'm going to try feeding a few cattle this winter and the wife claims she is going to go into the bee business next spring.

"I don't know why I never thought of this before, but some way the thing came to me plain as day as I lay in bed the other night. The mountain air seems to clear out your brain, and your troubles just fade into nothing at all."….

That first night in Banff we started out to find our old couple. We had trailed them fairly close all the way to Banff and then had gone off to have a swim and see the sights of the town, before making camp for the night. We found their location from the camp office, and after a little searching sighted the shiny new car, and the old couple sitting quietly on their folding chairs enjoying the evening. The woman's face had a new light; she was not worrying about the turkeys any more; she was fairly intoxicated with the sights she had seen that day; even the possible dangers of mountain driving did not bother her now. It was worth any chance they might have taken.

"I did not suppose anything could be as wonderful as that," she said with a catch in her voice.

We talked it over for a while. Was there more to see, were there other places to go?

But her mind was too long trained in the practical things of life to remain always in the clouds. Pretty soon she asked us if we would show "Pa" how we had our car fixed so we could sleep in it. We showed him how the backs of the front chairs came off, by removing two small bolts which were held in place by cotter pins, then the cushion of the back seat slipped forward to the front seats; the back cushion, which in the coach is loose, dropped down on the back seat, all the same as a sleeping car. It was done in a minute and the bed was ready for the blankets.

But their car was a touring model and did not have chairs in front, and the back cushion was nailed solid. So I told him how I had seen such cars fixed by cutting down the back of the front seat and putting it on a hinge. At the top it was secured by door hinges, and you just had to take out the pin, and the upholstered cushion dropped back, making a regular bed with springs all complete.

He thought that might be a good idea. It would save bothering with those beds and the tent. Of course the tent was nice to have along if a person were staying long in one place. But he would have to get things fixed up better by another year because he could see that "Ma" was going to make him come every summer—and he supposed they might as well.

"This is a long way ahead of ox teams," he added....

*Athabasca Glacier, Columbia Icefield, August 1941. Left to right: Henry House; MGE (with favourite Scotty); Henry George Glyde (painter). Both House and Glyde were affiliated with the Banff School.*
[GLENBOW ARCHIVES NA 5660-20]

# BANFF FINE ARTS SCHOOL

(FAMILY HERALD AND WEEKLY STAR, 24 SEPTEMBER 1941)

FROM THE FOUR CORNERS OF THE CONTINENT they come to the School of Fine Arts at Banff. Among these students there is contrast in superlative degree and at the same time a ridiculous similarity. Some stay for the month at the palatial Banff Springs Hotel; others at the camp grounds down by the Bow River; there are farm folks and westenders; there are Indians and whites; Southern accents and English evacuees; they come from California and Quebec; from Vancouver Island, Alabama, and Florida. But there is a common denominator for them all, their love of the arts and their desire to learn more. Rich and poor sit together on a rock or a campstool to sketch the Bow Falls or the mountain tops; they fraternize at the drama lectures and help each other choose colours for weaving or pottery, or to find an idle piano for practising.

Organized by the University of Alberta eight or nine years ago, it is still a new project, but its rapid development indicates that its conception was true. Donald Cameron, head of the extension branch of the university, is in charge, and he annually collects around him ranking teachers, some from the States and some from Canada. The art students have the services of three of the top flight Canadian artists: H.G. Glyde, ARCA, Calgary; W.J. Phillips, RCA, Winnipeg; Charles Fraser Comfort, ARCA, OSA, Toronto. This is Mr. Comfort's first year; the others are old-timers. Most popular of all the courses is the drama with five teachers, including Dr. Frederick H. Hock, head of the Department of Dramatic Art, University of North Carolina, now in his fifth year at the Banff School; Jos. F. Smith, head of the Department of Speech, University of Utah, who has been on the Banff staff since 1936; E. Maldwyn Jones and Sydney Risk from the University of Alberta staff; and Richard MacDonald, Edmonton, advisor in stagecraft.

The whole scheme started as a summer school for the theatre, and then in 1935 through co-operation of the School of Technology and Art, the art school was added. From the first, the drama school has had the largest following, but this year for the first time it looks as though drama would be overtaken by art. Music was added to the course in 1935 also, and this year, as a result of a grant from the Carnegie Foundation, courses have been added in weaving, design, modelling, and pottery. Right away they came in conflict with war priorities and had trouble in getting such materials as feldspar. The clays come from Medicine Hat. Weaving has proved particularly popular, due partly to the general interest in handicrafts and to the fact that Mary Meigs Atwater of Basin, Montana, is the instructor. Mrs. Meigs is head of the American Shuttlecraft Guild and dean of American hand-weavers. J.B. McLellan, graduate of the Glasgow School of Art, and now on the staff of the Provincial Institute of Technology and Art, Calgary, teaches modelling and pottery.

Jacques Jolas, director of Music Extension at Cornell College, Iowa, is back for the fourth year. Professor Albert L. Cru, head of the French department at the Teachers' College, Columbia University, heads up the French section and is assisted by Yvonne L. Poirier, also of New York.

There is a library division, a co-operative arrangement between the extension branch of the University of Alberta and McGill Library School. It is under the direction of G.R. Lomer of McGill, who has a staff of four with him.

LIVING PROBLEMS SOLVED

Donald Cameron organizes and administers the school. Mrs. Cameron, who has had much experience in these matters, looks after housing and sees that everyone has a bed. In addition to those who live in the auto camps and at hotels, there are a lot of others who wish to live cheaply and companionably. The school rents sixteen houses in the town for dormitories and conducts a dining hall. Those who live in dormitories get room and board for $36 a month. Students take their turn at waiting on table, so no waitresses are required. A trained kitchen staff is in charge of the cooking and the menus are the same as at the School of Agriculture. Those who live in their own tents in the auto park can get along even more cheaply; those who live at the Banff Springs Hotel can spend a lot more. But they all pay the same amount for tuition fees, namely, $25, so that those who live in dormitories could get by for the month on $75.

From the small beginning of two teachers back in 1934, the staff has grown to about twenty-five, and the number of students to 240, nearly half of them school teachers, others specializing in a hobby or merely wishing to make a creative use of leisure time. For those universities which have courses in art or drama, the Banff course ranks as a credit, and is also accepted for teachers' certification by all Departments of Education across Canada.

Learning to *parlez-vous*, or pot or paint at Banff is surely getting education in its most liquid and attractive form. As a locale for a School of Fine Arts, Banff is just a natural. It has everything from sky-high mountains to complacent bears down by the rubbish piles, rainbows that prop themselves up on spruce trees and property Indians in full feathers who hang around the CPR Hotel, willing to have their pictures taken at so much per; hordes of tourists who come on railroad trains, buses, Lincolns, jalopies, airplanes, or bicycles built for two; there is just room along the river bank for one of the most beautiful golf courses in the world, and if one must get serious, there are the hot, health-giving sulphur springs bubbling up from some uneasy spot in the earth's anatomy that has grown weary of holding a mountain on its stomach. There is scenery plus at Banff. Indeed, half a dozen of Canada's leading artists have established homes there.

Small wonder that folk come from all over the continent to attend the Fine Arts School at Banff. The first year it was in existence, most of the students came from Alberta; now more than half come from outside the province. It was a three-year grant of $10,000 a year from the Carnegie Corporation to the University of Alberta which made the school possible in the beginning, and the idea was to develop a program in the arts for Alberta. The grant was renewed for another two years, and since then the university has carried the project. Indeed, it may become self-supporting; it almost went over the top last year.

Headquarters of the school this year is the new auditorium. Banff had many hotels but no auditorium, something badly needed with a drama school coming regularly to town every summer. So as a result of a plebiscite taken by the Banff Public School Board in 1939, it was decided to build a $50,000 auditorium. The Dominion government donated the site and the architect's plans; Sir Edward Beatty gave $2,500; the university chipped in to build and equip what is probably the best stage in Western Canada. The hall seats 750 and there is plenty of room on the stage to put on any show short of a circus. But already the auditorium is outgrown.

Various scholarships have been established that provide free tuition. To this purpose, Alberta was divided into nine divisions and the best original work in watercolours, oils, charcoal, etc. from each of these units entitles the would-be artist to a scholarship. In drama there are four scholarships open to Alberta, two awarded for the best essay on "What does the High School Dramatic Society contribute to the community?"; the other two are awarded for the best one-act play. In Saskatchewan through the Department of Extension at the University and the Provincial Drama League, three scholarships are given, at least one to a rural group....

It is an old gag to a reporter when someone enthusiastically bursts out, "You meet such interesting people." Well. There are plenty of them around the Banff School of Fine Arts. It was flattering, on being introduced to Cecilia Cravens, of Riverside, California, to have her reply immediately: "Oh yes, I met you at the International Stock Show in Chicago 13 years ago." At that time she was running the Southern California Exhibition, and boasts that she introduced the Art department to that fair, but she can also talk about pigs and Percherons....

Several fine arts students have had their pictures hung in the National Gallery, but probably the greatest service of the students of the Fine Arts School has been the enriching of home communities. A new vitality has been given to community drama. With a little training and a sketch pad, aesthetic values become keener.

# NOTES

PREFACE

1. All quotations from this address, titled "Special Fields," are based on the unpaginated typescript in the Miriam Green Ellis Collection, Bruce Peel Special Collections Library, University of Alberta, Box 12, folder 1, item 4.
2. This passage supplies the title of this preface.
3. Two examples of Western Canadian academics from among Ellis's contemporaries will suffice. After scholarship study in Paris and a PHD in History from the University of Minnesota, Hilda Neatby (1904–1975) was appointed to the University of Saskatchewan in 1946, "a full twenty-one years after her first temporary appointment" (Corbett 174). She was the only woman member of the Royal Commission on National Development in the Arts, Letters and Sciences (the Massey Commission, 1949–1951), the first woman president of the Canadian Historical Association (1962), a fellow of the Royal Society of Canada, and a Companion of the Order of Canada. When addressing the Canadian Federation of University Women in Ottawa in 1952, Neatby rehearsed a theme that Canadian Women's Press Club members would have endorsed: "Women...are intellectually and emotionally competent, as they always have been. They now operate in a much larger social frame, and some women have not realized, perhaps, that the frame is larger. They are tempted to excuse themselves from action on the ground that women cannot do certain things....It seems to me that it is the job of the CFUW to help make women see themselves as individuals, free to work,

and to suffer, and to make mistakes. Free and responsible, they must sum up all their assets and liabilities of character, of intellectual ability, of knowledge and experience, of economic and social position; and they must then devote themselves disinterestedly and intelligently, without self-consciousness, to the difficult and arduous tasks that confront free people everywhere" (qtd. in Hayden 59). Neatby's colleague at the University of Saskatchewan, Mabel Timlin (1891–1976), supported herself as a secretary at the university for twenty years while she earned degrees. On the award of a PHD from the University of Washington in 1940, she was appointed to the Department of Economics. The first woman social scientist elected as a fellow of the Royal Society of Canada, she was also the first woman president of the Canadian Political Science Association and a Member of the Order of Canada.

DOWN NORTH

1. The Honourable Frank Oliver, Minister of the Interior in Sir Wilfrid Laurier's Liberal government, was the editor-in-chief of the *Edmonton Bulletin*. In partnership with telegraph operator Alex Taylor, Oliver (1853–1933) established the paper in 1880, the second newspaper in the Great Northwest. By 1911, there were three dailies in Edmonton, the others being the *Journal* and the *Capital*. Elected in 1896 as the first Member of Parliament from Alberta, he served in the federal Cabinet until his defeat in 1917.
2. Beginning in Great Slave Lake and flowing north into the Arctic Ocean, the Mackenzie River, the longest river in Canada, covers over 1,800 kilometres; its entire system extends 4,250 kilometres.
3. Norman Wells, Northwest Territories, was Canada's first major oil discovery; from 1920 until 2004 it produced 226 million barrels.
4. With the Norman Wells discovery, Fort Smith, on the Slave River near the Alberta/Northwest Territories border, became the site of an administrative building for the Northwest Territories, the first Court of Justice in the Mackenzie District, and, in 1922, the headquarters of Wood Buffalo National Park.
5. Home for centuries to the Dene people, the Nahanni River in the Northwest Territories flows from the Mackenzie Mountains, through the Selwyn Mountains, over the Virginia Falls, and empties into the Liard River.
6. The Alberta and Great Waterways Railway, intended to link Edmonton with Fort McMurray and thus with navigation on the Athabasca–Mackenzie River system, was incorporated in 1909 by the government of Premier A.C. Rutherford to stimulate the growth of the natural resource industry. Disputes about the award of

the contract led to Rutherford's resignation. A labour shortage during the war and impassable muskeg conditions beyond Lac La Biche slowed progress. By 1921, track had reached the Clearwater River, where the terminal was named Waterways. It did not reach the last few kilometres into Fort McMurray for almost two decades. By 1929, A&GWR joined the newly formed Northern Alberta Railways. The Waterways route was superseded by the Great Slave Lake Railway in 1964 (Lester et al.).

7. Horses or ponies.
8. Baggage or tramp's clothes.
9. "On board are Fullerton Waldo of the *Philadelphia Ledger*; Roland Holroyd of the Department of Botany of University of Pennsylvania; Harry Ransford, manager of the Dominion Bank, Edmonton; Willis J. West, manager of the Alberta and Arctic Transportation Line; Mr. and Mrs. J. Willison, bride and groom, going through to the Hudson's Bay posts; Father Grouard, going in to Chipewyan; John and Ethel Carley, Sharon, Pennsylvania; Mary Ellis Conlin, Edmonton; Gladys Patterson, going to Fort Norman to be married to Mr. Jackson; me; and some others including J.W. Crisall, Medicine Hat, who is going to McPherson where his son is Anglican missionary; Frank Morris who is giving shooting exhibitions of the Hudson's Bay posts" (Diary 1–2; 19 June.).
10. The botanist, who proves to be so disappointing as an identifier of plants, is Roland Holroyd.
11. Gladys Patterson's blithe trust that all will be well may have prompted Ellis's more ambivalent depiction of Rose in her short story "A War Bride's Return."
12. Ellis's diary recounts the "quaint remarks" of George the porter, who defends his telling the truth rather than the fabrications of "the porter down at Montreal." As George relates, "a passenger asked him the name of the river there and he said, it was the Mississippi. Surely not the Mississippi in Quebec, she said. Oh, yes, Miss, the Mississip is a powerful big river. Yous likely to find it most any place" (Diary 3; 19 June).
13. Émile-Jean-Baptiste-Marie Grouard, OMI (1840–1931), served in many mission posts in the Great North-West: Fort Chipewyan, Lac La Biche, Dunvegan, Mission Saint-Bernard (later called Grouard), among others. He served at Fort Chipewyan for thirteen years immediately following his ordination in 1862. His original huge bishopric of Athabasca-Mackenzie was divided in 1901, with Grouard retaining the bishopric of Athabasca, and Bishop Breynat assuming the position in Mackenzie. Grouard brought the first printing press to Athabasca

Country, and composed and printed catechetical texts in five distinct Indigenous languages.

14. Sometimes referred to as Red Deer's Lake, Lac La Biche derives its name from the red deer or wapiti (North American elk) called—without designating sex—"biche." Approximately 250 kilometres northeast of Edmonton, it was the site of the Oblate Mission of Notre Dame des Victoires, which, perched on a hill overlooking the lake, provided an ideal location for fishing and agriculture, activities at which the missionaries excelled. It was also the warehouse for the northern missions at a point of navigational access to Lake Athabasca and thus to sites in the immense Athabasca–Mackenzie region. Portage La Biche, charted first by the North West Company's David Thompson in 1798, along with his later discovery of the Athabasca Pass with linkage to the Columbia River, consolidated the importance of Lac La Biche as a vital hinge between Rupert's Land and Athabasca Country.

15. From its headwaters in Broach Lake, Saskatchewan, the Upper Clearwater River turns west at the Saskatchewan/Alberta border and ends in Fort McMurray at its confluence with the Athabasca River.

16. Thomas Draper, a Michigan manufacturer, secured a tar sand lease at Waterways in 1921, and, in 1922, opened The McMurray Asphaltum and Oil Company, which quarried the tar sands for road and sidewalk projects in Edmonton. Although Draper's interests were more commercial, he also supplied tar sands for the extraction research of chemist Dr. Karl Clark of the Alberta Research Council at the University of Alberta. Cam McEachern notes, "Draper's grievance was primarily with how the provincial government consistently ignored his activity in public comments that understated the sands' potential" (283).

17. Leggings or long stockings, originally shipman's hose.

18. Gerald Card was the Indian agent at Fort Simpson in 1911; his arrival with agricultural implements caused considerable suspicion among the Cree population, who feared that their land was going to be claimed for settlement and a demonstration farm, leading to the extinction of hunting and trapping. Card himself recognized the "doubtful legitimacy" of his presence. By 1920, he was the agent at Fort Smith, within Treaty 8 territory; he fulfilled roles as agent of the Canadian National Parks Branch, mining recorder, recorder of vital statistics, justice of the peace, and issuer of marriage licences (Fumoleau 172–73).

19. Dr. A.L. Macdonald, the first resident physician, arrived in Fort Smith in 1910 and remained when the Grey Nuns opened St. Anne's Hospital in 1914. His practice stretched from Fort McMurray to Fort Good Hope, a distance of 1,300 miles by water: "Dr. Macdonald is a treasure with his quaint manner and all

the knowledge of a native. He has been in the country twelve years. Says there is scarcely ever an operation necessary among the natives. Sometimes they cut themselves, but never has he known a case of appendicitis or anything like that.... He is a McGill graduate of 87" (Diary 11; 21 June).

20. The unpaginated appendix to Ellis's diary includes this statistic about Treaty 8: "Total annuitants under Treaty 8—3323."
21. Originally the site of a North West Trading post established in 1788, Fort Chipewyan on the northwest tip of Lake Athabasca is the oldest community in Alberta.
22. Water flows out of Lake Athabasca north via Rivière des Rochers and Chenal des Quatre Fourches to join the Peace River, together forming the Slave River which flows northwest to Great Slave Lake, drained by the Mackenize River to the Arctic Ocean. When the water level is high on the Peace River, Rivière des Rochers and Chenal des Quatre Fourches flow south, flooding the Peace–Athabasca Delta, which was declared a World Heritage Site in 1985.
23. "Had lunch and came over in the big red car to Fort Smith. Portage is sixteen miles or more long and they are doing considerable work on the road. It is rough in spots, but on the whole very good. Met a big caterpillar dragging several wagons and several smaller tractors and teams. Those going towards Smith all heavily laden. Coming the other way empty. The bull dogs are bad and the horses all have boudoir caps of bright colored calico" (Diary 19; 23 June).
24. The competition for riverboat and fur-trade business involved the Hudson's Bay Company, established in 1670, the Boston-based Lamson and Hubbard Company, which was registered in Edmonton in 1918, and the Northern Trading Company, located in Edmonton from 1913 following a takeover of a company that had been active in the Mackenzie from the 1880s (Ray 104–05).
25. Ellis's diary identifies the cook as "Doc. Grittin who has one year in the University of Chicago for medicine" (20; 23 June).
26. Guy Houghton Blanchet (1884–1966) was a mining engineer whose work on the Topographical Survey of Canada earned him the title of Dominion Land Surveyor. He related his adventures in *Search in the North* (1960; see Hoyle).
27. Ellis's diary entry for 24 June is more expansive on Ada Mary Conibear's trading post: "She has everything from a clothes wringer to fancy combs, oranges, lemons, cocoanuts, and said that last year she had brought in plums, the first she had seen in ten years....Her husband mushed into Norman last year. He is an engineer and she does all the housework and the trading. She is known about the settlement for having things that no one else had. She has cake pans, and snow shoes, fancy

hair pins and mocassins, bacon. At first the store was about eight foot square. Then they enlarged it to about three times that size, and now are building another addition" (25–26). Ellis details the Conibears' vegetable and flower gardens, their lawn, "made bit by bit by bringing in a little piece of sod as they found it here and there," the large organ, "the first brought into the country," and their family, one daughter and two sons (25–27). As she later clarified in her talk to the Rotary Club in Yorkton, "Canada Has Something," Ellis made arrangements with Nellie McClung and the Minister of Education first for correspondence courses and then for the completion of the Conibear children's high school education in Edmonton; all the Conibear children attended the University of Alberta. Mabel went on to study at the Sorbonne. Her son Kenneth, a Rhodes scholar from the University of Alberta in 1931, wrote several books about life in the North: *Northland Footprints* (1936), *Northward to Eden* (1939), and *Arctic Adventures with the Lady Greenbelly* (1943). Son Frank was also an author; among his titles are *Husky, the Story of Cap* (1940), *Water Trio* (1948), and *The Wise One* (1949). Retaining her original spelling of the surname, Ellis published "A Business Woman in the Far North—Mrs. Connibear of Fort Smith," in *Canadian Countryman* and the *Vancouver Sunday Province*.

28. Norwegian-born seaman and adventurer Storker Teodor Storkerson (1883–1940) married Uiniq (1895?–1931), known as Elwina, at Herschel Island in 1910. Both Storker and Elwina were recruited for Vilhjalmur Stefansson's Canadian Arctic Expedition (1913–1918), he as a cartographer conducting the first-ever hydrographic soundings, and she as a seamstress, making winter clothing and waterproof boots. In what proved to be abortive attempts to establish reindeer companies in the Arctic and then in Norway, Storker left his wife and three daughters, Martina, Aida, and Bessie, at St. Peter's Anglican Mission in Hay River. They never re-united (see D. Gray).

29. Thongs or thread made of rawhide. In her diary, Ellis explains, "an Eskimo babiche bag [is] made of fancily woven strips of leather that looks like twine and [is] trimmed with coarse bright colored wool and at the top a piece of leather ornamented with quill work" (27; 24 June).

30. Bishop Gabriel Breynat, OMI (1867–1954) served in the Mackenzie Vicariate from 1901 until his retirement in 1943. He established six hospitals: Fort Simpson (1914), Fort Smith (1916), Aklavik (1920s), Fort Rae (1938), Fort Resolution (1938), and Fort McMurray (1943), all of which were phased out after World War II.

31. Soeur Alice McQuillan, SGM, the founding Superior at Fort Resolution, served at this post from 1903 until 1925, when she went north to the mission at Aklavik. Ellis's diary notes that "Soeur McQuillan, who has been the teacher there for nineteen years and who founded that school, was down to New Brunswick for holiday" (36). Ellis's photo of Sister St. Rose and diary entry for June 29 evidence a particular fondness: "Sister St. Rose gave me some cakes and cookies with red sugar for my birthday" (43). Ellis also records that she "spent the evening reading of the Grey Nuns in the Far North" (37), a monograph by Pierre Duchassois, OMI, published in 1919.
32. Rear-Admiral Sir John Franklin (1786–1847), Arctic explorer, disappeared while navigating a section of the Northwest Passage.
33. Thomas William "Flynn" Harris, Indian agent at Fort Simpson, 1913–1930, and at Fort Good Hope, 1930–1933, impressed all visitors as a true eccentric. As Jean Godsell related, "A master of English, French, German, Spanish, Esperanto, Cree, Chipewyan and one or two other languages, he could quote the classics verbatim, had gone to school with Sir Robert Borden,...and would—but for his addiction to John Barleycorn—have been one of the leading criminal lawyers of his day" (112). When in his cups, Flynn "traded" false teeth with an official from Edmonton and allowed they were "the best fit [he] ever had" (see also MacLaren and LaFramboise 250). René Fumoleau's *As Long As This Land Shall Last* presents Flynn, a promoter and signatory of Treaty 11, as a lenient justice of the peace who attended to the special promises made to First Nations at Treaty Time (Fumoleau 203).
34. In 1902 in partnership with Clement Lewis, Poole Field, a former North West Mounted Police officer, established a trading post, Nahanni House, at the confluence of the Ross and Pelly rivers. Field later ran the Whitehorse-based fur trading post Taylor and Drury at Ross River. He also operated posts at Carmacks and Fort Norman. After the death of his first wife, Kitty Tom, in the flu epidemic of 1916, he married Mary Adele (Laferty) Atkinson (Kagan).
35. While using the Nahanni River as an alternate route to the Klondike, Willie and Frank McLeod disappeared in 1908; the brothers' headless skeletons were later discovered. Their companion, Bobbie Weir, who was never found, may have been the culprit.
36. In an area later named Deadmen or Headless Valley, the decapitated remains of Yukon prospector Martin Jorgensen were found in his burnt-out cabin in 1917 (Newton 267).
37. Native lead sulphide, common lead ore.

38. St. Peter's day school was established at Hay River in 1894; with federal assistance in 1900 it became the first Anglican Indian and Eskimo residential school, with students often travelling south as much as 1,500 kilometres from their family community. During Miss Samwell's time, the Reverend Alfred James Vale was principal (Anglican Church of Canada "St. Peter's School").
39. Identified in her diary as J.L. McCreary (58; 2 July).
40. Bishop James Richard Lucas of the Diocese of Mackenzie River established All Saints Anglican Mission in Aklavik in 1919. The first missionary, Reverend Edward Hester, also led day schooling in the small community of Inuvialuit, Gwich'in, and Metis peoples (Anglican Church of Canada "All Saints School"). For information on missionary rivalries, see Craig Mishler, "Missionaries in Collision: Anglicans and Oblates among the Gwich'in, 1861–65."
41. Frederick Victor Seibert (1885–1966), Dominion and Alberta land surveyor, was associated with the Topographical Surveys Branch of the Department of the Interior. In 1921–1922, he located food caches for the Hudson's Bay Company along the Mackenzie River on the route from the sixth meridian northward from the sixtieth parallel ("Fred Seibert"). About the dial at Fort Norman, Ellis's diary comments on Fred Seibert: "The H.B. had one with 13 hrs on one side and 11 hrs on the other. Said that was done to make Indians work a long day" (64; 2 July).
42. Her diary describes the "only horse held in captivity this far north" as "black and thin and apparently well pleased with a chew of smoking tobacco" (63; 2 July).
43. She records in her diary, "There were oil derricks on Bear Island and on either shore. On the East shore you could see the black streak running down to the lake" (63; 2 July).
44. In this fast-water section where the Mountain River joins the Mackenzie from the west, the river drops approximately twenty feet within a few miles.
45. This gorge of eleven kilometres formed within limestone bedrock is located on the Mackenzie River near Fort Good Hope.
46. Ellis writes,

> I finished dressing, had my breakfast and much against my tired inclination went up to see the R.C. Church. It shows great patience and much work but is considerably tawdry. There were only a couple little benches, no chairs at all.
>
> There was a choir loft which is apparently not used, the little organ being down stairs. The altar rail was painted to represent marble. The sanctuary light was burning in front of it and there were statues of St. Joseph and of St. Antoine....

The whole place is whitewashed and the effect as we saw it in the distance through the Ramparts was beautiful in the morning light and would have been more effective still had it not been so dull and cloudy.

It is built on the top of a high bank and there are long steps down to it. The Indians pack all the freight up those long steps. There were wooden nails in the sidewalks. (Diary 66–67; 2 July)

47. Missionary, artist, and early anthropologist, Émile Petitot, OMI (1838–1917) actually preceded Father Grouard in the Great Northwest. When they were both recuperating (Petitot from exhaustion and Grouard from voicelessness) in Paris in 1875, Petitot was Grouard's instructor in painting (Carrière 69–70).

48. William Copeland McCalla's *Wild Flowers of Western Canada* describes *Hedysarum mackenzii*: "From the axils of the upper leaves spring long racemes of numerous pale pink, rose, or purple flowers. Although the stems are stiff, the drooping blossoms and light foliage lend an air of elegance and grace to the plant. The drooping flowers are succeeded by drooping pods" (76).

49. The Gwich'in ("one who dwells") peoples of the Northwest Territories, the Yukon, and Alaska were referred to as "squinters" by the French and as Tukudh (another name for their language) by the Anglican missionaries who prepared biblical texts in this language. Gwich'in is part of the Athapaskan language family ("Old Crow").

50. Born in the Orkney Islands, John Firth (1854–1939), who served the Hudson's Bay Company at Fort McPherson from 1871 until his retirement in 1921, was widely respected for his physical strength and peacemaking initiatives among rival Gwich'in and Inuvialuit groups. He and his Gwich'in wife had ten children, four sons and six daughters. For pictures of Firth and his wife and of a winter dance at their home, see the photographs "Hudson's Bay Company Factor, John Firth and Wife, Fort McPherson, Northwest Territories" (1908; Glenbow Archives NA-513-19) and "Dance in Mr. John Firth's house, Fort McPherson, Northwest Territories" (ca. 1908–1909; Glenbow Archives NA-513-20), available at the Glenbow Museum website.

51. Inuit hunters Alikomiak and Tàtimagana were arrested for the murder of four Inuit at Coronation Gulf in 1921. While in custody at Tree River Alikomiak shot and killed RCMP officer W.A. Doak and Hudson's Bay Company employee Otto Binder. Both were sentenced to death; despite pleas for leniency, they were hanged in an abandoned whaling shed on Herschel Island (1 February 1924), the first Inuit to be condemned and executed under Canadian law (Coates and Morrison 144).

52. Jamaican-born Beresford Henry Segre, graduate in the civil engineering class of 1909 from the University of Toronto and veteran of the Canadian Expeditionary Forces of World War I, was Dominion Land Surveyor for the Topographical Surveys Branch of the Department of the Interior ("Notes by Classes" 268).

53. An adaptation of Robert W. Service's "Ballad of the Northern Lights": "We guessed and groped, North, ever North, with many a twist and turn / We saw ablaze in the deathless days the splendid sunsets burn" (lines 63–64).

54. Ellis identifies the "Copper River Eskimos" and "Mackenzie Delta Eskimos" as "Kogmollycs" (Diary 84; 5 July). At Fort McPherson, her diary details some activities of the Mackenzie Delta Inuit, relayed to her by Mrs. Wood, wife of the police inspector at Herschel Island: "The tribe to the East is called Kogmollycs....Most of them have gone down to the gulf to get Killilooak or white whales. They use the oil of this whale for nearly everything. In the winter they do not cook their food at all. They cut off the frozen chunks and dip their first two fingers in the bowl of oil, which is common to all the diners, and swab it down with their meat. They eat meat entirely....At dances Kogmollycs have an old woman in the middle singing while one of the others plays a drum, hitting first one side and then the other, a real man's job, too. When the one woman is exhausted, the others take up the tune" (71–72). The Copper Inuit relied on the native copper gathered along the Coppermine River and the Coronation Gulf. In his first Canadian Arctic Expedition (1908–1912), Vilhjalmur Stefansson discovered both that Victoria Island was inhabited and that so called "Blond Eskimos" lived among the Copper Inuit (Páalsson 200). Richard G. Condon suggests that "Rather than viewing the Copper Inuit as more primitive, people like Stefansson were more inclined to view them as uncorrupted by civilization" (108). As an anthropologist in the Second Canadian Arctic Expedition (1913–1918), Diamond Jenness lived with the Copper Inuit for two years, documenting their lives, languages and culture in *The People of the Twilight* (1928). The Roman Catholic missionary Raymond de Coccala referred to the people of Minto Island and Prince Albert Sound as "Krangmalit," "derived from the word 'kranga' meaning 'beyond'" (328). Among the intermarrying subgroups documented by Stefansson and Jenness are the Kogluktogmiut, inhabiting the Bloody Falls on the Coppermine River, the Kogluktualugmiut ("the dwellers of the place where there is pot stone") on the Tree River east of the Coppermine, and the Kogluktuaryumiut, located at the mouth of the Kogluktuaryuk River. These groups, singly or together, may have been the reference for the anglicized "Kogmolloycs" ("Copper Inuit"). In commenting on the inhabitants of Arctic Red River and Fort McPherson in 1908, Agnes Deans

Cameron also used the designation "Kogmollycs" to refer to Mackenzie Delta Eskimo (221, 241).

55. A selection of the bone objects (needle cases, bow case, seal toggle, child's toy), collected by Diamond Jenness for the Geological Survey of Canada, are on display at the Canadian Museum of Civilization's *Playthings and Curios: Historic Inuit Art* exhibit website. Copper Inuit materials are also housed in the Noice Collection at the Field Museum of Natural History in Chicago.

56. Stone, bone, or shell inserted in the lips.

57. Although in *The People of the Twilight* Diamond Jenness concludes that "no longer is infanticide tolerated" (247), during his two years of living with Ikpuck and his partner Icehouse, he did know of mothers "destroying their babes within an hour of delivery" (207) and presented a situational explanation:

> Terrible as their crime may seem, they should not be condemned too hastily....[T]he mother received little consideration, according to our standards, before and after the child was born....She performed all her usual tasks up to the moment of parturition and resumed them within a few hours of delivery....She carried the child everywhere on her back.... For three years and even longer, the mother furnished its nourishment from her own breast. Can we blame her if sometimes she shrank from the burden? Often she had no choice. It was physically impossible for her to raise twins, or children born within two years of one another. Surely it was kinder to stifle the infant in its first hour of extra-uterine life, before it knew pain or hunger, or could awaken by its cries and smiles the tender love that as yet lay sleeping in the mother's heart. (208-09)

58. When visiting the site of the mission and the proposed hospital at Aklavik, Ellis was particularly impressed by the pluck of Mrs. Hoare. She relates in her diary,

> Mrs. Hoare is a nurse from the Ottawa Protestant hospital and she and her husband are real honest to god folks. They look more like the real thing in missionaries than anything I have seen in the North. She had her baby with no one but her husband with her. Dr. Doyle was to have come to her, but his wife was very sick with her baby at the same time. (77-78; 5 July)

59. Sphagnum moss grown in boggy or swampy places and noted for absorbency.

60. McCalla's *Wild Flowers of Canada* observes, "the finding of a colony in bloom in the mossy spruce woods is the laying up of a treasure in memory" (62).

61. Daniel Defoe's novel *The Life and Strange Surprising Adventures of Robinson Crusoe, of York, Mariner* (1719) relates the hero's adaptative strategies for survival when he is shipwrecked on an uninhabited island; at length Crusoe is assisted by

a young native whom he saves from death and calls Friday because of the day on which he met him.

62. Ellis was not quite the first white woman to see the Salt Springs. In her journey to the Arctic, Agnes Deans Cameron records the visit she and her niece made to "one of the most marvellous salt deposits in the world," whose extent she detailed: "The Salt River winds in crescent curves through a valley wooded with aspen and spruce, and the Salt Plains six miles in extent stretch at the base of hills six or seven hundred feet high. The salt lies all over the ground in beautiful cubes—pure crystal salt. It is anybody's salt plain; you can come here when you will and scoop up all you want. These plains have supplied the North country with salt since first white men penetrated the country" (Cameron 158–59).

63. Edgar Rice Burroughs' *Tarzan of the Apes* (1914) introduces a twentieth-century folk hero, the son of an English nobleman abandoned in Africa in infancy and brought up by the apes, whose language he learns.

64. In 1922, W.L. Cassels completed his survey of an Indian Fishing Reserve on the Salt River (see Cassels 1922). Maxwell Graham, chief of the Animal Division in the Parks Branch, worked to establish a haven for Canada's remnant population of wood bison in Wood Buffalo National Park. However, when the thriving mixed herd of plains and wood bison at Wainwright, AB, was culled, cases of tuberculosis were discovered. His plans to ship up to 2,000 plains bison north to Wood Buffalo because of insufficient pasture at Wainwright were not adopted due to fear of interbreeding and disease (Foster 17–18).

A WAR BRIDE'S RETURN

1. Confinement to barracks, a form of punishment in the armed forces that would be noted in a soldier's record.
2. Above, the mother goes into the river to save a horse; this contradiction likely suggests that MGE had not finished revising the story for publication.
3. The Voluntary Aid Detachment was an organization that provided field nursing services, mainly in hospitals, beginning in 1909.

THE WOMEN GRAIN GROWERS OF SASKATCHEWAN

1. Women's Christian Temperance Union.

MEN ON RELIEF GO BACK TO LAND

1. The *Soldier Settlement Act (1917)* provided World War I veterans with free quarter-sections in Manitoba, Saskatchewan, and Alberta, and $2,500 in

interest-free loans. The expropriation of reserve lands for soldier settlement by Robert Borden's government in 1919 was partially addressed in the 1992 Treaty Land Entitlement Framework Agreement.

## THEIR SECOND HONEYMOON

1. The allusion refers to the well-known title of one of Henry W. Nevinson's *Essays in Rebellion* (1913). "The Daily Round, The Common Task" concerns a bachelor, accustomed to the attentions of a landlady, who decides mistakenly that he can look after himself when he house-sits for a friend. Unable to start the fire, make the bed, or feed himself, he concludes—with the wit of the time—that "a woman's place is the home" (175).

# WORKS CITED

Aberdeen, Marchioness of Aberdeen [Ishbel Gordon]. *Through Canada with a Kodak*. Introd. Marjory Harper. Toronto: University of Toronto Press, 1994. Print.

Anglican Church of Canada General Synod Archives. "All Saints School—Aklavik, NWT." *Mission and Justice Relationships*. Angican Church of Canada, 2008. Web. 7 July 2012. <http://www.anglican.ca/rs/history/schools/st-perters-hay-river.htm>.

———. "St. Peter's School—Hay River, NWT." *Mission and Justice Relationships*. Angican Church of Canada, 2008. Web. 8 July 2012. <http://www.anglican.ca/rs/history/schools/st-perters-hay-river.htm>.

"Another Heavy Passenger List for Far North." *Edmonton Bulletin* 16 May 1922: 2. Print.

Batten, Jr., Charles L. *Pleasurable Instruction: Form and Convention in Eighteenth-Century Travel Literature*. Berkeley: University of California Press, 1978. Print.

Beynon, Francis Marion. *Aleta Dey*. Introd. Anne Rich. London: Virago, 1988. Print.

Blanchet, Guy Houghton. *Search in the North*. Toronto: Macmillan, 1960. Print.

Blondal, Patricia. *A Candle to Light the Sun*. Toronto: McClelland & Stewart, 1960. Print.

Bugnet, Georges. *Nipsya*. Trans. Constance Davies Woodrow. New York: Louis Carrier, 1929. Print.

Burroughs, Edgar Rice. *Tarzan of the Apes*. 1914. 8th ed. London: Methuen, 1920. Print.

Cameron, Agnes Deans. *The New North: Being Some Account of a Woman's Journey through Canada to the Arctic*. New York: D. Appleton, 1910. Print.

Canadian Women's Press Club. "Constitution." Print. Accession 74. 56/6. Canadian Women's Press Club Miscellaneous Correspondence, PAA.

———. *Triennial Report*, 1959-62. Ottawa: CWPC, 1962. Print. Accession 74. 56/6. Canadian Women's Press Club Miscellaneous Correspondence, PAA.

Carrière, Gaston, OMI. *Dictionnaire des Oblats de Marie Immaculée au Canada*. Vol. 3. Ottawa: Éditions de l'Université d'Ottawa, 1979. Print.

Cassels, W.L. "Plan of Indian Fishing Reserve on Salt River, Northwest Territories, 1922." Indian Affairs Survey Record 2026. *Indian Reserves—Western Canada*. Microfiche no. 6165, record no. 2137, LAC.

Coates, Ken, and William R. Morrison. *Land of the Midnight Sun: A History of the Yukon*. Montreal: McGill-Queen's University Press, 2005. Print.

Coccala, Raymond de, and Paul King. *The Incredible Eskimo: Life Among the Barren Land Eskimo*. Surrey, BC: Hancock House, 1986. Print.

Condon, Richard G. *The Northern Copper Inuit: A History*. Norman: University of Oklahoma Press, 1996. Print.

Conibear, Frank, and J.L. Blundell. *Water Trio*. London: Peter Davis, 1948.

———, and J.L. Blundell. *The Wise One*. New York: W. Sloane, 1949.

———, and Kenneth Conibear. *Husky, the Story of Cap*. London: Peter Davis, 1940.

Conibear, Kenneth. *Arctic Adventures with the Lady Greenbelly*. 1943. Victoria, BC: Trafford, 2000. Print.

———. *Northland Footprints*. London: Lovat Dickson, 1936.

———. *Northward to Eden*. London: Peter Davies, 1939.

"Copper Inuit." *Wikipedia*. Wikimedia Foundation, Inc., n.d. Web. 15 October 2010.

Corbett, Mike. "I Dreamed I Saw Hilda Neatby Last Night: *So Little for the Mind* after 50 Years." *McGill Journal of Education* 39.2 (2004): 159-81. Print.

"Cornelia." "Magic Journey North to Land of Midnight Sun: Miriam Green Ellis Gives Fascinating Lecture to University Women." *Toronto Telegram* 28 November 1923: n. pag. Print.

Cram, J.S. "Retiring Editor Honored." *Family Herald and Weekly Star* 15 January 1953: 7+. Print.

CWPC. *See* Canadian Women's Press Club.

Defoe, Daniel. *The Life and Strange Surprising Adventures of Robinson Crusoe, of York, Mariner*. 1719. Rpt. as *Robinson Crusoe*. Ed. Evan R. Davis. Peterborough, ON: Broadview, 2010. Print.

Derrida, Jacques. *Archive Fever: A Freudian Impression.* Trans. Eric Prenowitz. Chicago: University of Chicago Press, 1996. Print.

Downie, Mary Alice, and Barbara Robertson with Elizabeth Jane Errington, eds. *Early Voices: Portraits of Canada by Women Writers, 1639–1914.* Toronto: Natural Heritage–Dundurn, 2010. Print.

Dufferin, Marchioness of Dufferin and Ava. *My Canadian Journal, 1872–78: Extracts from My Letters Home While Lord Dufferin Was Governor-General.* New York: D. Appleton, 1891. Print.

Edmonton Bulletin. Advertisement. *Edmonton Bulletin* 29 December 1921: 13.

Ellis, George. "Report of Inspector Ellis, Edmonton." *Annual Report of the Department of Education of the Province of Alberta, 1906.* Edmonton: Jas. E. Richards, Government Printer, 1907. 52–55.

———. "Report of Inspector Ellis, Edmonton." *Second Annual Report of the Department of Education of the Province of Alberta, 1907.* Edmonton: Jas. E. Richards, Government Printer, 1908. 39–40.

———. "Report of G. E. Ellis, Edmonton Inspectorate." *Third Annual Report of the Department of Education of the Province of Alberta, 1908.* Edmonton: Jas. E. Richards, Government Printer, 1909. 40–41.

Ellis, Miriam Green. "Aggie Stag Banquet." [Speech.] 11 November 1948. Ts. Box 12, folder III, item 4. Miriam Green Ellis Collection, BPSC.

———. "Alone." Ts. Box 2, folder III. Miriam Green Ellis Collection, BPSC.

———. "Banff Fine Arts School." *Family Herald and Weekly Star* 24 September 1941. Print. Box 8, folder II. Miriam Green Ellis Collection, BPSC.

———. "A Business Woman in the Far North—Mrs. Connibear of Fort Smith," *Canadian Countryman* 12 December 1925: 15; *Vancouver Sunday Province* 10 April 1927: 3.

———. "Canada Has Something." [Speech given at Rotary Ladies' Night, Yorkton, SK.] 27 November 1939. Ts. Box 12, folder VIII. Miriam Green Ellis Collection, BPSC.

———. Diary [of trip 1922]. [Notes on Mackenzie trip.] Ts. Box 3, folder 1. Miriam Green Ellis Collection, BPSC.

———. "Down North." Ts. Box 3, folder II. Miriam Green Ellis Collection, BPSC.

———. "From Aberdeen to Alberta." *Family Herald and Weekly Star* 21 May 1930. Print. Box 8, folder I. Miriam Green Ellis Collection, BPSC.

———. "Men on Relief Go Back to Land." *Family Herald and Weekly Star* 7 June 1933: 3, 5. Print.

———. "My Car 'Finnigan' and I." *Grain Growers' Guide* 7 April 1920. Print. Box 14, folder XIII. Miriam Green Ellis Collection, BPSC.

———. *Pathfinders*. Canadian Women's Press Club, 1956. Print. Box 2, folder x, item 12. Miriam Green Ellis Collection, BPSC.

———. "Special Fields." [Speech given at the Triennial CWPC, Calgary, AB.] 1932. Ts. Box 12, folder I, item 4. Miriam Green Ellis Collection, BPSC.

———. "Sun Dance at Hobbema." Ts. Box 14, folder VII. Miriam Green Ellis Collection, BPSC.

———. "Their Second Honeymoon." *Family Herald and Weekly Star* 11 January 1928. Print. Box 8, folder I. Miriam Green Ellis Collection, BPSC.

———. "The Tragedy of the Regina Plains." *Family Herald and Weekly Star* 30 September 1931: 3, 5. Print.

———. "University of Manitoba [Collecting News], 4th Year English Class." March 1934. Ts. Miriam Green Ellis Collection, BPSC.

———. "A War Bride's Return." Ts and ms. Box 2, folder IV. Miriam Green Ellis Collection, BPSC.

———. "Watching Other People Farm." [Address to University Women's Club, Saskatoon, SK.] 15 January 1945. Ts. Box 12, folder III, item 1. Miriam Green Ellis Collection, BPSC.

———. "Western Homes I Have Seen." [Speech to the Manitoba Horticultural Association.] 17 February 1943. Ts. Box 12, folder II, item 7. Miriam Green Ellis Collection, BPSC.

———. "The Women Grain Growers of Saskatchewan." *Woman's Century* March 1915: 11. Rpt. in *Feminism and the Periodical Press, 1900–1918*. Ed. Lucy Delap, Maria DiCenzo, and Leila Ryan. Vol. 1. London: Routledge, 2006. 431. Print.

———. "World's Best Wheat from Bush Land: Jack Canuck Returns from Chicago." *Family Herald and Weekly Star* 18 December 1929. Print. Box 8, folder I. Miriam Green Ellis Collection, BPSC.

Errington, Elizabeth Jane. "The Diversity of Voices." *Early Voices: Portraits of Canada by Women Writers, 1639–1914*. Ed. Mary Alice Downie and Barbara Robertson with Elizabeth Jane Errington. Toronto: Natural Heritage–Dundurn, 2010. 21–29. Print.

"Fast Arctic Steamer Service Via Waterways Is Arranged Alberta and Arctic Line Announces Plans." *Edmonton Bulletin* 25 March 1922: 2. Print.

Ferguson, Emily. *Janey Canuck in the West*. Toronto: Cassell, 1910. Print.

Fiamengo, Janice. *The Woman's Page: Journalism and Rhetoric in Early Canada*. Toronto: University of Toronto Press, 2008. Print.

Foster, Janet. *Working for Wildlife: The Beginnings of Preservation in Canada*. 2nd ed. Toronto: University of Toronto Press, 1998. Print.

Frazier, Ian. "The Magic of Crazy Horse." *New York Review of Books* 24 February 2011: 32–34. Print.

"Fred Siebert." *Canadian Surveyor Supplement* June 1966. *Alberta's Land Surveying History*. Association of Alberta Land Surveyors, n.d. Web. 4 November 2010. <http://www.landsurveyinghistory.ab.ca/Characters/Seibert_FV.htm>.

Freeman, Barbara. "'Every Stroke Upward:' Women Journalists in Canada, 1880–1906." *Canadian Woman Studies / Les cahiers de la femme* 7.3 (1986): 43–46. Print.

———. *Kit's Kingdom: The Journalism of Kathleen Blake Coleman*. Ottawa: Carleton University Press, 1989. Print.

Fumoleau, René. *As Long As This Land Shall Last: A History of Treaty 8 and Treaty 11, 1870–1939*. Calgary: University of Calgary Press, 2004. Print.

Gillilan, Strickland W. *Including Finnigin: A Book of Gillilan Verse*. Chicago: Forbes, 1914. Print.

Glenbow Museum. "Archives Photographs." Web. 5 November 2010. <http://ww2.glenbow.org/search/archivesPhotosSearch.aspx>.

Godsell, Jean W. *I Was No Lady: The Autobiography of a Fur Trader's Wife*. Toronto: Ryerson, 1959. Print.

Gorham, Deborah. "Pen and Buckskin: Women Journalists in the West Who Knew Wheat and Justice." *Content* 85 (1978): 22–23. Print.

Grahame, Kenneth. *The Wind in the Willows*. 1908. Oxford: Oxford University Press, 1999.

Gray, David. *The Story of the Canadian Arctic Expedition, 1913–1918*. Canadian Museum of Civilization, 22 October 2009. Web. 7 July 2012. <http://www.civilization.ca/cmc/exhibitions/hist/cae/pe0612e.shtml>.

Gray, James Henry. "Our World Stopped and We Got Off." *The Prairie West: Historical Readings*. 2nd ed. Ed. R. Douglas Francis and Howard Palmer. Edmonton: University of Alberta Press, 1992. 631–39. Print.

———. *The Winter Years: The Depression on the Prairies*. Saskatoon: Fifth House, 2003. Print.

Hacker, Carlotta. *E. Cora Hind*. Don Mills: Fitzhenry and Whiteside, 1979. Print.

Haig, Kennethe Macmahon. *Brave Harvest: The Life Story of E. Cora Hind*. Toronto: Allen, 1945. Print.

Hayden, Michael, ed. *So Much To Do, So Little Time: The Writings of Hilda Neatby*. Vancouver: University of British Columbia Press, 1983. Print.

Hendry, Peter. "End of an Era–I." *Family Herald and Weekly Star* 12 September 1968: 4. Print.

Henisch, Heinz K., and Bridget A. Henisch. *The Painted Photograph, 1839-1941: Origins, Techniques, Aspirations*. University Park: Pennsylvania State University Press, 1996. Print.

Herring, Frances E. *Canadian Camp Life*. London: T.F. Unwin, 1900. Print.

Hind, E. Cora. "Crop Conditions." *Manitoba Free Press* 19 July 1913: 1; 26 July 1913, 1. Print.

———. *My Travels and Findings*. Toronto: Macmillan, 1939. Print.

———. "R.P. Roblin, Wheat Speculator." *Manitoba Free Press* 13 September 1904: 4. Print.

———. *Seeing for Myself: Agricultural Conditions Around the World*. Toronto: Macmillan, 1937. Print.

———. "Shaunavon Has Splendid Crop." *Manitoba Free Press* 27 August 1918: 1. Print.

———. "Sixty Per Cent of Wheat Is Cut." *Manitoba Free Press* 6 September 1904: 1. Print.

———. "Will Be Enormous Yields in Swan River Valley Districts." *Manitoba Free Press* 21 August 1918: 2. Print.

Hoyle, Gwynyth. *The Northern Horizons of Guy Blanchet, Intrepid Surveyor*. Toronto: Natural Heritage–Dundurn, 2007. Print.

Humphries, Steve. *Victorian Britain Through the Magic Lantern*. London: Sidgwick and Jackson, 1989. Print.

Jackel, Susan. "First Days, Fighting Days: Prairie Presswomen and Suffrage Activism, 1906–1916." *First Days, Fighting Days: Women in Manitoba History*. Ed. Mary Kinnear. Regina: Canadian Plains Research Center, University of Regina, 1987. 53–75. Print.

Jephson, Lady [Harriet J. Campbell]. *A Canadian Scrap-Book*. London: Marshall Russell, 1897. Print.

Jenness, Diamond. *The People of the Twilight*. New York: Macmillan, 1928. Print.

"John D. Hunt Is Honor Guest at Women's Press Club Soiree." *Edmonton Bulletin* 3 February 1919. 74.56 / 9. PAA.

Jones, David C. "'There Is Some Power about the Land': The Western Agrarian Press and Country Life Ideology." *Journal of Canadian Studies* 17.3 (1982): 96–108. Print.

Kagan, Norman E. "A History of Ross River." *ExploreTheYukon.com*, 2008. Web. 7 July 2012. <http://explorenorth.com/yukon/ross_river-history.html>.

Kesterton, W.H. *A History of Journalism in Canada*. Toronto: McClelland & Stewart, 1967. Print.

LaFramboise, Lisa. "Miriam Green Ellis, 1881–1964." *The Small Details of Life: Twenty Diaries by Women in Canada.* Ed. Kathryn Carter. Toronto: University of Toronto Press, 2002. 301–22. Print.

Lang, Marjory. Message to Patricia Demers. 29 April 2010. Email.

———. *Women Who Made the News: Female Journalists in Canada, 1880–1945.* Montreal: McGill-Queen's University Press, 1999. Print.

Lester, Geoffrey, ed. *Atlas of Alberta Railways.* Electronic text only. Edmonton: University of Alberta Press, 2005. Web. 7 July 2012. <http://railways.library.ualberta.ca/>.

Lutes, Jean Marie. *Front-Page Girls: Women Journalists in American Culture and Fiction, 1880–1930.* Ithaca: Cornell University Press, 2006. Print.

Macbeth, Madge. *Shackles.* Ed. Peggy Lynn Kelly. Ottawa: Tecumseh, 2005. Print.

MacEwan, Grant. "Miriam Green Ellis: The Lady with the Notebook." *...And Mighty Women Too: Stories of Notable Western Canadian Women.* Saskatoon: Western Producer Prairie Books, 1975. 169–74. Print.

MacLaren, I.S., and Lisa LaFramboise. Introduction. *The Ladies, the Gwich'in, and the Rat: Travels on the Athabasca, Mackenzie, Rat, Porcupine, and Yukon Rivers in 1926.* Eds. I.S. MacLaren and Lisa LaFramboise. Edmonton: University of Alberta Press, 1998. xv–xlix. Print.

Marriott, Anne. *The Wind Our Enemy.* Toronto: Ryerson Press, 1939. Print.

McCalla, William Copeland. *Wild Flowers of Western Canada.* Toronto: Musson, 1920. Print.

McClung, Nellie L. *The Stream Runs Fast: My Own Story.* Toronto: Thomas Allen, 1945. Print.

———. "Why Boys and Girls Leave the Farm." *Nor-West Farmer* 5 September 1913: 1105. Print.

McEachern, Cam. "Time's Grip along the Athabasca, 1920s and 1930s." *History, Literature and the Writing of the Canadian Prairies.* Ed. Alison Calder and Robert Wardaugh. Winnipeg: University of Manitoba Press, 2005. 283–84.

"Miriam Green Ellis, Dean of Canada's Newspaper Women, Visiting Here." *Honolulu Star-Bulletin* 10 May 1950: n. pag. Print. Box 14, folder VI. Miriam Green Ellis Collection, BPSC.

Mishler, Craig. "Missionaries in Collision: Anglicans and Oblates among the Gwich'in, 1861–1865." *Arctic* 43.2 (1990): 121–26. Web. 4 November 2010. <http://arctic.synergiesprairies.ca/arctic/index.php/arctic/article/view/1601/1580>.

Nevinson, Henry W. *Essays in Rebellion*. London: James Nisbet, 1913. *Project Gutenberg*. 2004. Web. 15 July 2012. <http://www.gutenberg.org/files/11079/11079-h/11079-h.htm>.

"New River and Lake Maps Will Be Used by North Captains." *Edmonton Bulletin* 11 May 1922: 7. Print.

Newton, Michael. *The Encyclopedia of Unsolved Crimes*. 2nd ed. New York: Facts on File, 2009. Print.

"Northern River Steamers Are Making Fast Time Due to Good Stage of Water." *Edmonton Bulletin* 19 June 1922: 8. Print.

"Notes by Classes." *University of Toronto Monthly* 22.6 (1922): 266–72. Print.

"Old Crow: Some of the Vuntut Gwitchin Language." *Old Crow—Yukon: Home of the Vuntut Gwitchin First Nation*. Vuntut Gwitchin First Nation, 2010. Web. 5 November 2010. <http://www.oldcrow.ca/language.htm>.

Oliver, Marjorie S. *Canadian Women's Press Club Golden Jubilee 1904–1954, Newspacket*. Toronto, 1954. Print. GA 94, accrual 1991, file 1. Toronto Women's Press Club Fonds, Doris Lewis Rare Book Room, University of Waterloo, Waterloo, ON.

Orders in Council. 161 / 06. Print. Alberta Justice Fonds, PAA.

Páalsson, Gisli. *Anthropology and the New Genetics*. Cambridge: Cambridge University Press, 2007. Print.

Pettipas, Katherine. *Severing the Ties That Bind: Government Repression of Indigenous Religious Ceremonies on the Prairies*. Winnipeg: University of Manitoba Press, 1994. Print.

*Playthings and Curios: Historic Inuit Art*. Canadian Museum of Civilization, 2010. Web. 15 October 2010. <http://www.civilization.ca/cmc/exhibitions/tresors/art_inuit/inart31e.shtml>.

Pratt, Mary Louise. *Imperial Eyes: Travel Writing and Transculturation*. 2nd ed. London: Routledge, 2008. Print.

"Press Club Entertains in Honor of Miss Cora Hind." *Edmonton Journal* April 1919: n. pag. Print. Accession 74. 56 / 9. PAA.

Rasmussen, Karl. *Trail Blazers of Canadian Agriculture*. Ottawa: Agricultural Institute of Canada, 1995. Print.

Ray, Arthur J. *The Canadian Fur Trade in the Industrial Age*. Toronto: University of Toronto Press, 1990. Print.

"Record of Major George Ellis, Textual Document Canadian Expeditionary Force Personnel." Print. RG 150, accession 1992–93/166, box 2882-40. Veterans' Affairs Fonds, LAC.

Rex, Kay. *No Daughter of Mine: The Women and History of the Canadian Women's Press Club, 1904-1971*. Toronto: Cedar Cave, 1995. Print.

Riding, Laura. *The World and Ourselves*. London: Chatto & Windus, 1938. Print.

"River Navigation Preparations Are Hustled in North." *Edmonton Bulletin* 10 April 1022: 2. Print.

Roy, Wendy. *Maps of Difference: Canada, Women, and Travel*. Montreal: McGill-Queen's University Press, 2005. Print.

———. "Primacy, Technology, and Nationalism in Agnes Deans Cameron's *The New North*." *Mosaic* 38.2 (2005): 53-79. Print.

Service, Robert William. "Ballad of the Northern Lights." *Ballads of a Cheechako*. Toronto: W. Briggs, 1909. 20. Print.

Steedman, Carolyn. *Dust: The Archive and Cultural History*. New Brunswick, NJ: Rutgers University Press, 2002. Print.

Strong-Boag, Veronica. "Pulling in Double Harness or Hauling a Double Load: Women, Work and Feminism on the Canadian Prairie." *The Prairie West: Historical Readings*. 2nd ed. Ed. R. Douglas Francis and Howard Palmer. Edmonton: University of Alberta Press, 1992. 401-23. Print.

"Sun Dance of the Crees at Hobbema: By Special Permission of Government Red Men Observe Wierd [*sic*] Ceremony." *Edmonton Journal* 21 July 1923: 3. Print.

Taylor, Elizabeth R. "Articles Found Useful on My Mackenzie River Trip." *The Far Islands and Other Cold Places: Travel Essays of a Victorian Lady*. Ed. James Taylor Dunn. St. Paul, MN: Pogo, 1997. 59-62. Print.

———. "Up the Mackenzie River to the Polar Sea: A Lady's Journey in Arctic America." *The Far Islands and Other Cold Places: Travel Essays of a Victorian Lady*. Ed. James Taylor Dunn. St. Paul, MN: Pogo, 1997. 50-58. Print.

Taylor, Georgina. *H.D. and the Public Sphere of Modernist Women Writers, 1913-1946*. Oxford: Clarendon, 2001. Print.

"Three Years' Growth." *Manitoba Free Press* 12 September 1904: 12.

Tory, Henry Marshall. "Convocation Address." *Edmonton Bulletin* 14 October 1908: 13-16.

"Voice of the Farm." *Family Herald and Weekly Star* 26 September 1968: 4-6.

Voisey, Paul. *High River and the Times: An Alberta Community and Its Weekly Newspaper, 1905-1966*. Edmonton: University of Alberta Press, 2004.

*Vox Lycei: 1887-1937, Lisgar Collegiate Institute Year Book*. Ed. John Fraser and Dick Barber. Ottawa: Lisgar Collegiate Institute, 1937.

Vyvyan, Clara. *Lady Vyvyan's Arctic Adventure. The Ladies, the Gwich'in, and the Rat: Travels on the Athabasca, Mackenzie, Rat, Porcupine, and Yukon Rivers in 1926*.

Ed. I.S. MacLaren and Lisa LaFramboise. Edmonton: University of Alberta Press, 1998. 1–187.

Warner, Michael. *Publics and Counterpublics*. New York: Zone, 2005.

"Wireless Equipped Surveyors Leaving for Far North." *Edmonton Bulletin* 20 April 1022: 5.

"Woman Reporter Once Shocked Toronto Society." *Regina Leader-Post* 12 January 1963: 12.

Wood, Louis Aubrey. *A History of Farmers' Movements in Canada: The Origins and Development of Agrarian Protest, 1872–1924*. Toronto: University of Toronto Press, 1975.

Zeman, Brenda. *88 Years of Puck Chasing in Saskatchewan*. Regina: WDS Associates and Saskatchewan Sports Hall of Fame, 1983.

# INDEX

*Page numbers in italics refer to illustrations. "MGE" refers to Miriam Green Ellis.*

Aboriginal people *see* Eskimos; Indians; Native people
aesthetic values, lxvii
Aggie Stag banquet, xxii
agriculture
    assisted settlement, 141–142
    experimental farms, 26–27, 129
    markets, 122
    MGE on, xiv, lv, lxix, lxxi
    in MGE's fiction, 117–118
    in MGE's journalism, 18
    as news topic, xxxiv
    northern, 26, 139, 142–143
    reporters, xiv, lxviii–lxix, 18
    *see also* women, farm life
aircraft, *xxxix*, lxiv

Aklavik, 51–59, 190n40
Alberta and Arctic Transportation Company, xxxvii, xxxviii
Alberta and Great Waterways Railway, xxxvii, xl, 184n6
Alexandra Falls, 25
Alikomiak, xli, 45–46, *47*, 191n51
Alix, Alberta, 130
"Alone," l, lii–liii, 73–90
Arctic *see* North
arts, *41*, 178–181
asphalt, 11, 186n16
assisted settlement, 141–142, 194n1("Men on Relief")
Athabasca Glacier, *176*
Athabasca [Athabaska] Indians, 14–15
Athabasca [Athabaska] River, 8, 10, 13
Atwater, Mary Meigs, 178–179
auto camps, 170–171, 174–175, 179
automobiles *see* auto camps; cars

back-to-the-land movement, 141–147
Banff, 171, 174, 177, 180
"Banff Fine Arts School," 177–181
Banff School of Fine Arts, lxvii, 177–181
bees, 131, 174
Binder, Otto, 46, 191n51
birdwatching, 13
bison *see* buffalo
Blanchet, Guy Houghton, xxxviii, 20, 187n26
boat travel
    conditions, xlii, 10–14, 17–19, 21, 23–24, 187n25
    fuel, 21, 23, 33
    Indians', 31
    motor boats, 58
    navigation, 50, 63
    pictures of, *10*, *41*
    transfers, 65–66
    York boats, 25
botanist *see* Holroyd, Roland
botany *see* wildflowers
Breynat, Gabriel, 17, 25, 188n30
buffalo, 19–20, 66–71, 163, 168, 194n64
Bugnet, Georges, xliii–liv
butter, 122

cabin, *xxxv*, xxxvi
Cameron, Agnes Deans, xlv–xlix, 194n62
Cameron, Donald, 178, 179, 180
Cameron, Mrs. Donald, 179
camping, 68–69, 170–171, 174–175, 179
"Canada Has Something," lxvii, 188n27
Canadian Women's Press Club, x–xvi, xxii–xxiv, xxxvi, xlv, lxviii–lxix, lxxi, 183n3

canoes, 31, *32*, 69
Card, Gerald, 14, 20, *20*, 186n18
Card, Mrs. Gerald, 20
Carley, Ethel, xxxviii, 185n9
Carley, John, xxxviii, 185n9
cars
    camping, 170–171, 174–175, 179
    in the Depression, 136–137
    MGE's, *xxxiv*, lxv–lxvi, 150–158
    northern, 18, 187n22
Cassels, W.L., 67, 194n64
cattle, 18, 27
Chaplin, 8
Chief Nahanni, 82
Chipewyan *see* Fort Chipewyan
Christmas, 59
churches, 17, 24–25, 34, 40, *41*, 45, 59, 190n45
    *see also* missions
Clearwater River, 8, *10*, 185n6, 186n13
Columbia Icefield, *171*
Comfort, Charles Fraser, 178
Conibear, Ada Mary, 20, 187n27
convents, 30, 164
country life *see* cabin; rural life; women, farm life
Cree people, lxvi–lxvii, 17, 161, 186n18
Crisall, James Mordant, 45, 186n9
Cru, Albert, 179
curling, xxxii

dances, 43, 59, 161–168, 192n54
democracy, lxviii–lxix
dentistry, 27, 58
Depression, 134–140, 141–142
"dirt farmers," xxii
discourse, lxviii–lxix

Discovery Well, 36
Doak, W.A., 191n51
doctors, 14, 20–21, 27, 186n19
dogs, 26, 45, 59, 99, *171*
domestic abuse *see* marriage
Dominion Day, 33
"Down North," xxxvi–xxxviii, xlii–xliii, *1*, 3–71, 185n9
drama, 178
Draper, Thomas, 11, 186n16
driving *see* cars
drought, 134–136
drumming, 165, 166, 168, 192n54
dust bowl, 134–136

*Edmonton Bulletin*, 184n1
*Edmonton Journal*, lxvi
Edson, Alberta, 126
education, 173, 178–179, 180, 181, 188n27
  *see also* schools
eggs, 122
Ellis Collection, xxiv–xxv
"Eskimo Stories," xxxviii
Eskimos, 17, 24, 25, *47*, 51–59, 192n54

*Family Herald and Weekly Star*
  MGE's career at, xxii, lx–lxii
  MGE's works in, 125, 129, 133, 141, 169, 177
farm organizations, xxxii, xxxiii
farmers, xxii, 172
  *see also* agriculture; Depression; soldier settlement; women, farm life
feminism, lxiii–lxiv
Field, Mrs. Poole, 28, 30, 189n34

Field, Poole, 28, 189n34
"Finnigan," *xxxiv*, lxv, *150*, 151–158
First Nations *see* Indians
Firth, John, 43, 191n50
Firth, Mrs. John, 43
fishing, 24–26, 31, 33, 53, 54, 55
Fitzgerald *see* Fort Fitzgerald
flies, 65, 68, 153, 187n23
flowers *see* wildflowers
flying *see* aircraft
fodder, 139–140
Fort Chipewyan, *16*, 17, 187n21
Fort Fitzgerald, 18
Fort Good Hope, 39–42, 63
Fort McMurray, *9*
Fort McPherson, xli, 42, 43–50, *44*, *48*, 191n50
Fort Norman, 20–21, 27, 33–39, 63, 190n41
Fort Norman Company, 36
Fort Providence, 25
Fort Resolution, 21, *22*, 65
Fort Simpson, 26–28, 186n18, 189n33
Fort Smith, 14, 18–20, *20*, 65–66, 184n4, 186n16, 186n19, 187n23
Fourth of July, 42, 49
French language, 179
"From Aberdeen to Alberta," 129–132
funerals, 157–158
fur trade
  history of, 187n21, 187n24
  Indians trading, 29, 34
  in MGE's fiction, 109
  pelts, 46, 53–54
  transportation, 19
  workers, 6
  *see also* Hudson's Bay Company

galena, 30
gardens
    northern, 20, 24, 25, 55, 65, 187n27
    at schools, 123
Gaudet family, 40
Glyde, Henry George, *171*, 178
gold, 28–29, 64, 76, 77, 80
Graham, Maxwell, 67, 69
grain, 17, *20*, 27, 71, 133, 134, 137, 140
*Grain Growers' Guide*, 151
graveyards, 40, 45
Great Depression *see* Depression
Great Slave Lake, 19–20, 21, 23, 65
Grey Nuns, 20, 25, 186n19, 189n31
Gritten, Doc., 187n25
Grouard, Émile-Jean-Baptiste-Marie, 6, 7, 15, *16*, 185n9, 185n13
Gwich'in people, 191n49, 191n50
    *see also* Loucheux people

Haig, Kennethe, xxii
Harris, Thomas William "Flynn," 26–27, 189n33
Hay River Mission, 24–25, 31, 190n38
Hay River (river), 25
health *see* doctors; illness; nurses
Hind, E. Cora, x, xii–xiii, xvii–xviii, lxvii–lxix, 123
Hoare, Mr., 59
Hoare, Mrs., 56, 58, 59, 193n58
Hobbema Reserve, lxvi, 162–163
Hock, Frederick H., 178
hockey, *xxxi*, xxxii
Holroyd, Roland, xl–xli, 6, 18, 24, 36, 46, 62, 185n8–9
home, xxi–xxii
honey, 131

horses
    MGE riding, 67–69
    in MGE's fiction, 194n2
    northern, 36, 185n7, 187n23, 190n42
    on ranches, 129–130
    at Sun Dances, 165
hot springs, 30, 180
House, Henry, *171*
Hudson's Bay Company
    competition, 187n24
    dentists, 58
    employees, 40, 43, 46, 185n9, 191n50
    houses, 33
    and Nahanni Indians, 29–30
hunting, 34, 53

identity and belonging, l
illness, 14, 27, 56, 58, 146
Imperial Oil Co., 21, 27, 36, 63
Indian agents, 14, 26–27, 186n18, 189n33
Indians
    health, 14
    MGE on, 43, 162–163
    in MGE's fiction, 74, 85, 97–98, 105, 109
    pictures of, *16, 22, 32, 37–38, 44*
    see also particular groups by name; schools; treaty payments
Inuit *see* Eskimos

Jamieson, Peter, Jr., 130–132
Jamieson, Peter, Sr., 130–132
Jenness, Diamond, 192n54, 193n55, 193n57

Joe (Indian guide), 67-70
Jolas, Jacques, 179
Jones, E. Maldwyn, 178
Jorgensen, Martin, 28-29, 189n36
journalism, xxii, lv
  see also Canadian Women's Press Club
Justice Creek, 64

Klondike [Klondyke], 23

Lac La Biche, 6, 186n14
Lacombe airstrip, *xxxix*
Lacombe, Alberta, 129-139
Lake Athabasca [Athabaska], 13
Lake Louise, 171
"The Land of the Midnight Sun," *xxvi-xxvii*, xlix
Laura, xli, 59-60, 61-62
lead, 29-30, 189n37
lectures, xxii, xxiv, *xxvi-xxvii*, xlix, lvii, lxiii, lxviii, 183n1, 188n27
Liard River, 27, 184n5
libraries, 179
"Limberlost," xxxv
Loucheux people, 24, 43, *44*, *48*, 191n49
  see also Gwich'in people
Louise Falls, 25
Lucas, James Richard, 17, 34, 55, 190n40

Macdonald, A.L., 14, 20, 18619
MacDonald, Richard, 178
Mackenzie Delta Eskimos, 53-59, 192n54
Mackenzie diocese, 17

Mackenzie River
  description, 25-26, 51, 184n2
  fishing on, 26
  Indians of, 15, 17
  MGE's travel on, 19, *32*
  pictures of, *32*, *41*
Mackenzie River delta, 49-51
MacNaughton, Mrs. John, 122
Manitoba Farm Women, xxxiii
*Manitoba Free Press*, lvii-lix
marriage, xli, liii, lv, lxiv, 60, 118, 144, 171
  see also MGE, marriage
May, Wilfrid "Wop," *xvii*, xxxix
McCleary [McCreary], Mr., 33-34, *35*, 190n39
McClung, Jack, *xvii*, *150*
McClung, Nellie, x, xv, xxxix, lvi, 188n27
McLellan, J.B., 179
"Men on Relief Go Back to Land," 141-147
MGE
  appearance, xii, xliii, lxiv, lxix, 12, *22*, *42*
  birth, xxix
  career, x, xxxiii-xxxiv
  context, xvii-xviii, lxviii-lxix
  diaries, xxix, xxxviii, xxxix, l, 5
  journalism topics, xxiv, xxxiv, xlix, lxvii, 18
  marriage, xxx, xxxiii, xxxvi, lxx
  as naturalist, xliii, xlviii-xlix
  nicknames, *xxxiv*, xxxvi
  parents, xxix, 5
  personality, x, xii-xiii, xlix, lxiii-lxv, lxix-lxx
  photography, xxiv-xxv, *xxvi*, 18, 50

INDEX   211

pictures of, *xi, xvii, xxiii, xxxi,*
　　　　*xxxv, xxxix,* 20, 69, *150, 177*
　　private life, xxviii
　　reading, xxxvi
　　reputation, x, xvi
　　retirement, xxii–xxiii
　　schooling, xxix–xxx
　　self-portraits, lxiv
　　signature, *xi,* xxxvi
　　sports, *xxxi,* xxxii, *32*
　　travels, xxiv, lxiv
　　unpublished works, xxix, l–lv
　　works *see* individual works by title
　　writing process, xxxviii–xxxix
　　writing style, xxix, xliv, xlix, lx–lxii,
　　　　lxxi
midnight sun, 40, *41,* 43, 49–51, 60, *61*
Minchen, Frank, 24–25
minerals, 23, 28–30, 71
mining, lxxi, 23, 33
Miriam Green Ellis Bursaries, lxiii
missionaries
　　Anglican, 45, 191n49
　　medical, 56, 186n19
　　rivalries, 190n40
　　Roman Catholic, xl, 63
　　support by farm women, lvii
missions
　　Anglican, 17, 24, 33, 34, 55, 59,
　　　　190n38, 190n40
　　farms, 65
　　orphanages, 164
　　Roman Catholic, 17, 20, 25, 33, 40,
　　　　*41,* 190n46
　　schools, 24, 25, 27, 30, 31, 109,
　　　　190n38
moccasins, 31, 43

mosquitoes *see* flies
motor camps, 170, 174
Murphy, Emily (Ferguson), lvi
music, xxx, 178, 179
　　*see also* drumming
"My Car 'Finnigan' and I," 151–158

Nahanni Indians, 29–30, 74
Nahanni River, 4, 28, 29–30, 74, 184n5
Native–non-Native relations, l, lii–liv
Native people, xlii, l, liii
　　*see also* Eskimos; Indians
nature, xlviii–xlix
*The New North,* xlv–xlviii
nipâhkwêsimowin, lxvi
*Nipsya,* xliii–liv
Norman [Oil] Wells, 4, 6, 23, 184n3
the North, *xxvi–xxvii,* xxxvi–xlix, 3–4,
　　60
　　*see also* "Down North"
North West Company, 187n21
Northern Trading Company, 59, 187n24
Northwest [North West] Territories, 19
nuns, 164
　　*see also* Grey Nuns
nurses, 56, 58, 59, 122

oats, 127
Oblates, xl
oil industry
　　claims recording, 19, 33
　　future of, 71
　　important discoveries, 184n3
　　oil wells, 36, 39, 190n43
　　prospecting, 25, 36, 39
　　uses of oil, 11

*see also* particular oil companies by name; tar sands
Oliver, Frank, xl, xlii, 4, 26, 184n1
Outrement, Henri, xliii–liv

paternalism, lxvii–lxviii, lxx, 12
*Pathfinders*, x, xii, lvii
Patterson, Gladys, xl, liii, 6, 185n9, 185n11
Peace River, 126
Peel River, 42, 49
Persons Case, xiii–xiv
Petitot, Émile, 40, 191n47
Phillips, W.J., 178
Pickford, 8
piloting, 17–18
pipes, 166
politics, xiii–xiv
post offices, 20
"Press Club Entertains," xxxvi
Prince Albert Collegiate Institute, *xxxi*, xxxii
prospecting, 23, 25, 28–29
Pure Oil Company, 25

railways, 144
  *see also* Alberta and Great Waterways Railway
rainbows, 62
the Ramparts, 39
Rapids of the Drowned, 18
"A Recipe for Remembrance," *xi*
Red Cross Service, 139
Red River carts, 169, 171
Reed, Frank, 129
*Regina Leader-Post*, xxxiv
relief, 137, 138–139, 141–147

relief commissions, 139
religion, 164, 168
  *see also* missions
reverse dynamic, xl
Richardson, Dr., 14, 17, 33, 34
riding *see* horses
Risk, Sydney, 178
Rivière des Rochers, 17–18, 187n22
Rodona Farm, 131
Rotary Clubs, 188n27
Royal Canadian Mounted Police, 43, 45, 55, 59, 76, 191n51
Royal Winter Fair, xii
rural life, xl, lv–lvii
rural rehabilitation, 141–142
Russian thistle, 135

salt, 11–12, 194n62
Salt Plains, 67, 194n62
Salt River, 71
Salt Springs, 66–71, 194n62
Samwell, Miss, 31, 33, 190n38
Sans Sault Rapids, 39
Saskatchewan, 121, 134
saw mills, 19, 27
School of Technology and Art, 178
schools
  arts, 177–181
  in the Depression, 139
  farm children, 122, 123
  gardens, 123
  northern day schools, 15, 27, 190n40
  residential, 24, 25, 190n38
Segre, Beresford Henry, 49, 192n52
Seibert, Frederick Victor, 36, 67, 190n41
Service, Robert W., 192n53
Slave Delta, 21

Slave River, 21, 187n22
Slavey [Slavi] Indians, 34
Smith, Jos. F., 178
Smith, Joseph H.B., 126–128
Smith's Landing *see* Fort Smith
soldier settlement, 144, 194n1 ("Men on Relief")
"Special Fields," xiii, lxiii, 183n1
speeches *see* lectures
St. Rose, Sister, 25
steamboats *see* boat travel
Stefansson, Alex, 57
Stefansson, Mrs., 52
Stefansson, Vilhjalmur, 51, 188n28, 192n54
Storkerson, Storker Teodor, 188n28
Storkerson, Uiniq (Elwina), 24, 188n28
Stransberg, Pete, 54
suffragist principles *see* votes for women
"Sun Dance at Hobbema," lxvi–lxvii, 161–168
Sun Dances, lxvi–lxvii, *160*, 161–168
sun dials, 36, 190n41
surveyors, xxxviii, 20, 49, 66, 187n26, 190n41, 192n52
sweetgrass, 166
swimming, xlii, 31, *32*

tar sands, xlii, lxx, 11, 186n16
teachers, 15, 180
temperance, lvii
"Their Second Honeymoon," 169–175
Thirst Dance, lxvi
"The Toad," *xxxiv*
"Toad Hall," *xxxv*, xxxvi
tourists, 170, 180
traders *see* fur trade

"The Tragedy of the Regina Plains," 133–140
train travel, 5–6, 8, 185n12
travel, 173–174
travel writing, xxxviii–xl, xliii–xlix
treaties, 14–15, 17
Treaty 8, 14–15, 186n18, 187n20
treaty payments, 14, 31
Trelle, Herman, 126

Uiniq *see* Storkerson, Uiniq (Elwina)
United Farm Women of Alberta, xxxiii
United Farmers of Canada, 139
University of Alberta, xxxi–xxxii, 178, 180
University of Manitoba, xxii, lxix
University Women's Club, xxiv, *xxvii*, lxiii
urban life, lvi

Vale, Canon, 24
veterans *see* World War I
votes for women, xxxii–xxxiii, lvii, lx, lxviii, 123
    *see also* Persons Case

war *see* war brides; World War I
war brides, 6, 91
"A War Bride's Return," liii–liv, 91–118, 185n11
"Watching Other People Farm," lxiii–lxiv
Waterways, xl, 8, *9*, 185n6, 186n16
Wembley, Alberta, 126
the West, xxix
wheat, 124–128
Whittaker, Archdeacon, 55

Whittaker, Mrs., 55
wildflowers, 18, 21, 23–24, 33, 34, 36, 40, 42, 46, 62–64, 191n48
wildlife, 51
Winnipeg Board of Trade, 145–146
Wolf Creek, Alberta, 126
*Woman's Century*, xxxiii, 121
women
    Canadian Women's Press Club on, 183n3
    clothing, 11
    election of, lxiii
    Eskimos, 193n57
    farm life, lvi–lvii, lx, 144, 172
    MGE championing, xxix, lx, lxvii–lxviii, 195n1
    in politics, xiii–xiv, lxiii
    at Sun Dances, *160*, 163
    as writers, xliv–xlix, lxviii–lxix
Women Grain Growers, xxxiii, lx, 121
"Women Grain Growers of Saskatchewan," xxxiii
"The Women Grain Growers of Saskatchewan," 121–123
Women's Institute, 139
women's organizations, 123
    *see also* specific organizations by name
women's rights, xliii, lvii, lxx, 123, 183n3
    *see also* votes for women
Wood, Inspector, 43
World War I
    effect on MGE, xxxii
    and female journalists, xxxiii
    German missionaries, 63
    memorials, 17, 24–25
    in MGE's fiction, 114–116
    soldier settlement, 144, 194n1
    *see also* war brides
"World's Best Wheat from Bush Land," 125–128
"World's Wheat King," 125–128
Wrigley, 64
writing, xxii

Other Titles from The University of Alberta Press

### THIS WILD SPIRIT
*Women in the Rocky Mountains of Canada*
COLLEEN SKIDMORE, Editor

508 pages | B&W photographs, colour section, bibliography, index
Mountain Cairns: A series on the history and culture of the Canadian Rockies
978-0-88864-466-4 | $34.95 (T) PAPER
978-0-88864-587-6 | $27.99 (T) EPUB
Women's Studies/Canadian History

### NAHANNI JOURNALS
*R.M. Patterson's 1927–1929 Journals*
RAYMOND MURRAY PATTERSON
RICHARD C. DAVIS, Editor
JUSTIN TRUDEAU, Foreword

316 pages | B&W photographs, maps, preface, foreword, introduction, notes, bibliography
978-0-88864-477-0 | $29.95 (T) PAPER
Adventure Travel/Tourism

### PEOPLE OF THE LAKES
*Stories of Our Van Tat Gwich'in Elders/Googwandak Nakhwach'ànjòo Van Tat Gwich'in*
VUNTUT GWITCHIN FIRST NATION & SHIRLEEN SMITH

456 pages | Full-colour throughout, 125 colour images and B&W images, maps, notes, glossary, bibliography, index
978-0-88864-505-0 | $34.95 (T) PAPER
Native Studies/Oral History/The North